THE COMPLETE BOOK
OF OUTDOOR COOKERY

The Complete Book

BY JAMES A. BEARD AND

PERENNIAL LIBRARY

HARPER & ROW
PUBLISHERS, New York

GRAND RAPIDS, PHILADELPHIA, ST. LOUIS, SAN FRANCISCO
LONDON, SINGAPORE, SYDNEY, TOKYO

# of Outdoor Cookery

HELEN EVANS BROWN

foreword by

JEREMIAH TOWER

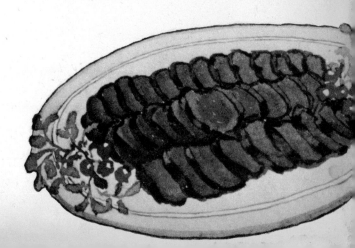

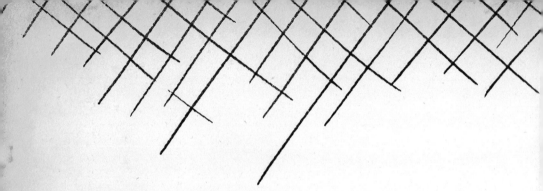

For John Schaffner

First PERENNIAL LIBRARY edition 1989.

Designed by Barbara DuPree Knowles

LIBRARY OF CONGRESS CATALOGUE CARD NUMBER: 88-45923

ISBN 0-06-097206-8

89 90 91 92 93 DT/RRD 10 9 8 7 6 5 4 3 2 1

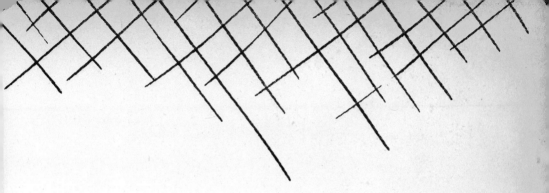

CONTENTS

v

FOREWORD

James Beard and Helen Evans Brown do not age. The preface to the first edition of this book says that "in recent years all America has become enchanted with outdoor cookery," a statement just as valid now as then to introduce the book.

Nowadays a reader might expect the book to be filled with some of the culinary bad habits or fashions of the times, but these two cook–authors are really good. They are the best, and the quality shines through. To be sure, there are outmoded bits of information but it is fascinating how few there are. There is no onion powder, or garlic salt, or cans of this and that to make sauces, no bouillon cubes and dried soup packages. No, this is a mouth-watering book that makes one want to go out immediately and start cooking its wonderful food.

Today, I would wax less enthusiastically about charcoal briquets (although I still prefer them to a gas grill). I do remember going to the docks in Montauk, Long Island in 1963 and buying a three-inch-thick pink swordfish steak, taking it back to the beach in front of our summer place, and sipping cool white wine while the sun set over Montauk lake, quite unencumbered with guilt at the smell of those briquets I was waiting patiently to turn white-ashed. Now, over twenty years later, I would definitely try a couple or three supermarkets looking for real charcoal, or build a driftwood fire. If

I were really organized I would have remembered to have packed my own charcoal to bring along.

Also, I would not agree with the comment that pork (loin) "should not be eaten until well done," and would recommend 155 degrees as the internal point to reach, and I would personally emphasize a bit more the high temperatures needed for cooking fillets of fish. I am glad the authors mention frozen meat because better to know how to deal with it than not; I would love to be able to talk to Jim in his kitchen in Greenwich Village about the pros and cons of salting food before, during, and after cooking. In one place the authors make a point of not salting food before cooking as good general advice, but the old recipe for an entrecôte Bercy that they admire very much calls for salting the steak before cooking. I would, as a last and fairly feeble complaint, point out that the times and doneness table for steaks is a bit on the overcooked side for modern tastes. I think the readers' tastes have changed toward the more rare of medium rare.

All this aside, this is a really good book. And it is timeless. The authors were never geared to fashion, only to what worked and what was realistic at the time, as it still is according to common sense and classical principles. They do not favor California wines over European wines (or vice versa) as so many people do, but choose whichever wines make the most wonderful match with the food.

One of the reasons this book is so rich in material and engaging in its scope is that Beard and Brown do not see outdoor cookery as limited to dishes that are "necessarily prepared over coals." This book shows how to bring the full scope of a kitchen—and of dining room quality eating—out of doors. And this is an intelligent book. Each chapter is crammed with practical advice and personal insight, all of it stylishly larded with sensuality and a friendly desire to eat the food they are talking about. When talking about "steak au poivre," one word tells us all about the cooks and the book opening up in front of us. "When it is cooked to your liking," they say, already setting the tone that this is a book for the reader, put on the steak "a large dollop of sweet butter, which should melt and drool over the surface": an instruction that has me drooling and rushing out to buy a steak and some Tellichery peppercorns. And I say intelligent because as I read the book I kept saying out loud to myself (much to the consternation of my neighboring airline passengers), "yes, yes, someone has finally said it." Well, of course, I temporarily forgot that 1955 publication date. Take the paragraph called "Lamb Chops" at the head of Chapter Six. They say it as it should be and don't leave anything out. Especially about chops being cut thick or otherwise the cook is wasting time and money: "If you need to pinch the pennies, don't have chops."

I have a certain reputation for having revived the practice of grilling in restaurants in the United States, but when I read this book now, I know I could only have imagined to have "revived" or "rediscovered" the art of grilling and outdoor cookery. It is all here, to the point where it does not have to be done again, except for more new recipes. The overall picture and feeling is totally intact, and so are all the details, down, for example, to something like reminding the reader to have a pair of pliers for tightening or loosening the wing nuts on spits. Most people interested in outdoor cooking are not that familiar even with spit cooking and its infinite variations, let alone informed enough to remember to bring the pliers.

But for me the personal thrill was, in the "Guide for Charcoal Broiling and Roasting," at the very end, in the entry "Whole Fish, Roasted on a Spit." I was completely happy that throughout the book they use the term "to roast" correctly, but it was the fish on a spit that truly thrilled me. I thought I had invented that—with a large fish, anyway.

My staff and I were doing the Tribute to James Beard "Meals on Wheels" benefit at Rockefeller Center in New York. We needed something dramatic and not seen before to be a showpiece to our exhibit of grilled foods. We decided to do a spit-roasted marlin or tuna, whichever one hundred-pound fish we could find. It was a mad idea, but it worked. It caught the eye of national morning television news, "Lifestyles of the Rich and Famous," and just about everyone else. It was also delicious. On the plane back to San Francisco, I opened up *The Complete Book of Outdoor Cookery,* since I was to write the foreword to the reprinted edition. Just barely into the book, as we cruised along at forty thousand feet, there it was, using an albacore tuna as an example: "Whole fish, roasted on a spit." I had been fairly much up in the clouds already with our gastronomic and public victory, but as I put the book down, a deeper, most relaxed feeling of satisfaction swelled up in me—the old man and his co-author had done it first. We are still their students.

Jeremiah Tower

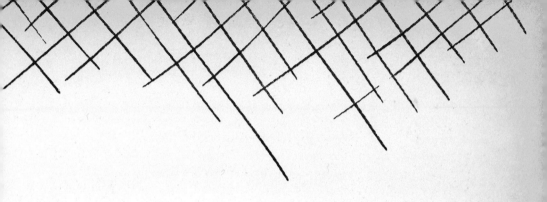

PREFACE

This book is for you, whether you do your charcoal cookery in a portable grill, on the deck of your yacht, or on a stack of bricks in a city back yard. Such cookery may be limited to an occasional campfire at the beach, or it may be that cooking and dining al fresco is the order of your summer day. In any case, you will find information here that will suit your every need.

In recent years all America has become enchanted with outdoor cookery. We love the informality of such a meal, our keen outdoor appetites, and the joy of watching the meat as it cooks to mahogany perfection. But most of all we marvel at the flavor of the food. Restaurateurs, taking heed, were quick to install charcoal broilers and rotisseries in their establishments, and to boast of their foods "from the grill." The family cook was not far behind. Although most coals cookery is still done under the sky, more and more luxurious residences are being equipped with kitchen or playroom fireplaces which include grates for broiling, spits for roasting. What's more, many a family has taken to using a hibachi or other portable grill in the fireplace, and enjoying charcoal-cooked meals throughout the year.

We know that, though cooks may be "born" ones, they're not born with experience, and that that's also true of the charcoal cook. It is our hope that this book will keep them from the mistakes that novices at the grill sometimes make, but we want it to be helpful to the old hand as well. For this reason we include everything, from making a fire to roasting a goose and smoking pastrami. When we didn't know the answers, we either experimented until we found them or turned to experts on the subject. To them, and to Philip Brown who did much of our testing and tasting, we give our thanks.

Though we do not attempt to give directions for everything that could be cooked *out of doors,* we do present some recipes for dishes that are not necessarily prepared *over coals.* These include dishes that go well with grilled foods and may be cooked in the kitchen oven or in an electric device near the scene of the grilling. There are also recipes for salads which need no heat of any kind. We give many suggestions for menus, including what wines go best with them. Chapters on "Camp Cookery," "Picnics and Cook-outs," "Galley and Trailer Cooking" are here, as well as a section on sauces that are as right for the patio as they are for the dining room noted for its *haute cuisine.* Broiling and roasting have always been high in the field of gastronomy, and it is our aim to introduce more of you to the thrill of the grill.

Helen Evans Brown
James A. Beard

THE COMPLETE BOOK
OF OUTDOOR COOKERY

"Charbonadoes, or carbonadoes, is meat broyled upon the coals, of divers kinds according to men's pleasures."

—GERVASE MARKHAM, *The English Housewife*, 1649

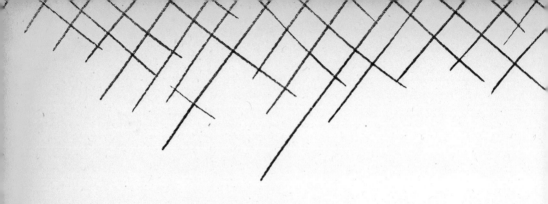

{ *Recipes for items printed in* **bold face**
may be located by consulting the Index. }

CHARCOAL GRILLS
AND GRILL EQUIPMENT

charcoal grills

So great has become the urge to cook over charcoal that the manu-
facture of barbecue equipment has become big business. However,
an elaborately engineered grill is not necessary to enjoy this newest
form of recreation. Your broiling facilities may be a piece of gridded
iron, salvaged from an old stove and propped up on a pile of rocks,
or it may be a gorgeous stainless steel cookery unit, complete with
an adjustable firebox, an electric spit, and other such luxurious
accouterments. Whatever your financial circumstances, whatever
your available space, you can find some device that will fit your
needs, at a cost of from a few cents to several hundred dollars.

MAKESHIFT GRILLS

A grate from an old oven, propped up on bricks, makes a good one
if yard space is available. Another popular one is a Chinese *wok,* or
the top of an old hotwater tank, set on a tripod or propped steady
with bricks or stones. With this type of grill it's wise to put a few
inches of sand in the bottom to make the fire bed level and to raise
it a bit.

PORTABLE GRILLS

These are of several types, and there are many of them. There is the folding type, usually with a trough-shaped firebox and folding legs, and the bucket type, an insulated pail with a grill top and a cover. The latter offers the advantage of being able to carry the fuel to the picnic, ready to light on the spot. The Japanese hibachis, at least those made of cast iron, may be a little heavy for toting any distance, but they are easily moved from patio to indoor fireplace, or to station wagon. A hibachi is a little portable charcoal stove or "fire bowl," which has been used in Japan for centuries, mostly for heating purposes and keeping tea water hot and hands warm. It has captured the fancy of the American hostess, and hibachis are everywhere. A very small portable grill that sells for a few dollars is designed for individual use—an amusing if not too practical idea. The firebox is necessarily small, so only hors d'oeuvre or minute steaks or hamburgers can be cooked on them. A larger portable grill, one that folds and fits into a carrying case, is useful over outdoor fires or for persons who want to cook in their fireplaces but lack storage space. Then there's a folding device that is light in weight and low in cost. It uses aluminum foil for added heat through reflection.

WHEELED GRILLS

This is probably the most popular kind of barbecue grill. There are four general types. One, the brazier, has a large shallow round firebox with a grill which may or may not be adjustable. Some of these are equipped with spits, either hand or electrically turned. Many families have used and enjoyed this type of barbecue for years. Another is the cart, or wheeled table.

This may be a simple grill with a firebox beneath, or a de luxe job that includes shelves under the firebox, a hood, a warming oven, cutting boards, and a spit, either manual or motor-driven. This is probably the most practical of all grills. We believe that the very fancy ones are no more functional than the simpler ones, but we also think that, if you do more than very occasional charcoal grilling, it is wise to purchase a well-made one with a grill sufficiently large to accommodate food for your usual number of guests, and with an electric spit if you intend to do any roasting. Manually operated spits are picturesque but too laborious for fun. We also believe that a stainless steel grill is a good investment. It requires a modicum of care and will look handsome for years. We recommend one that can be removed from its wheeled base, so that it may be transported in a car or used in brick or stone fireplaces inside or out.

The third type is the vertical grill. With this, the food cooks in front of the fire rather than over it. Some cooks like this idea, claiming that as the fat or baste cannot drip into the coals there will be no flare-up. This we admit to be true, but we believe that neither will there be flaming of the fire if it is properly controlled and, though we do not go all out for *smoke* cookery, we feel that a little flavor of the charcoal adds greatly to the palatability of the meat.

Still another grill is the one with multiple spits. Originally designed for skewer cookery, this type proves very useful for cooking meats and vegetables at the same time. For instance, potatoes can roast on one spit, spareribs on another, and onions on a third. Or lamb chops can broil on a grill while an eggplant and some green peppers turn on adjoining skewers.

Another type of charcoal grill is growing in popularity: the kitchen grill, the very newest thing in the modern home. These are being installed not only in palatial summer residences but in year-round suburban places and winter apartments. Charcoal cookery, it seems, is more than a fad.

Besides your charcoal grill, you will need a few other necessities and perhaps some niceties. Although the market is flooded with trick gimmicks which, supposedly, no charcoal chef can live without, we have kept our list down to a minimum. Few pieces of special equipment are necessary for outdoor cookery. These few, however, are invaluable.

NECESSITIES

✔ A TABLE. This may be a makeshift one, but it should be sturdy and a good working height. One with a hardwood cutting surface is ideal.

✔ GLOVES. Both canvas work gloves and fireproof gloves are all but indispensable. The work gloves are for handling charcoal, a method we think far more efficient than the use of tongs. The fireproof gloves are for use when adjusting spit or roast over the fire, moving the grill, spreading the fire, or other hot jobs.

✔ TONGS. These are invaluable for turning steaks and other broiling foods, and for lifting potatoes from coals, corn from grill, and pots from hooks. They are inexpensive, so it's smart to have more than one pair.

✔ THERMOMETERS. You will see in **Chapter 3,** under the heading **"Temperature of Finished Meat,"** why we consider these important. One should be attached to the spit so that, when turning, you will know the heat to which your meat is subjected. The other thermometer, even more important, is one to determine the interior temperature of the meat that is cooking. We prefer one with a round dial—it is easy to read without performing gymnastics to do so. Regular meat thermometers have one great disadvantage—their lowest temperature marking is usually 140°, making it impossible to get a proper reading for rare meat. We use, instead, a thermometer that registers from 0° to 220°, thus enabling the cook to know when the meat has reached room temperature as well as the cooking one.

✔ SPRINKLER BOTTLE. A large bottle with a sprinkler top, such as is used for dampening clothes. This to douse overexuberant flames.

✔ BASTING BRUSH. We sometimes use a faggot of parsley or other herbs, but we have to admit that a good long-handled pastry brush does a better if not so picturesque job. We both reject, and violently, the use of a cotton dish mop as a swab.

✔ PLIERS. These are necessary for tightening the holding forks, if your spit is round, or for squaring up the spitted meat before balancing, if your spit is square.

✔ HINGED BROILERS. One will do, but three is the ideal number:

1. A basket grill—a sort of shallow hinged box made of wire with a long handle—is perfect for thick, whole fish, lobster, chickens, and other foods that may be difficult to turn. It is also obviously quicker to turn five or six at one time than to do them individually.

2. A hinged grill with medium grids for thinner pieces of tender meat, such as fish fillets or steaks, sweetbreads, and such.

3. A hinged broiler with fine grids for such small tidbits as oysters, kidneys, chicken livers, and shrimps.

✔ DRIP PANS. These are essential for all spit roasting. Properly placed, they will catch all the drippings from a roast as the spit turns, preventing the fat from dropping into the coals and causing a conflagration, as explained in **Chapter 2**, under the heading "**Flaring.**"

✔ SKEWERS. These are necessary for shish kebab, shaslik, and all foods cooked *en brochette*. They may be simple ones of metal or wood, or elaborate steel ones with wooden or decorative handles. Heavy wire with an end looped for a handle is a satisfactory improvisation. Also inexpensive bamboo chopsticks may be split and used, though they should be soaked in water 1 hour to prevent their burning.

NICETIES

✔ UTENSILS. It is fine to have special knives and long-handled forks and spoons for your outdoor cooking, but ordinary utensils, borrowed from the kitchen, will do nicely. Better your pet sharp kitchen knife that can be honed to razor sharpness than the indifferently bladed one with a fancy handle in a matching "barbecue set."

✔ SALTS AND PEPPERS. A large pepper mill that grinds coarsely, or, even better, one that can be regulated from fine to very coarse is helpful. Also a large shaker with big holes for coarse salt. We like kosher salt because it *is* coarse.

✔ APRONS. We see the advantage of an apron, but we think that a plain bibbed one, made of heavy duck or denim, can be used both indoors and out. As for those with "funny" slogans and decorations, we don't find them irresistible.

✔ TOWELS AND POT HOLDERS. These are important, but again may come from the kitchen. Large pot holders with rings, for hanging close by the grill, are indeed handy, and so is a towel rack within reach. Paper towels, as in the kitchen, are invaluable.

✔ CARRYALL. It is nice to have a handled wicker or wire basket, or one of the wooden tool trays that carpenters carry. Herbs and other seasonings and all small utensils may thus be carried to the scene of the cooking.

✔ CARVING BOARDS. These, too, may come from the house, but they are important for both cutting meat before and carving it after the cooking. Have good sturdy ones of hardwood—perhaps two or three of different sizes.

electrical equipment

Electrical equipment has an important place in outside cooking. Porch, patio, and terrace are all close enough for connections, and the use of many of the new portable appliances will give added pleasure and ease to dining al fresco. They serve two functions: the cook is enabled, if there is but one, to officiate at the charcoal grill and at the same time to enjoy the guests and prepare such last-minute dishes as are not cooked over charcoal; and the food will be freshly made and piping hot come serving time.

THE ELECTRIC BROILER AND ROTISSERIE

Perhaps the most popular of appliances for outdoor use is the electric broiler and rotisserie. This either to take the place of the charcoal unit or as an auxiliary to it. There are many families who enjoy cooking and eating outside but who, for one reason or another, are unable or unwilling to use a charcoal fire. The electric broiler and rotisserie is their next best bet. Almost all the recipes for broiled and roasted foods given in this book may be used in this kind of electrical unit, and in most cases the cooking times are the same. The only exception is in roasting large pieces of meat, for there are few rotisseries on the market that will accommodate a 20-pound turkey or a 5-rib roast. Watching a piece of meat turn in an electric rotisserie is almost as enchanting as when the fuel is charcoal. The only real difference is in the lack of charcoal flavor in the food. This deficiency some cooks attempt to overcome by seasoning the meat with charcoal salt or liquid smoke. We reject this method because, to us, it has an artificial flavor. What's more, we see no need for it —most meats either broiled or roasted in these infrared appliances are sensationally good eating. For using them, follow the instructions that accompany them and use the recipes in this book.

ELECTRIC SKILLETS AND FRYING PANS

These appliances are most useful for outdoor dining. Anything that is to be sautéed may be done in them, and in addition the deeper kind may be used as "cookers," for casserole dishes, beans, stews, spoon breads, and the like. They are also invaluable for **sukiyaki,** a dish that fits beautifully with the informality of eating outside. What's more, they have controlled heat, so that they require less attention than range- or grill-heated skillets or saucepans. When recipes in this book may be prepared in one, we indicate the fact.

DEEP FAT FRYERS

Here's another kitchen appliance that takes to the great outdoors. French fried potatoes and freshly fried doughnuts are two deep-fried foods that go perfectly with outside eating—the first with any and all grilled meats and fish; the second for breakfast, lunch, or supper served under the sky. The deep fryer has other uses, of course: delicate corn fritters to serve with broiled chicken, tiny savory croquettes that make perfect appetizers, delectable *beignets des fruits* for summer desserts . . .

ELECTRIC COOKERS

This is an auxiliary appliance that will serve you well. For soups, especially those hearty soup-stews that are so right for outdoor appetites; for casserole dishes, too, long- or short-cooking ones. The electric cooker (and the electric bean pot, as well) will produce many main dishes, or dishes that are perfect accompaniments for the yield of the grill. Recipes will be found in **Chapter 16.**

CHAFING DISHES

We include here chafing dishes that are heated by alcohol as well as electric ones. The latter, however, are faster and so more suitable for actual cooking, while the slower ones do nicely for keeping food warm. Also, the deep-type automatic skillet makes a fine electric chafing dish—actually better than most, because the heat can be regulated. You will find the chafing dish ideally suited for meat sauces (see **Chapter 20**), as well as for appetizers, meat accompaniments, and desserts.

HOT TRAYS AND TABLES

These electrically heated trays, and the wheeled tables with their tops heated the same way, are niceties for outdoor service. Dishes prepared either inside or out can be kept at eating temperature. Dishes kept warm by candles serve the same purpose, but not so efficiently. They are, however, far better than risking cold food.

OTHER ELECTRIC APPLIANCES

To say that the electric blender and the electric mixer are especially adapted to the outdoors would be to exaggerate, but certainly both are useful in the preparation of food indoors, and many cooks use the blender for iced summer drinks and cold soups that are made on the scene. The coffee maker is as useful outdoors as it is in, and the electric grill, toaster, and waffle maker are all ideal for breakfasting on the porch or patio.

PRESSURE COOKERS

Although this is not electric (at least we don't *know* of an electric one), the pressure cooker is invaluable for some types of outdoor cooking. Campers, especially those vacationing at high altitudes, find they make cooking far easier and quicker, and save fuel as well. Yachtsmen, trailer travelers, and other cooks who are handicapped by a shortage of fuel find a pressure cooker of great value. Recipes for its use will be found in **Chapter 22.**

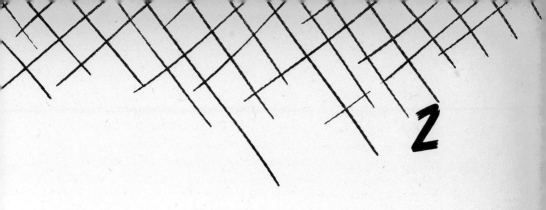

FIRE
AND FUEL

Anyone who can cook cannot necessarily cook over coals. What came naturally to our ancestors—the making of a cooking fire—has been almost entirely supplanted by the use of gas and electricity. Yet a generation that eagerly discarded the coal range as a nuisance has just as eagerly taken up cooking over charcoal. That these new enthusiasts sometimes go to unnecessarily laborious lengths to achieve a proper fire is unfortunately true. Actually the task should be an easy one, and will be if this simple method is followed.

FUEL

There are three customary fuels for cooking over coals. *Wood,* not often used, is ideal. It should, however, be sweet-tasting and non-resinous, such as wood of any fruit or nut tree, or grapevine, or a hardwood such as hickory, oak, or maple. *Charcoal,* made from hardwood and available in various-sized chunks, is perhaps the most frequently used fuel. Lastly, there are *briquets,* which may be made of charcoal, anthracite, or some by-product such as fruit pits.

Which is best? Wood is fine and what's more it's fun, but it does take time to burn into a deep bed of coals. If both it *and* time are available, by all means use it. Charcoal is the favorite of many.

Its only disadvantage is that the different-sized pieces sometimes make an evenly burning fire a little difficult. This may be avoided by making little pieces out of the big ones. Charcoal briquets are probably the most satisfactory of all. We have been using them almost exclusively of late. There are, however, several different kinds. The kind we prefer are made from hardwood charcoal. They are available in boxes and bags of various sizes. If you do a lot of charcoal cooking, the largest will be the economy size. The anthracite briquets have recently appeared in small bags, complete with a starter. Just light the bag and forget it until the coals are ready. For ease and cleanliness of handling these are excellent, especially for small portable grills. The third type are briquets made from by-products, such as fruit pits. These are fine, but they burn very hot, so care must be taken in their use. It is well to get to know one type of charcoal and stick to it. This because there is considerable variation in the heats they produce.

KINDLING

Gone are the days when fire building started with wood chopping and ended with much huffing and puffing to get the thing going. However, this method is still sometimes resorted to, and should be understood. Crumple newspaper sheets into balls and pile 5 or 6 in a heap. Around them lay slender dry sticks of wood, tepee fashion, and light. When the wood is burning merrily, chop some charcoal into the flames. Add to the fire by putting more fuel around the edge and raking it in as it ignites.

THE EASY WAY

Use a commercial kindling fluid, tablet, flare, or jelly, but make sure it's an odorless one. Unpleasant fumes are apt to linger and add their odor to the meat. We use, and highly recommend, an odorless paint thinner which we buy by the gallon at any paint or hardware store. Make a heap of charcoal or briquets (or of small logs, if you are using wood). It is best to build up the charcoal into a pyramid, using, for the average fire, about 35 to 40 briquets, or the equivalent in charcoal. Pour about ½ cup of the fluid over the top of the heap, allowing it to stand for 2 or 3 minutes before lighting. The fire should be ready to use in half an hour, or when the fuel is completely ignited and a little white ash begins to show.

Another good way to light any charcoal fire is to put briquets or pieces of charcoal in a can and fill with the thinner or other kindling fluid. Cover tightly and let stand anywhere from an hour to several days. Put a few of these "marinated" briquets in a little heap, pile more fuel over them, and light. This is a particularly safe way when using a portable grill that might leak if the fluid were poured directly on the fuel.

FIRE SIZE

We have discovered that most charcoal cooks make much larger fires than necessary. We have also found that a fire may be added to at will, as long as it is not allowed to die too low. The original size of the fire is regulated by two factors: the capacity of the firebox and the size of the food to be cooked. A small portable grill or hibachi will need only 12 to 24 briquets to cook the portions to which it is adapted. For a larger wheeled or permanently fixed grill, a fire of from 30 to 40 briquets (or a like amount of charcoal) is usually sufficient to begin with. If the roast is a large one, such as a turkey, more fuel must be added later. This is done by edging the burning coals with more briquets and raking them in as they ignite.

FIRE FOR COOKING

Half an hour or a little longer after lighting, the fire is ready for cooking. It should be spread evenly with a poker or other such device, so that the space covered by the burning coals is a little greater than the surface of the meat. The cooking should start with the fire at the greatest distance from the food, so that as it cools it can be adjusted closer for more heat—unless, of course, you want first to sear whatever you are cooking.

FIRE AND HEAT CONTROL

Here's where many charcoal cooks have trouble. Unless your grill has either an adjustable firebox or grill (one that may be raised or lowered), you will have to control the heat (and consequently the speed of cooking) by spreading the coals or by dousing a too hot fire with water. Another way is to cook in a long-handled hinged broiler, which may be raised or lowered by hand, but this makes a chore of what should be a pleasure. Of course makeshift devices such as bricks propped under the grill may be used. Often, if the fire seems too low as the cooking is nearing completion, a little extra heat may be generated by brushing or flicking the white ash from the top of the dying coals.

COOKING TEMPERATURES

Low temperatures are best for most cooking over coals. The temperature for broiling should be greater than that for roasting. We have, with the invaluable help of General Harold Bartron, done much experimenting with the actual temperatures of the coals at both fire and grill level, and have found it surprising how those temperatures vary. Just above the coal level a fire may be 600°, while at the grill level (6 or 7 inches away) it will be closer to 350°, and a pyrometer which is actually in the coals will register 1200° or more. For most charcoal broiling, 275° to 375° is a good all-around heat to maintain at grill level. A thermometer fixed to the spit and turning with it will usually register from 225° to 275°. This is because it cools as it turns away from the fire, then heats up again as it nears the fire.

Although we advocate the use of a spit or grill thermometer for judging the temperature of a fire, we admit that, just as Grandmother could judge her oven with her hand, so an expert can judge his fire heat. One such expert, Jorge Ramirez, who ran the Acme Barbecue College in Alhambra, California, taught his "students" to judge fire by counting. A slow fire (one of 275° or less), he said, is one over which you can hold your hand at meat level for 4 seconds, a medium fire (300°) takes a 3-second count, and 2 seconds indicate a fast (325°) fire. Ramirez counted seconds by saying, "Hippopotamus one, hippopotamus two," and so on.

FLARING

Sometimes, when the food is fat, or when an oily baste is used, the charcoals will flare into flames. This is not good except when a real "char" on the outside of steaks, or an especially crispy skin on poultry, is wanted. In that case, many chefs allow flaring or even encourage it, until the outside of the meat is all but black. We like ours crisply, darkly brown, but will stop this side of the cinder stage. To control this unwanted flaring, douse with water from a sprinkler-top bottle, or from a spray gun filled with water. Of course the best way to control flaring is to prevent it, by keeping fat from falling into the hot coals. Trimming excess fat is one way to do this; another is to be sure that the spit turns away from you at the top of the turn, so that the meat is coming toward you and the front of the grill at the bottom of the turn. It is at this point that the grease drops, so the fire may be pushed back of this spot and the fat caught in a narrow shallow pan or a double fold of aluminum foil, just under the drip. In this way no grease will go into the coals. Another way to catch the grease is to have a circle of coals with a drip pan in their center. Many cooks use this system when broiling as well as roasting.

TECHNICALITIES

Cooking over charcoal, once thought to be mastered only by years of practice, is becoming as much a science as an art. Certainly, as in any other form of cookery, technique improves with practice, but there are a few facts and mechanical aids that the novice will find invaluable and the experienced cook may also welcome. They relate to temperature and timing. The temperature of the fire has already been discussed in **Chapter 2.** The internal temperatures of the foods before and after cooking are even more important.

TEMPERATURE OF FOOD
BEFORE COOKING

It stands to reason that a piece of meat, fish, or poultry, taken directly from the refrigerator and being, therefore, about 40° throughout, will take longer to cook than a like piece of meat at room temperature (70°). Which is best?

The answer is: "It depends." That, we assure you, is not evasive. If you are cooking a thin steak, say a flank, and want it crisply brown outside and juicily rare within, take it directly from the refrigerator to the grill. On the other hand, a very thick steak, handled in a like manner, may still be cold inside though the outside looks and smells superlative. The thick steak should be cooked after it has reached room temperature. The crispiness of its outside can be regulated by the heat of the fire. Room temperature is also recommended if you like your meat cooked evenly throughout. So it depends, you see, both on your personal preference for rare or well-done meat and on the thickness or contours of the food to be cooked. Large pieces of meat, especially roasts, should usually be started at room temperature.

TIME REQUIRED

Remember that it takes a long time for a large piece of meat to reach room temperature after it has been taken from the refrigerator, and a much longer time when it has been frozen. A medium-sized refrigerated turkey, for instance, will take as long as 8 hours to reach room temperature, while a frozen one will take 24 hours or more. The meat thermometer which we describe below, because its graduations begin at zero, will be of tremendous help in determining when your meat is ready for cooking. In case you have not allowed enough time for the warming up, cook more slowly than usual.

FROZEN MEAT

Although we prefer unfrozen meat for charcoal cooking, we realize that many persons depend upon their freezers for much of their meat and all of their game. It is therefore necessary to discuss it. While it is often recommended that meat be put in the oven in the frozen state, to preserve the juice, we don't feel this is a good idea when cooking over charcoal. The loss of juices will not be great if the meat doesn't stand too long after thawing, and it will be much easier to spit and cook evenly after reaching that point. This applies to roasts and other large pieces of meat. With thin steaks it's different. Unless you like them evenly cooked all the way through, they may go from freezer to grill with success, though the time required to cook them is necessarily much longer. We took three identical steaks—Spencers (steaks cut from the ribs) 1 inch thick —for an experiment. (Too thin for good eating, but we were proving a point.) One steak was put on the grill frozen solid, one was thawed but at refrigerator temperature, and the third was at room temperature. To reach the same degree of rareness, the first took 25 minutes, the second 13 minutes, and the third only 8 minutes! So you see . . .

TEMPERATURE OF FINISHED MEAT

This is an important subject, and one not too well understood by most cooks. One reason for this, according to Mr. Ben Levy, long in the meat business, is the meat thermometer used in most home kitchens. Mr. Levy introduced us to one used in laboratories. It is more accurate, reacts faster, and its graduations go from 0° to 220°.* As we discovered for ourselves, and both Mr. Levy and General Bartron confirm, beef not removed from the grill until it reaches 140° is *not* rare. There are two reasons for this: one is that the meat continues to cook after it leaves the fire; the other is that even 140° is too well done for people who like blood-rare beef. Therefore, in our charts, we include an extra category—very rare.

We can't be too emphatic about recommending the use of a meat thermometer when cooking large pieces of meat over charcoal. With smaller pieces, such as steaks, the knife test may be used (cutting and looking). Even if you don't agree with the recommended temperatures on a meat thermometer, you can take (and write down) the temperature of the roast you consider perfectly cooked. Cook it to within ten degrees of that temperature, lower the heat to 100° or less, and let it "coast" until you're ready to eat. Be sure, however, that the thermometer is inserted in the thickest part of the meat, and is not touching either fat or bone.

TIMING IN CHARCOAL COOKERY

Here is another big IF. Accurate timing is absolutely impossible, even as it is, we feel, in oven cookery. The main reasons are those already discussed—the temperature of the food when it starts cooking and the temperature of the fire. When cooking outdoors, still another element enters—the temperature of the atmosphere and the prevailing winds. Over two fires of apparently the same temperature, on identical grills, we have cooked two identical **Spencer** roasts—same size, same temperature—and had one take half an hour longer to cook to the same degree as the other. Why? One grill was turned so that the meat on it had more breeze than the meat on the other.

* Thermometers that register from 0° to 220° are now readily available.

BROILING OVER CHARCOAL

This is the simplest form of charcoal cookery, and is the only one practiced by many outdoor cooks. A proper fire for broiling usually registers, at grill level, about 350°. It is not so important to have an exact temperature as it is to have one that doesn't fluctuate too much. If it is desirable to have a brown crust on the outside of the food, it should be seared first by broiling close to the coals, then finished by adjusting the grill at a greater distance. (For a real char, relished by many, allow a period of actual flaming.) If, on the other hand, evenly cooked meat is desired, use the same temperature throughout the cooking, and turn often, using tongs instead of a fork. (Meat pierced with a fork may lose some of its juices.)

SALTING

Two other questions come up often when charcoal broiling is discussed. One is, "When do you salt?" We believe that salting before cooking may start the juices running, so that it is better to reserve that task until the meat is almost, or completely, done.

BASTING

The other question, and this one is fought bitterly over many a grill, is whether to baste or not to baste. When it comes to beefsteak, we say—and say again—*don't*. To ruin the flavor of a good piece of beef with highly seasoned barbecue sauces is, to us, a culinary crime. (However, if you *like* your own basting sauce, use it by all means!) We would rather melt a great dollop of butter on our steak and let its molten gold mingle with the ruddy juices. Or, if sauce we must have, we choose a classic one (from **Chapter 20**). The above advice does not, however, apply to all meats (as explained in **Chapter 7**).

ROASTING OVER COALS

Many experts claim that this is the only true roasting, that meat cooked in an oven is baked. Certainly, charcoal-roasted meat tastes better than meat cooked any other way. Our ancestors cooked their meat before a fire and laboriously turned the spit so that the roast would brown evenly. Later they employed the unwilling services of a spit dog, and still later invented clock spits that did the job effectively. Today we have electric spits, and it is a beautiful sight to see a roaster or a chicken turning on one, and acquiring a heavenly brown glaze as it evenly bastes itself with its own juices. It looks effortless, and so it is, once the roast is properly spitted and balanced.

✔ SPITTING THE MEAT. This, we are frank to admit, takes experience and practice. The object is to have the meat secured to the spit so that, as nearly as possible, it is in balance (the spit passing through the center of gravity), and so that it is compact and well fastened, turning with the spit, not slipping around on it. This means not only that the meat should be tied or trussed securely but also that the holding forks on the spit must be properly placed and tightened. The trick, of course, is to have the wings and/or legs held close to the body, so that they will not dry out but will baste along with the rest of the bird or animal. When cooking boned and rolled roasts, chances are that you will have your meat man tie them for you, though it is a simple matter to do it yourself.

✔ BALANCING THE MEAT. This procedure is the most important part of spit roasting. If the meat is not in balance, the spit will turn jerkily, the food will brown unevenly, and there's a good chance that the motor, unable to stand the strain, will stop. With a manual spit, perfect balance is not important, but the whole business is so laborious that the operator may stop.

There are two necessary procedures in balancing, in addition to proper tying and trussing. The first is, as we said above, to have the spit as nearly as possible through the center of gravity of the meat. This, we believe, is best shown in the diagrams. The other trick, one that we learned from General Bartron, is to use a compensator. Several such devices are on the market, but we have seen none like the one he designed. It consists of a threaded rod fastened to the holding fork, on which compensating weights may be screwed. The big advantage of General Bartron's compensator is that balance may be adjusted *during* cooking, without the messy and tedious task of respitting. As fat renders out while the meat cooks, such readjustment is often necessary.

Do have your meat balanced before you put it over the fire. This can be judged by balancing it between the hands, or between two props of equal height. If using a compensator, spit the meat so that the heavy part is at the bottom, then add weights until the compensator rod is horizontal.

The roasting procedure is very much the same as that for broiling, except that a slightly lower temperature (about 250° at spit level) is recommended. As in broiling, the salt is better added toward the end of the cooking, and the matter of basting depends upon the fat—or lack of it. Like steaks, roasts shouldn't be pierced any more than absolutely necessary and some excellent cooks recommend leaving the meat on the spit for half an hour or so after it is removed from the fire, so that withdrawal will not waste the juices.

A GUIDE FOR CHARCOAL BROILING AND ROASTING

time and temperature

These approximate times are figures for food that is at room temperature (70°) and for a fire that registers about 350° at grill level, or 250° on the spit thermometer. (Internal temperatures are marked with an asterisk.)

STEAKS

THICKNESS	VERY RARE 120°–130°*	RARE 130°–140°*	MEDIUM 140°–160°*	WELL DONE 160°–170°*
1 inch	6–10 min.	8–12 min.	12–15 min.	Up to 20 min.
1½ inches	8–12 min.	10–14 min.	14–18 min.	Up to 25 min.
2 inches	14–20 min.	18–30 min.	25–35 min.	Up to 60 min.
2½ inches	20–30 min.	30–35 min.	35–45 min.	Up to 75 min.
3 inches	*Allow a little more time for this size steak. As it is almost roast-thick, it may be judged by its internal temperature, marked with asterisk.*			

roasts

STANDING RIB ROAST

These times are figured for a 5-rib standing roast. Because the diameter of this cut of meat is almost the same no matter what its length, the timing doesn't vary much with different-sized roasts. (It may be a slightly shorter time for ribs cut from the small end, and vice versa.) Let your meat thermometer be your guide. With the internal temperature being judged from the middle of the roast, the smaller slices will be slightly better done than the larger ones. That's fine, as everybody doesn't have the same taste. A rolled rib roast will take a few more minutes to cook than the standing one.

VERY RARE, 120° to 130°*	1¾ to 2¼ hours
RARE, 130° to 140°*	2 to 2½ hours
MEDIUM, 140° to 150°*	2½ to 3 hours
WELL DONE, up to 170°*	3 to 4 hours

SPENCER ROAST

A whole Spencer roast (a rib roast with the bone removed) will weigh about 16 pounds, and will take from 1½ hours to cook very rare, to 3¼ hours for a well-done roast. Use the meat thermometer and cook to the temperature recommended for **standing rib roasts.**

EYE OF THE RIB

This is just the lean round piece in the middle of the rib—the Spencer with the outside meat and fat removed. It will take from 1½ to 2¾ hours. Cook like a **Spencer,** but lard it.

TENDERLOIN

A tenderloin may be either spitted or cooked right on the grill. In the latter case, cook it as you would a steak of like thickness. Spitted, it will take about 25 minutes for very rare, if not larded. A tenderloin that is both larded and barded (wrapped with sliced salt pork) may take much longer—up to an hour. Use the meat thermometer and you won't be disappointed.

ROAST LEG OF LAMB

RARE, 140°*	1 to 1¼ hours
MEDIUM RARE, 145° to 150°*	1½ hours
MEDIUM, 150° to 160°*	1½ to 2 hours
WELL DONE, up to 175°*	2 to 2½ hours

BONED SHOULDER OF LAMB

RARE, 140°*	1 to 1¼ hours
MEDIUM RARE, 145° to 150°*	1½ hours
MEDIUM, 150° to 160°*	1½ to 2 hours
WELL DONE, up to 175°*	2 to 2½ hours

NOTE: Mutton should be eaten rare, lamb rare to medium rare, in our opinion.

ROAST TURKEY

A turkey may be roasted either stuffed or not, as you wish. The cooking time may be a bit longer when it is stuffed, because the heat strikes from the outside only. An unstuffed turkey of approximately 15 pounds, eviscerated weight, will take about 3 hours to roast on the spit. A meat thermometer may be used, but a more accurate test is to pull the leg. When it moves easily, the turkey is done. If a thermometer is used, cook to 170° and allow to coast until 180° is reached—this with the thermometer in the thickest part of the thigh.

ROAST CHICKEN

A chicken or duck, spit-roasted, will take from 1 to 1½ hours, depending on the size. Use the leg test for doneness (see **roast turkey**, above).

OTHER POULTRY

DUCKLING, 4–6 lbs.: 1 to 1½ hours

CORNISH GAME HENS, about 1½ lbs.: ¾ to 1 hour

GOOSE, 10 to 15 lbs.: 2 to 3 hours

SQUAB, ¾–1¼ lbs: ¾ to 1¼ hours

RABBIT, 3–5 lbs.: 40 minutes to 2 hours

WILD DUCK, 1–2½ lbs.: 20 to 30 minutes

WILD GOOSE, 5–8 lbs.: 45 minutes to 1¼ hours

FRESH LOIN OF PORK

As pork should not be eaten until well done, we have no variations as to cooking time. A loin, over a medium low fire, will take about 2 to 2½ hours to cook to 160°. It is then coasted until it reaches 165°, which gives you a perfectly cooked piece of meat, with white juicy flesh. (All danger of trichinosis is eliminated when the temperature reaches 150°.)

ROAST FRESH HAM

A 12-pound fresh ham (leg of pork), over a medium low fire, will take about 4 hours to reach 160°. Coast to 165°.

ROAST VEAL

A rolled roast of veal, weighing about 3 pounds, will take about 45 minutes to 1 hour to roast to 160°. It should then coast, and be eaten at 165° to 170°.

LAMB AND MUTTON
CHOPS AND STEAKS

THICKNESS	RARE 140°*	MEDIUM RARE 145°–150°*	MEDIUM 150°–160°*	WELL DONE UP–175°*
1 inch	5–6 min.	6–14 min.	14–18 min.	18–25 min.
1½ inches	6–8 min.	8–16 min.	12–20 min.	20–30 min.
2 inches	9–12 min.	12–20 min.	20–25 min.	25–35 min.

NOTE: We believe that mutton is best served rare, lamb rare or medium rare. Thus the latter category is added here.

VEAL CHOPS AND STEAKS

Veal should be well done but not dried out. Therefore it should be cooked to the minimum allowed for "well done" in the **chart** for **lamb and mutton chops**. The meat thermometer, if the cut is large enough to use it, should read from 165° to 170°—never over. Properly cooked veal is white, but not gray-white, and should be juicy.

PORK CHOPS AND STEAKS

THICKNESS	TIME
1 inch	25–30 min.
1½ inches	30–45 min.
2 inches	40–60 min.
2½ inches	55–75 min.

NOTE: Pork should always be cooked until well done, but not dry. As today's pork is quite lean, care must be taken to keep it moist. Baste frequently with a blend of white wine and melted butter or oil.

BROILED POULTRY

CHICKEN, split: 25–45 min.

DUCK, split: 30–50 min.

SQUAB, split: 25–35 min.

TURKEY, 3½ to 5½ pounds, split: 40–50 min.

TURKEY STEAKS, 1 inch thick: 30–45 min.
2 inches thick: 1 hour

HAM STEAKS

THICKNESS	TIME
¾ inch	25–30 min.
1 inch	30–35 min.
1½ inches	35–45 min.
2 inches	45–60 min.

LIVER

THICKNESS	RARE	MEDIUM	WELL DONE
½ inch	6 min.	8 min.	12 min.
1 inch	10 min.	12 min.	18 min.
1½ inches	15 min.	18 min.	22 min.
2 inches	18 min.	22 min.	25 min.

fish

These times are approximate only, because of variable conditions. To test fish for doneness, use a fork—if it flakes easily and has lost its translucent look, it's done.*

FISH STEAKS

THICKNESS	TIME
1 inch	6–9 min.
1½ inches	8–12 min.
2 inches	10–18 min.

FISH FILLETS

6–18 min., depending on thickness

SPLIT FISH

SMALL: 8–12 min.

WHOLE FISH

SMALL: 12–18 min.   SMALL *(foil wrapped):* 18–25 min.

WHOLE FISH, large: 30–60 min. ⎫ or until flesh
SPLIT FISH, large: 20–40 min. ⎭ flakes easily

WHOLE FISH, ROASTED ON SPIT

A firm-fleshed fish, such as an albacore, weighing about 10 pounds after cleaning and with head and tail removed, will take from 50 to 70 minutes. Cook to internal temperature of 130° to 135°.

* In later years Beard adopted the Canadian Fisheries Council rule for cooking fish by any method, which is: Cook for ten minutes per inch of thickness, measuring fish at the thickest point.

STEAKS

5

Think of charcoal broiling and almost everyone thinks first of steaks. This is not for lack of imagination, but rather that they are such good eating. So, though we cook almost everything else on the grill as well, we begin with this prime favorite. It's our contention that, though a plain and perfectly broiled steak is beef perfection, even that delight may pall if served too often. Therefore we give you variations—classic recipes that taste even better outdoors than in a distinguished restaurant.

selection of steaks

When buying a beefsteak, consider the number of people to be served, the cooking area of your grill, and the amount of money you plan to spend—which means what cut and grade you'll purchase.

✔ SERVINGS. For the average appetite, ½ to 1 pound of steak is not too much to allow. Minute steaks and filets mignons do run smaller—about 6 ounces each—but they are usually served at lunch or for lighter meals. Frankly, ½ pound each has rarely seemed enough for the hearty appetites of our friends.

✔ COOKING AREA. If your grill is small and your party large, cook one large thick steak, as it can be sliced to make the rounds. If a large grill is available, or the party small, individual steaks are in order.

✔ GRADES. Sometimes it is wiser to buy a less choice *cut* of top-grade meat than a preferred cut of lower grade. Sometimes vice versa. Cozy up to your butcher and discuss the matter with him. If he realizes you know what you want and are willing to pay for it, he'll probably be your slave. Certainly U.S. Prime Grade beef is the best for steaks. However, Choice Grade is also excellent—in fact it is the best grade available at most markets.

You can, of course, use a meat tenderizer with the tougher cuts of beef and get most satisfactory results. And if you do use one, use just a little more than the directions suggest and let it stand a shorter time for the best results. We prefer to purchase the non-seasoned variety, so that we won't lose the fine flavor of the beef itself.

Aging of beef is something of prime importance to the cook; aged beef is tenderer, it is better-flavored. The comparatively small shop of Arsène Tingaud in New York for many years did a very special aging job for several of the famous eating houses of the metropolis, and was known to age and send beef to restaurants and individuals as far away as the British West Indies. In the big box at Tingaud's, you could see short loins and racks hanging, in all degrees of aging. Some—and these were for one of the top restaurants—had green mold on the outside an inch long. Others had to hang so many weeks after they arrived in Tingaud's shop.* Nowadays packaged meat departments have largely supplanted the custom cutter, so it is increasingly hard to know your butcher. But in every town of any size there are a few left who know and love good meat. It will be worth your while to seek out one of them.

CUTS

Look for well-marbled, cherry-red, velvety-looking beef, with a creamy fat which is rather flaky in spots. (That is especially true so far as the kidney fat is concerned.) The following are the cuts to look for:

* Editor's note: Beard's custom butcher in the latter part of his life was Jefferson Market in New York.

✔ TENDERLOIN. This is considered to be the top steak to serve, although many think that other cuts have finer texture, better flavor, and certainly the blessing of good fat. The lower-grade tenderloins are better buys, for they have less fat and, some claim, more flavor. A whole tenderloin is a fine buy for a large party—it can be cooked whole and sliced to great advantage. It is boneless and usually has a minimum of fat, so its price is within reason. Its several cuts—tournedos, Chateaubriands, filets, and filets mignons —we will discuss later.

✔ PORTERHOUSE and T-BONE. These are practically the same cut, and are often confused. They are cut from the short loin, and the porterhouse comes from the part nearest the round, or hind leg. Next comes the T-bone, then the club steak. Therefore, the porterhouse is the steak with the greatest amount of tenderloin, the club having none. Porterhouse or T-bone should be cut thick—2 to 3 inches—and when cut should weigh from 3 to 4½ pounds.

✔ RIB STEAKS. Sometimes known as entrecôtes, club steaks, minute steaks. For minute steaks they should be cut about ½ to 1 inch thick. For club steaks, about 1½ to 2 inches thick. The gauchos of the Pampas used to cut their steaks one whole rib per person, with bone. The bone was the only utensil used for eating, and very handy it was, too. Try them for an outdoor boys' party.

✔ SPENCER STEAKS. These are rib steaks with the bone removed; sometimes, also, with the coarser meat and fat removed, leaving only the "eye" of the rib. They are very choice. Have them cut 1 to 2 inches thick and cook like tenderloin steak.

✔ BONELESS LOIN or STRIP STEAK. Sometimes called contra filet. This is the strip of meat, with or without bone, which is left when the filet is removed from the short loin (the porterhouse without the filet and bone). It is what is usually served in restaurants as loin strip New York cut—a name, by the way, which is unknown in that city. For one person the steak should be cut 1½ inches thick—a very generous portion. For two persons, cut this steak 2 to 2½ inches thick, and for four diners either broil two of these, or have one cut about 4 inches thick and carve it in thinnish diagonal slices.

✔ RUMP STEAK. Steak cut from the rump of a young steer is boneless as well as being delicious and tender, and broils exceedingly well. In fact, in many European countries, it is considered one of the choicest cuts for grilling. Have rump steak cut from 2 to 3 inches thick, from top-grade beef.

✔ BONELESS TOP SIRLOIN. In today's method of meat-cutting, such cuts as pinbone and wedgebone sirloin, as well as whole sirloin steaks, are practically obsolete and have been replaced by the boneless top sirloin, which is often offered whole, in Cryovac, at very special prices. It is from the end of the loin and is of excellent quality, with perhaps the best flavor of any steak cut from the loin. It may be cut into individual steaks or cut thick and sliced for serving. It is excellent for steak sandwiches, and makes an admirable roast as well.

✔ CHUCK STEAK. Chuck steak cut from top-grade beef can be broiled successfully, especially if it is marinated or tenderized in advance. It is meat of excellent flavor and good texture, which is usually considerably less in price than other cuts. It may be cut thick or thin.

✔ FLANK STEAK. This is a triangular-shaped piece of meat cut from the inside of a flank of beef.

broiling beef steaks

BROILED TENDERLOIN OF BEEF
(FILET DE BOEUF GRILLÉ)

This is party fare, although not so extravagant as you may think (see description under the heading "Cuts" in this chapter). Purchase a whole filet or several pounds of the cut in one piece. Have the butcher tie it for you or, if you are adept at such things, do it yourself so that you have a well-formed roll of meat. Grill the meat over the coals until properly rare—use your meat thermometer. It is wise to baste the filet or brush it with butter fairly often; this lubricates the meat, which might otherwise become a little dry. Salt and pepper it when it is just about ready to serve. Remove from the grill to a hot platter or board, and serve in fairly thick slices. Be sure to catch the juices as you are carving and spoon them over the meat. Serve with great baked potatoes and a tray of accompaniments such as grated cheese, sour cream, chives, crumbled bacon.

CHÂTEAUBRIAND

Originally this steak was a preposterous extravagance: a thick tenderloin was grilled between two lesser steaks, after which the latter were discarded. Today it is still luxurious, but wonderful for a fancy outdoor party. Have thick (2 to 2½ inches) steaks cut from the heavy part of the tenderloin, broil to your liking, and serve with **Châteaubriand** or **Béarnaise sauce.** With them have shoestring potatoes, made outdoors if you wish, in your electric fryer, and tiny green peas cooked with little lettuce leaves and bits of ham. A good red wine is in order.

TOURNEDOS BÉARNAISE

Don't give this dish to your fanciest friends—they no doubt have it frequently. Serve them grilled eel or roasted kidneys, and save this to delight those friends who seldom enjoy such treats.

A tournedos is cut from the filet after it has been surrounded with a blanket of pounded suet and tied well. Each one should be cut about 1½ or 2 inches thick, and grilled over charcoal not too long. Salt and pepper them to taste and serve with **Béarnaise sauce,** tiny new potatoes smothered in butter and sprinkled with chopped parsley and chives, tender green beans cooked whole and served with slivered almonds, and a bottle of Vosne Romanée or a Pinot Noir. Finish off with chilled melon with a dash of port wine, and plenty of coffee.

FILET MIGNON

This is not what everyone thinks it is—a tenderloin steak. It is, rather, the small end of the tenderloin which sometimes is triangular in shape and has to be flattened or rolled. It is a tender morsel, and if rolled and wrapped with a thin sheet of suet or with strips of bacon, it makes a delicious treat for the outdoor grill. Brush the small filets with butter and broil very quickly, being certain that they get a chance to brown but remain rare and juicy on the inside. Salt and pepper them, and serve with a **potato casserole,** and perhaps a great salad of mixed greens with or without an oil dressing. Sometimes merely mixed greens with salt and pepper and lemon juice are pleasanter than the usual dressed salad.

FILET MIGNON, TARRAGON

Melt 4 tablespoons of butter and add 1 teaspoon of salt, 3 tablespoons of white wine, and 1 teaspoon of dried tarragon or 1 tablespoon of fresh tarragon. Brush the filets mignons with this mixture during the broiling process, and after they have been removed to hot plates. Serve with hot French bread, lavishly buttered, **Cognac beans,** and, if you want to bother with deep fat frying, drop 1 or 2 bunches of parsley into hot fat. It comes to the top of the fat when it's done, and that's almost at once. It's delicious with this type of steak. Drink a bottle of chilled rosé wine, preferably a California one.

BROILED PORTERHOUSE, T-BONE, OR SIRLOIN

Have your steak well aged and cut about 2 or more inches thick. If it is from heavy beef, it should be trimmed of some of its fat (save it, chop fine, and use for frying potatoes). Grill over coals, allowing about 6 to 10 minutes per side for rare, slightly more for medium rare, if at room temperature when you start (**see chart, Chapter 4**). If you want a charred crust on your steak, let the fire flame up around the meat after it has been browned and is well on its way to being done (**see Chapter 2**). Salt and pepper the steak, top with a generous piece of butter, and keep hot on an also hot platter or plank until ready to carve.

Carve the bone completely out of the steak with a sharp knife and hide it for yourself, then cut the meat in diagonal slices as thick as you wish. Slice right across the filet and the contra filet, so that everyone gets a fine piece of each part of the steak. Serve this delectable meat with thinly sliced potatoes sautéed in the beef suet, which has previously been rendered until the little pieces of fat are crisp and flavorsome. A huge bowl of watercress and a bottle of fine red Burgundy will round this out to perfection. Good French bread and some cheese to finish off the wine make this a pretty remarkable meal.

BLUE CHEESE BROILED STEAK

Crush a clove of garlic in a mortar or heavy bowl. When it is reduced to all but nothing, add ½ pound of blue cheese and mash well. Select a thick steak (2 to 2½ inches) and grill it in your best manner. When it's brown on one side, turn it, and spread the top side with the cheese mixture. When it's done on the bottom the cheese should have melted into an unctuous and savory sauce. Serve it with ash-roasted potatoes, and with a cole slaw made with sliced raw cauliflower instead of cabbage. Have charcoal-toasted rye bread, too, with a robust wine such as Grignolino.

RIB STEAK, BORDELAISE
(ENTRECÔTE BORDELAISE)

This manner of preparing rib steak is typical of the Bordeaux region, renowned for its magnificent wines. One rib steak will probably serve 1 or 2 persons, depending on its size.

Grill the steaks to your delight, then remove them to a hot plank or platter and top them with thin slices of beef marrow which has been poached in a little boiling salted water. Cover the steaks with **Bordelaise sauce,** or serve it separately, and have plenty of it. The sauce may be made at the grill or in the kitchen.

Try a fine red Bordeaux with this. Have plenty of French bread to sop the sauce, and a large platter of cold or hot asparagus with either a plain **butter sauce** or **vinaigrette sauce.**

ENTRECÔTE BERCY

This delightful version of the rib steak is one from a very old French cookbook, which tells us that it demands to be cooked and eaten outdoors. "It must," says the now forgotten but great authority, "to be a genuine entrecôte bercy, be cut medium—not too thick or too thin." Salt and pepper both sides of the cut well and grill over a brisk fire until done. While it is grilling, heat a platter or board on or near the grill, and mix 3 tablespoons of butter as it melts with plenty of finely chopped parsley, chervil (using tarragon if chervil is not available), and shallots. Cream well together, and when you remove the steak, turn it quickly in the sauce, top with another piece of butter, and sprinkle with chopped parsley. "Serve at once to two people, with a bottle of Hermitage, and plenty of French bread and some green beans which have been mixed with marrow slices after they are cooked."

STEAK DIANE

If you have an electric skillet or chafing dish, this is a wonderful showpiece for the garden or patio dinner. It may also be done in a skillet over the grill. Have 2 sirloins ½ inch thick and grill them rare. For each steak, heat ½ cup of finely chopped shallots or, failing these, chopped green onions. When they have cooked for just a minute, add salt and pepper to taste, 2 tablespoons of Worcestershire sauce and 2 tablespoons of meat glaze of reduced stock. Let this blend, add the steaks, which have been sliced, with another ounce or two of butter, and turn the slices very quickly. Add 4 ounces (½ cup) of Cognac and set ablaze. This, of course, is more effective after dark. Serve the steaks while still flaming to eager and hungry guests, along with some julienne potatoes, a great mound of fresh asparagus with grated cheese and crumbs, a green salad, and a bottle of good claret—say a Château Lascombes, or a Cabernet Sauvignon. Dessert might be glamorous, too, for this dinner, say a combination of fresh pineapple, raspberries, and blueberries, with sugar and a fine dosage of kirsch or *eau de vie de framboise.* And, of course, a vat of caffè espresso, or your favorite black coffee.

STEAK MOYEN ÂGE

The reason for this cognomen is simple. Mary Meerson, who did much research for a number of French movies, including *Carnival in Flanders,* found during her work a great many old Flemish recipes. This one intrigued her so much that she grilled one over the fire in her studio. The result was as sensational as the picture itself. Here it is—and *not* in the original Flemish!

Allow 12 to 14 ounces of sirloin steak for each serving. A half hour before you grill the steak, press in thoroughly as much leaf rosemary as possible, using the heel of your hand. Let the steak rest with this herbing for about 15 minutes, then grill it as you like it. Remove to a hot platter, where it should be salted to taste and well buttered for that additional richness.

We think that the accompanying food should be rather simple. Plain boiled new potatoes with just a bellyband of the skin removed, butter, salt, and sour cream will take care of the starch department. And a huge bowl of green onions and cucumber fingers is nice instead of a green or a salad. Some good ale, and for dessert sliced peaches with brown sugar and rum, and plenty of strong coffee.

STEAK AU POIVRE

Though this is traditionally pan-broiled and flamed with Cognac, we found it delicious when cooked over charcoal. Choose a sirloin or rib steak about 2 inches thick. For a 3-pound steak use about 1½ tablespoons of peppercorns, which should be crushed in a mortar or rolled with a rolling pin until they are in coarse chunks, not as finely ground as the pepper that comes from the average mill. With the heel of your hand, press the pepper firmly into the steak on both sides. Let the steak stand thus for 30 to 45 minutes, then grill according to you, or to the rules given above. When it is cooked to your liking, remove the steak to a hot platter or board and top with salt to taste and a large dollop of sweet butter, which should melt and drool over the surface before you carve it.

With this steak, serve **foiled potatoes,** or potatoes baked in the oven if it is handier. Crisp French bread for a mopper-upper, and artichokes with a simple butter sauce, if you serve them hot, or with a French dressing if they are cold, are excellent with the spiciness of the steak. We like a robust wine such as Barbera with this, or a good ale. Cheese seems to be the logical follow-up, or perhaps fruit topped with sherbet of some kind.

SALT BROILED STEAK

Charm's charming Charlotte Adams, the food editor, has long been a good friend. Years ago Charlotte became an enthusiastic griller with salt. This is her own special version of broiling a steak. Charlotte's recipe is for a 2- to 3-pound sirloin, cut thick.

"Wipe the steak and season with freshly ground black pepper.

Next, spread over it a thin coating of prepared mustard, then dampen ½ cup of salt with water, just enough so that it can be spread with a knife, over the mustard. This keeps the juice from running out and causes the steak to blacken on the outside when cooking. It does not taste salty. Turn the steak frequently and be sure to have a wooden board handy to place it on for carving, and, before that, for testing its degree of doneness. We like it rare. Put plenty of butter on it before carving."

MINUTE STEAKS

There is no particular reason for calling these cuts "minute steaks" because they will not cook in a minute, neither are they really *minute*. Where the terminology originated we have no idea. They are thin cuts from the strip, the sirloin, the rump, the Spencer, or the ribs. Usually they are about 6 to 9 ounces of meat. Minute steaks must be broiled quickly, pan-broiled, or sautéed. They should be watched very carefully lest they overcook and become dull and as tasteless as well-done steak can be. Serve them with any of the sauces we have mentioned, or just as they are.

MINUTE STEAK SANDWICHES

This is a very easy way to serve 10 or 12 persons if you have a large grill which will accommodate that many steaks at one time, or enough individual grills to go around. Grill the steaks as usual and serve between slices of well-buttered toast. Accompany with sliced tomatoes, sliced red onions, and ripe olives, and with potato chips. Eat with fingers or with knife and fork, as you wish. Onion rolls, split, toasted, and buttered, make a wonderful service for these steak sandwiches.

MINUTE STEAK, CHARLIE'S FASHION

This is simple, hearty, and very turn-of-the-century. It is merely a well-grilled minute steak on a hot plate, with a blanket of sautéed onion rings to cover it, and a good helping of home fried potatoes on the side. Plenty of beer with this dish, and for dessert there is only one thing—green apple pie with cheese, and steaming mugs of coffee with cream.

OLD-FASHIONED MINUTE STEAK
SMOTHERED IN MUSHROOMS

Sauté 1½ pounds of mushroom caps in ¼ pound of butter, with the chopped stems added when the caps are almost cooked. Add a clove of garlic, finely chopped, 6 tablespoons of chopped parsley, and, just before serving, 1 cup of sour cream, which should heat through but not boil. Grill your steaks as you will, and top with this mushroom sauce. Serve with hashed brown potatoes and a chilled rosé wine, and for dessert ripe pears and a selection of good cheeses.

DEVILED STEAKS

Use minute steaks for this—you will no doubt serve one to a person. You will also need about 1½ to 2 cups of toasted buttered crumbs for 4 people, and about ¼ pound of butter, and a devil sauce. Grill the steaks quickly, but undercook them a little. Spread the hot steaks with butter and roll them in buttered toasted crumbs, pressing the crumbs in. Replace them on the grill for just a minute, for the crumbs to brown and crisp. Serve with the **sauce diable** and plain boiled potatoes, and a **cucumber salad.** Ale or stout goes very well with this.

MARINATED STEAKS

You may use minute steaks, top sirloin, or rib steaks for this. Marinate your steaks in olive oil to cover the bottom of the dish in which you marinate—about 1 cup of olive oil for 4 steaks. To each steak add 1 small clove of garlic, finely chopped, and the juice of ½ lemon. Let the steaks stand for 12 to 24 hours, turning frequently. Add more oil to the dish if you see that the previous amount has been absorbed. Grill these steaks as usual, adding salt and pepper to taste when they are just about cooked. Serve this delicious variation with a great bowl of sautéed mushrooms, sprinkled heavily with chopped parsley. Drink a bottle of Beaujolais, Julienas, or Gamay, of rather recent vintage, with this. Afterward, a large bowl of fresh cherries.

STEAK MARCHANDS DE VIN

This, tradition tells us, is the favorite dish of the vinous merchants in Bordeaux, who would give a little of their noonday bottle for the sauce. It is as simple as any sauce to make, but its mingled flavor has a particular fascination for good aged beef. Use a fine rump steak, cut around 1½ to 2 inches thick. Broil as usual although, grilled over dried trimmings of the vine, it tastes even better. Transfer this perfectly cooked morsel to a hot platter or plank, top with a good pat of butter, and serve with sautéed potatoes. Follow with a large plate of fresh asparagus and, of course, the sauce of the wine merchants (**marchands de vin**) to anoint the meat.

FLANK STEAK

Flank steak is a much misunderstood cut of meat, as most people think it has to be braised to be good. Not at all. A broiled flank steak is unbelievably delicious. It is known in good eating places as a London broil. The secret is to have a good grade of meat, cook it rare, and carve it deftly in *very* thin diagonal slices.

Have the steak at refrigerator temperature, or at least cold. Remove the tough membrane on the outside, if the butcher has neglected to do so, and slash any fat at the edge, to allow it to render. Brush with a little oil or melted butter and broil for about 8 minutes over a good fire, turning once during the cooking. Slice at a very long diagonal, so that a large, temptingly red center will be framed with an appetizing brown crust. London broil is excellent served on buttered toast with some **French fried onions** on the side. Beer seems to be in order with this dish. It is also good with **wine-shallot steak sauce.**

SKIRT STEAK ORIENTALE

The skirt steak is not too common a cut. (It is the piece back of the flank.) If it is from a top-grade beef, it is a delicious morsel when broiled. Follow the recipe for **deviled skirt or flank steak,** or try it this way.

Let it stand in a mixture of equal parts of soy sauce, sherry, and oil, with added garlic or grated ginger, if you like. Turn it frequently so that both sides are well treated to the flavors. After an hour or two in the marinade, broil quickly over a brisk fire until nicely browned and quite rare in the middle—not more than 8 minutes.

Serve with heated potato chips, edible-pod (Chinese) peas cooked quickly in a little butter and garnished with finely cut green onions, French bread, and a bottle of ale.

DEVILED SKIRT OR FLANK STEAK

Brush the steak with prepared mustard and sprinkle with freshly ground black pepper and paprika. Broil quickly, turning once or twice, and if necessary dribble a little oil over the steak so that the mustard does not char. Serve with buttered noodles to which you have added a clove of garlic and a goodly portion of grated cheese.

ANOTHER DEVIL

Place 1 flank or 2 skirt steaks on a deep platter or pan. Grate a large onion over them and spread it evenly on the surface of the meat. Add ½ teaspoon of dry mustard, 1 tablespoon each of vinegar and Worcestershire sauce, 1 teaspoon of salt, 1 crushed clove of garlic, and 1 teaspoon of freshly ground pepper. Turn the steak in this mixture several times, and let it stand for 1 hour. Broil it quickly, painting the surface with the marinade during the broiling. Serve thinly sliced, on toasted, buttered French bread, to 3 or 4 persons, with a cold vegetable salad of tomatoes, cooked green beans, peas, beets, raw onions, artichoke hearts—all these arranged on a bed of shredded greens and served with a Russian dressing.

HAMBURGER STEAK

For 4 persons you should have 2 pounds of ground beef chuck, top round, or top sirloin. Form the meat, being certain that you handle it lightly, into a large cake about 2 to 3 inches thick. Salt and pepper it well, and place it in a long-handled grill or on a small gridiron over the coals. Broil it very quickly, really just sear it well on each side, and get it crusty on the outside and soft and rare in the center. Remove to a hot platter, cut in wedges, and serve. It is good with **roasted corn** and slices of raw onion which have been vinegared and salted and allowed to marinate for an hour or two.

SALISBURY STEAK, BÉARNAISE

This is also hamburger, formed into a large, thick, steak-shaped loaf and grilled as above. Serve it with **Béarnaise sauce** and with **fettuccine Alfredo.** Cherry tomatoes would make a nice substitute for salad, and the dessert might well be ripe pears and Gorgonzola cheese.

GERMAN HAMBURGER CAKES

Hamburger is supposed to have originated in Germany. This version is made into individual oval cakes weighing about 6 ounces each, and broiled to a fine crusty brown, then topped with a fried egg and a few capers. Elegant, really, with **German fried potatoes** and beer.

MORE HAMBURGERS

Other ways with hamburgers are these:

1. Form meat into balls, poke a pat of butter and a filbert-sized chip of ice into each, and flatten enough to broil. This makes the meat extra juicy.

2. Form meat into thin flat cakes and sandwich a thin slice of onion between each two. Grill as usual.

3. Hamburgers may also be stuffed with thin slices of Cheddar cheese, pitted ripe olives, herb butter balls, squares of blue cheese, or deviled ham, before broiling.

CHULETAS

This is one of Elena Zelayeta's superb recipes. That it is also frugal makes it no less enticing. Combine 2 pounds of ground beef with 2 cups each of minced parsley and minced onion. Add 2 large eggs, 1 tablespoon of salt, ½ cup of grated Parmesan cheese, and some freshly ground pepper. Form in balls (this will make 2½ dozen) and pat each ball on a board that has been covered with 3 cups of dry sifted bread crumbs. Turn so that the patties are covered on each side—they should be about 4 inches in diameter, and thin. If desired, they may be shaped oblong instead of round. Chill well, then cook on a well-greased, fine-meshed grill, not more than 3 minutes to a side. Serve with **salsa fria** and **frijoles refritos.**

SUKIYAKI

This dish has three things to its credit: (1) it happens to be spectacular; (2) it's easy to prepare; and (3) it's one of the most delicious concoctions on the roster.

For 6 servings, you'll need two medium-sized skillets or one jumbo-sized. And have the various ingredients ready at hand on a platter. These will include 1½ pound sirloin or fillet of beef, cut in 2- by 3-inch paper-thin strips; 2 medium onions, sliced thin; 12 mushrooms, sliced thin; 1 cup thinly sliced bamboo shoots; 2 large bunches of washed and drained watercress; 10–12 scallions cut in small pieces; and 1 cup or more cubed bean curd. All these should be arranged in a colorful pattern on the platter or tray, for the color and the method of preparation of sukiyaki is a great part of its charm.

Plus all the above, have a package of long rice [cellophane noodles], washed and soaked in warm water for 30 minutes; 2 or 3 strips of beef fat; 2 tablespoons sugar; ½ cup soy sauce; ¼ cup of sherry; ½ cup of beef stock (or a beef bouillon cube dissolved in hot water); 6 eggs and cooked white rice.

Heat skillets or skillet, and rub well with beef fat. When smoking hot, add a little of the onion and stir to prevent browning. Add meat strips and sear on both sides. Add the sugar, the soy sauce, and the sherry. Let it come to a boil and add the rest of the onions, the mushrooms, and the bamboo shoots. Cook for a few minutes, then add the stock, all the greens, and the long rice.

When the long rice is just transparent, a very short time, add the bean curd. Blend all the ingredients well but do not overcook. The vegetables should still be crisp and bity.

Give each person a plate for the sukiyaki and white rice and a small bowl into which he can break a raw egg. Stir the egg a bit with chopsticks. Each mouthful of sukiyaki is dipped into the raw egg and then eaten with the rice.

HAM STEAKS

While we feel that baking a ham on the spit over the coals is more or less a waste of time, there is a good deal to be said for the idea of grilling a fine juicy thick ham steak. Not the thin slice of ham which passes in most markets for steak—that's what really used to be considered a breakfast slice. The real ham steak has to be 1 or 1½ inches thick, and should be treated tenderly; it will then make one of the pleasantest of outdoor meals. Of course the cooking time depends on how the ham has been processed, but a so-called "tenderized" but not "precooked" ham, 1 inch thick, will take about 30 to 40 minutes to cook, while a 2-inch one will take from 45 to 60 minutes. As today's hams are inclined to be rather lean, you may want to baste the steak with a little peanut oil from time to time. Try serving it with **charcoal-roasted yams** and **roasted onions.**

MARINATED HAM STEAK

Gash the fat on the ham so that it will broil without curling. Brush with melted butter and grill over a fire of low temperature, basting it a little with pineapple juice, white wine, or vermouth from time to time. The ham should be nicely browned and thoroughly cooked. If you wish, you may increase the heat for the last 15 minutes of grilling in order to give it a more crusty surface. Slice in fairly thin diagonal slices, and serve with toasted and well-buttered **corn bread** or corn muffins, **broiled pineapple,** and **cole slaw.**

DEVILED HAM STEAK

Choose a fine center cut of ham about 1½ inches thick and cover with a good brushing of English mustard (combine 1 tablespoon of dry mustard with ¼ teaspoon of salt, and enough white wine or wine vinegar to make a paste). Grill the steak over a low fire, turning it fairly often. It should take about 45 minutes at slow cooking. About 5 minutes before you feel that the ham steak is ready for the table, brush both sides with a mixture of the mustard and honey—1 teaspoon of mustard to 2 tablespoons of honey is about the right proportion. Turn the ham several times to allow this mixture to form a glaze. Slice in medium-thin diagonal slices, and serve it with **California lima bean casserole** and **charcoal-roasted bananas.** Beer with this is pretty special. Ham is also good basted with the syrup from a jar of preserved ginger.

PORK STEAK

Is it that the aroma of grilling pork is so tantalizing, or is it just the best of the meats when it is cooked simply? We sometimes think it is—richly crisp at the edge, succulent and sapid within. The true flavor of pork needs no tampering, no addition of herbs and spices, sauce or wine.

This much-neglected delicacy is a superb dish when cooked this way. The steaks should be cut from the leg, and should be about 1 to 2 inches thick. As with all pork dishes, a pork steak needs careful slow cooking, so build your charcoal fire well ahead and get the temperature fairly low. Brush the pork steak lightly with butter, and place it on the grill, letting it coast along slowly, browning evenly and cooking through. Turn it every 10 minutes until the steak is pleasantly browned and tender, and thoroughly cooked. Salt and pepper it well, and serve on very hot plates, along with some sautéed apples in the French fashion: peel and slice very thinly 3 to 5 very tart apples. Sauté them in butter or in fresh pork fat fairly quickly until the edges are lightly browned. Add about 2 teaspoons of sugar, and toss the pan so that the sugar is evenly distributed. Do not let the apples overcook, for they should hold their shape and be crispy at the edges and slightly firm in the thicker part of the slices. **German fried potatoes** are excellent with this as well. And beer—wine, unless it is a rosé, seems not too complementary to pork.

LAMB STEAKS

These are usually cut from the leg, sometimes from the shoulder, and are, if properly cooked and flavored, a top choice for charcoal grilling. The wisest way to buy them is to purchase a whole leg and have the butcher cut the choicer sections into 1½ inch steaks for you. Use the rest for braising or stewing, or for **shaslik.**

Lamb is always the better for the addition of a little garlic, and the steaks are no exception. Rub them with a garlic clove, or crush a garlic clove in a small amount of coarse salt and then rub the salt onto the steaks. Brush them with oil, and grill the steaks over a medium fire until they have achieved a pleasant pinkness and are not overcooked, for nothing is quite so uninteresting as too well-done lamb steaks—unless it be well-done beefsteaks (**see chart, Chapter 4**). At least, that's our opinion. Serve the lamb steaks very hot on piping plates or planks. Serve with **white beans, country style,** and with quantities of crisp celery and ripe olives. Have, too, a bottle of chilled rosé wine, and perhaps some pineapple with rum for dessert.

LAMB STEAKS WITH TARRAGON

Marinate lamb steaks in a bath of white wine, generously laced with fresh or dried tarragon leaves. (To 1 cup of white wine add 2 teaspoons of dried tarragon, or 2 tablespoons of fresh leaves.) Let the steaks absorb this for 2 hours. When you remove the steaks, transfer them to a piece of absorbent paper. Melt 6 tablespoons of butter in a small saucepan, add the wine and tarragon, and heat it. Reserve this. Rub the steaks with a little butter and grill them over medium-hot coals, brushing them from time to time with the wine-butter-tarragon mixture. When they are done to your liking, serve them on very hot plates, accompanied by **rice with nuts** and **string bean salad.** Drink a bottle of chilled white wine—an Alsatian Gewürztraminer or one from California, perhaps—and have some crisp French rolls, and a fine strawberry shortcake with heavy cream for dessert.

LAMB SHOULDER STEAKS

Although lamb steaks cut from the leg are neater-looking and certainly easier to handle, don't overlook the wonderful taste of those from the shoulder. Appearance isn't everything, and a penny saved is flavor gained. Cook them just as you do the steaks from the leg, above.

MUTTON STEAKS

The best of the mutton steaks are cut from the leg, and preferably from well-aged heavy mutton. They should be at least 1½ inches thick, and better yet, 2 inches. Trim the fat fairly close to the meat and rub the surface lightly with garlic. Grill over a medium charcoal heat; it will take 20 minutes for a 2-inch steak to cook medium rare, 30 minutes medium well done (see chart). We think it is a better deal to have it on the rarer side, rather than too well done. Salt and pepper to taste, and serve with a good **Béarnaise sauce** and with **broiled mushrooms** and **boiled potatoes**. Good, too, with a purée of white beans, possibly kept hot in a chafing dish or electric skillet.

MUTTON STEAKS, MACAO

Marinate thick mutton steaks with soy sauce, fresh grated ginger, garlic, and a touch of thyme. Turn them well in the mixture, and let them absorb flavor for 6 to 8 hours. Grill, brushing from time to time with the marinade, until nicely browned and rare in the middle. Serve with rice, **broiled tomatoes** or fried green peppers, and a bottle of California rosé.

MUTTON STEAK À L'ESTRAGON

Combine 1 cup of white wine, 2 teaspoons of dried tarragon, 1 teaspoon of salt, and 3 tablespoons of olive oil. Marinate mutton steaks in this mixture. Broil as above. Serve with **German fried potatoes** and a **celery salad.**

MUTTON STEAKS ESPAÑOL

Broil as usual. Melt ⅛ pound of butter with 2 finely crushed cloves of garlic, 2 tablespoons of wine vinegar, and 3 tablespoons of capers. Heat and pour over the steaks as you serve them. Boiled white beans with butter and seasonings and a little juice might go well with this. So does a new dish we just dreamed up—mashed white turnips topped with sautéed mushrooms.

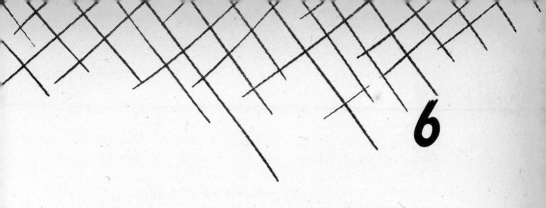

CHOPS

6

We both confess to a weakness for a good substantial chop. Besides its succulence, savor, and speed of preparation, a chop is a great comfort to the dieter—a category in which many of us, unhappily, find ourselves.

lamb chops

Lamb chops are never cheap, so we feel that if you are going to have them you might as well shoot the works and buy the absolute tops. Any chop is better when cut thick; this is especially true when you buy for outdoor grilling. U.S. Prime or Choice are the grades to look for. Shoulder chops, less expensive than the others, are not so compact and have more bone, but the flavor is delicious and they are not to be despised. Select them anywhere from 1 to 2½ inches thick, according to your taste or your pocketbook. If you need to pinch the pennies, don't have chops.

BROILED LAMB CHOPS

If you broil a chop over charcoal, we hope you will want it well pinked inside and nicely crisped on the outside. Give lamb time to broil slowly for best results (see chart, Chapter 4). The fat must cook through, and if you are wise you will have the fire quite moderate when you put the chops on. Turn them and test by cutting close to the bone to see if they are done. If you want more char, bring the heat up or adjust your grill for the last few minutes of cooking. You may follow any of the recipes given for **lamb steaks,** or try the ones below. Serve with **California lima bean casserole** and with sliced tomatoes dressed with olive oil.

LAMB CHOPS WITH GARLIC (À L'AIL)

Slit the chops with a sharp knife to make a small pocket. Cream together (for 6 good thick chops) ½ cup of butter, 2 well-chopped garlic cloves, and 3 tablespoons of chopped parsley. Stuff each chop with a little of this mixture and reserve the rest; secure the chops with small skewers or with toothpicks. Broil in the usual manner and season with salt and pepper. Top each chop with a little more of the butter, just as you serve. **A mushroom and potato pie,** peas, and a good rosé wine are right for this delightful meal.

LAMB CHOPS STUFFED WITH CHICKEN LIVERS

Use loin chops, or if you can find large rib ones, have them cut double and make a slit or pocket between the bones. Sauté chicken livers and chopped shallots in butter, season with a whisper of rosemary or tarragon, and stuff the cavities. Fasten as in the recipe for **lamb chops with garlic,** if you are using loin chops—the rib chops will not need skewering. Broil to suit you, and serve with **barley and mushroom casserole.**

ENGLISH LAMB CHOPS

Correctly speaking, these are cut from the saddle, and should be very thick. (That is, the part which would be covered by a saddle if the lamb wore one.) Sometimes, however, they are thick (2½ to 3 inches) loin chops. Although it is not necessary, we think they taste better if a kidney is rolled into each chop and a strip of bacon fastened around it with a small skewer of wood or steel. Grill slowly to get a good color on both sides and a fine pinkness in the center (see chart, Chapter 4). Salt and pepper well, and serve with baked potatoes with cheese or sour cream and chives, and a good **cole slaw**. Ale and beer are natural allies of this dish.

mutton chops

The best mutton chops run very heavy, and we like them better than lamb. There is a goodly covering of fat, which should be well trimmed, as mutton fat has a not too pleasant flavor. Buy a chop from 1½ to 3 inches thick for each person, with or without the kidney. Rub the chops well with garlic and brush with a little melted butter. Grill over a medium fire. Take it easy—you don't want to rush the process. It is smart to turn the chops on the fat edge for a bit of their cooking time, as well as on the two fleshy sides. Test for doneness by cutting close to the bone. Salt and sprinkle with coarsely ground pepper. We like a mutton chop with **potato and turnip casserole,** string beans, and stuffed olives. Also a great deal of ale.

✔ ENGLISH MUTTON CHOPS. Are cut and cooked the same way as **English lamb chops.**

HERBED MUTTON CHOPS

Sprinkle the chops with thyme, rosemary, or tarragon before broiling. Press the herb well into the flesh, so that it will flavor the meat while cooking. Some cooks like to throw some of the herbs on the fire just before the chops are done. Chops cooked this way are delicious with **garlic loaf,** a salad of green beans and artichoke hearts with a bland French dressing, and ale or stout. If you prefer wine, select a robust red one—maybe a Charbono. For dessert some fine ripe pears and a good Stilton cheese, if available. If not, a fine French Roquefort or a Danish Blue.

TURKISH MUTTON CHOPS

This is an interesting and delectable way with mutton chops. Make a small pocket in each of 4 chops. Crush 2 cloves of garlic with ¼ cup of pine nuts, 4 tablespoons of chopped parsley, 2 teaspoons of chopped fresh mint, and ¼ cup of butter. Mix with a mortar and pestle, or with a heavy spoon in a bowl, so that the nuts become crushed into the mixture. Stuff a spoonful of the mixture into each pocket. Broil the chops as above, salt and pepper them to taste, and serve with **broiled eggplant** and **broiled tomatoes.** A red wine with this. For dessert, ripe mangoes or, if they are not available, good melon.

pork chops

Is there anything better? For outside cookery, use the best loin, or if it is heavy pork, the rib chops as well. Have the chops cut 1½ to 2 inches thick, or thicker if you wish. Pork, having to be well done, should cook rather slowly (**see chart, Chapter 4**). Fast cooking is apt to harden the fibers and make the meat dry. Serve with fried green tomatoes and **hominy spoon bread,** or with applesauce made with sweet vermouth.

FARMYARD PORK CHOPS

Soak the chops in milk to cover, which has been seasoned with salt and coarse black pepper to taste, and 2 cloves of garlic, finely chopped. Let the chops soak for several hours. Remove them from the marinade and grill slowly over the coals (**see chart, Chapter 4**). Use the milk to make a real old-fashioned cream gravy, with some of the drippings from the chops, in a chafing dish. Serve baked potatoes with the gravy, which might be enriched with sour cream, if you like. We'd like **charcoal-roasted apples,** too.

HERBED PORK CHOPS

Here's a recipe that is out of the ordinary—we think you'll go for it. Cover pork chops with tomato juice which has been well seasoned with salt and coarsely ground black pepper, and plenty of crushed basil leaves. Let the chops marinate in this for several hours, remove carefully, making certain that the basil clings to the chops here and there. Broil them slowly and use the tomato juice as a base for the sauce. This should have a generous blessing of garlic, a little olive oil, and the seasonings to your taste. Serve with a huge pan of sliced onions sautéed in pork fat or in butter until just soft and golden brown. Plenty of crisp bread and a bottle of chilled Orvieto from Italy complete this repast.

veal chops

Loin chops of young tender veal may be broiled if the process is a slow one, with low heat and some lubrication. Have the chops cut 1½ to 2 inches thick, and see that the veal is young and tender, with some fat. Butter or oil the chops well, or roll a strip of bacon around each one and secure it with a small skewer. Grill slowly over low-temperature coals, and turn often (see chart, Chapter 4). Salt and pepper to taste when they are removed from the fire. Serve with tiny buttered new potatoes and sautéed green pepper strips, which should be flavored with a touch of wine vinegar at the last moment, just before rushing to the table. Drink a bottle of good Gewürztraminer with this.

HERBED VEAL CHOPS

An interesting and delicious way to do veal chops, this. Roll fresh young chops in oil or butter, and then in a mixture of chopped chives, parsley, and tarragon. Let them stand for an hour thus, and grill over low heat until the meat is cooked through. Serve with fettuccine Alfredo. Have some crisp radishes and celery for greenery, and drink a bottle of soft delicate Pouilly Fumé with the meal. Follow with a huge bowl of fresh raspberries with kirsch. Elegant eating!

venison chops

Venison can, just like any meat, be deliciously tender or as tough as an old goat. For broiled chops, we hope most fervently that yours is a young buck. If not, you'd best choose another method of cookery. Cut the chops from the loin, 1½ to 2 inches thick, and broil them good and rare, if you want them at their best. Season well with salt and pepper, and serve up very quickly with some fried slices of **polenta,** nicely browned. Pour some extra-fine Burgundy (in fact this is a wonderful excuse for indulging in your best wines), such as a Richebourg, or a great Clos Vougeot, or a fine Pinot Noir from California. Have some crisp greens, too, and follow with some really ripe pears, a piece of good cheese, and some walnuts. Naturally, a repeat on the wine is in order. More **venison recipes** will be found in **Chapter 12.**

MARINATED VENISON CHOPS

We think, if the deer is a young and tender one, it is a pity to marinate the chops. The flavor of the marinade is apt to overpower the taste of the meat. If you *must,* however, do it for a day or two in red wine with a touch of wine vinegar, a carrot, an onion stuck with cloves, and a little thyme. Grill the marinated chops as above, basting a good deal with the marinade. Serve with a sauce made by sautéing 6 or 8 chopped green onions in 4 tablespoons of butter, and adding about ½ cup of the marinade and bringing it to a boil. Add ½ teaspoon of freshly ground black pepper, lastly stir in 1 cup of sour cream, and let it heat through but not boil. Sprinkle lavishly with chopped parsley. Serve with some crisp watercress, and shell macaroni, boiled *al dente* and buttered, to be used as a sop for the sauce. Give the macaroni a sprinkling of black pepper and a dusting of paprika as well. Have a fine bottle of Hermitage from the Rhône Valley, or what you will. This dish is also exceptionally good when served with a purée of chestnuts. In this case, crusty bread is in order for the sopping.

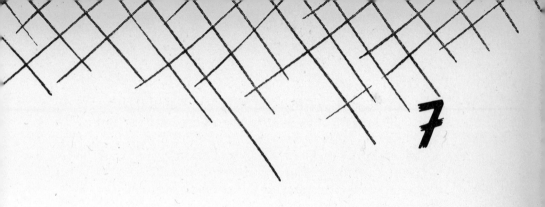

7

ROASTS

A roast is perhaps the best choice for entertaining out of doors—this for several reasons. The sight of it, turning over a charcoal fire, fascinates everyone and stimulates the appetite. It is, compared with steaks and chops, an economical dish, and it is also possible to feed a larger crowd using the same-sized grill. But most important of all is the fact that the roast actually tastes better, cooked this way, than you've ever had it from the kitchen range.

beef

Of all the roasts, beef comes first with everyone. As in beef steaks, the meat should be heavy, well aged, and liberally marbled with fat. U.S. Government grading makes it easy to buy the best every time (see **Chapter 5,** under heading **"Selection of Steaks"**).

STANDING RIB ROAST

In America, the favorite roast of beef is a standing rib one, consisting of from 3 to 5 ribs (though all 8 may be used for a large party), with the bones left on. The first 4 or 5 ribs are sometimes called *prime* ribs, and are preferred. Connoisseurs esteem the standing rib roast because of the extra flavor the bones impart to the meat.

✔ SELECTING. When selecting a standing rib roast, allow from ¾ pound to 1 pound per person, with perhaps extra allowed for ample outdoor appetites, or for cold roast beef tomorrow. Have your butcher cut the ribs short—7 inches is about right. The back cord and feather bone should be removed and, if you wish, the chine bone. However, fat tied on the outside may cause too much flaring during the roasting. It also makes sense not to buy a roast that is too large for your spit. Some people, including the authors, like to roast a standing 5-ribber, then remove (and hide) the bones before carving for the guests. The bones later become **deviled beef ribs,** and are they ever wonderful!

✔ SPITTING. If one side of the roast is much heavier than the other (and it usually is), spit it diagonally across from the rib end to the top of the eye. This will give you a better balance (**see Chapter 3**). If the meat is compact and seems well-balanced, run the spit parallel to the top part of the ribs.

✔ ROASTING. Roast the beef over a fairly slow fire, according to directions in **Chapter 3**—the spit thermometer should register about 250°. When using a meat thermometer, be sure that it is in the thickest part of the meat and not touching a bone. Assuming you like your beef rare, don't cook it over 125°, then douse the fire or lower it far from the meat, and allow it to coast for 20 to 30 minutes. (We cook ours to 120° for very rare—it coasts to 130°.) This coasting has two advantages: it allows guests (and cook!) to have another drink before dinner, and it gives the juices in the roast time to develop. A heavy 5-rib roast will take about 1¾ to 2½ hours to cook rare. This is also true of a 3- or 4-rib roast, as the thickness of the meat is about the same. Serve rib roast with almost any of the dishes in **Chapter 16**.

ROLLED RIB ROAST

Often a more economical buy than a standing rib roast, this cut is easy to spit, either through the center or on a diagonal. It's also a cinch to carve. Cook it as above, and serve it with a casserole and salad.

SPENCER ROAST

This roast, from the ribs with the bone removed, is ideal for a party. It usually weighs about 16 pounds when the whole length of the rib section is used, and should serve 16 to 20 persons. It is not rolled but is spitted the long way, going through from corner to corner. Cook as above. It will take from 1½ to 2½ hours to cook rare.

EYE OF THE RIB

The eye of the rib is just that—the center portion of the rib, with all bone and outside meat removed. Thus it is smaller in diameter than the Spencer. Many people prefer it to a tenderloin. It is spitted lengthwise. It weighs about 8 pounds and should serve 12 people, as there is no waste. It will take from 1¼ to 2½ hours to cook rare. This is often called a Spencer roast, so when ordering be sure to explain what you want. Because the fat has been removed, we advise basting this roast with a little olive oil or other fat. Try it served with **garlic rice** and with broccoli.

SALTED RUMP ROAST

Rump should not be overlooked, either broiled or cooked this way. Select one 2½ inches or more thick (we suppose it could be called a steak as well as a roast), and spread one side ½ inch thick with coarse salt that has been moistened with one fourth as much water. Cover the salt with aluminum foil, turn, and repeat on the other side—the easiest way to do this is in the hinged broiler in which the meat is to cook. Broil over hot coals. This will be very rare in 9 minutes for each side. A thicker cut may be cooked the same way. It will take from 12 to 18 minutes on a side, for rare, or until the thermometer shows it done **(see chart, Chapter 4).** Serve with **Elena's rice with green chilis and sour cream,** and for dessert, have a huge glass bowl filled with a fresh fruit compote.

SIRLOIN ROAST

Many people prefer the sirloin for roasting. It is a luxury cut but has little waste. If it is a boneless one, cook it as you would a **Spencer or eye of the rib.** If the bone is in, spit it, and cook as you would a **standing rib roast**. Try it with **Nevada chili beans** and **celery salad**.

ROAST BEEF SANDWICHES

Any of these roasts may be cut thin and used for sandwiches for a large informal party. Use toasted French bread, fresh homemade bread, rolls, or even rye bread, all well buttered. If you wish you may use an herb butter, such as **tarragon** or **rosemary**. At any rate, lay on the slices of beef lavishly, and let each man salt or sauce his own **(see Chapter 20 for sauces)**. The sandwiches may be closed or open, though the first are, perhaps, easier to eat.

ROAST TENDERLOIN OF BEEF

This is sheer luxury, but it is boneless and almost fatless, so it goes a long way. What's more, a lower grade of beef is acceptable—by some, even preferred—when it's tenderloin. Spit the meat through the center, butter or oil it, and roast for 25 to 45 minutes. We believe that here the knife rather than the thermometer is best for testing doneness. Serve any of the sauces suggested for roast beef in **Chapter 20** and **Cognac beans**.

LARDED AND PIQUED TENDERLOIN

If the above is sheer luxury, this may seem almost ostentatious, but it's fun to splurge a bit at times. Have your butcher lard the tenderloin with ¼-inch strips of salt pork (or do it yourself). Roast as above and, just before serving, pour ¼ cup of Cognac over the meat and ignite. Serve with **mushroom and potato pie** and **Béarnaise sauce**.

lamb and mutton

"Gently stir and blow the fire,
Lay the mutton down to roast;
Dress it quickly, I desire,
In the drippings put a toast.
That I hunger may remove—
Mutton is the meat I love."

—SIDNEY SMITH

Mutton takes beautifully to roasting over charcoal—so, too, does lamb. The latter is more popular in this country, and certainly a roasted baby one is a gastronomical delight. Still, we feel that mature mutton is even more so, particularly when cooked so that it is still pink and juicy inside. Unfortunately, yearling lamb is the closest many of us can come to mutton, but perhaps concerted and continuous yowls from food lovers will produce some American mutton that compares with that of Canada. Because mutton is scarce, we are not giving separate recipes for it. It may, in every case, be cooked in the same manner as the lamb.

For boned lamb or mutton, allow ½ to ¾ pound a serving; if the bone is in, ¾ to 1 pound each.

LEG OF LAMB OR MUTTON

A leg may be boned or not, as you wish. As both lamb and mutton go well with garlic, it is a good idea to make several incisions in the flesh with a sharp knife and in them insert slices of fresh garlic, pushing them well in. If you wish, rub the lamb well with rosemary or basil, then spit. Roast over a medium fire until done to your liking. We feel that both lamb and mutton should show definite rareness. We stop cooking lamb at 140° to 150°, mutton at 130° to 140°. You may not agree on lamb, but we think you will on mutton. Roast leg of lamb is good served with asparagus or spinach with tarragon, crisp French bread, and a Grenache rosé. Mutton is wonderful with puréed white beans or with turnips.

ROLLED SHOULDER OF LAMB OR MUTTON

The shoulder, though more difficult to carve than the leg, is full of fine flavor, and perfectly adapted to roasting, which is nice, as it is an economy cut. Have it boned and rolled, if you prefer, and roast it as you do the leg. Serve it with **white beans.**

MARINATED SHOULDER OF LAMB

If you wish, you may marinate the shoulder as for **marinated saddle of venison** before roasting, in which case try it with **kidney bean casserole.**

STUFFED SHOULDER OR
LEG OF LAMB OR MUTTON

Bone the meat or have your butcher do it. Combine ½ cup of butter, 2 cloves of garlic, finely chopped, 1 teaspoon of tarragon, ½ teaspoon of salt, ¼ teaspoon of pepper, ¾ cup of chopped parsley, 1 egg, and 1 cup of bread crumbs. Spread on the meat, roll, and tie securely. Roast as for the leg, and serve with **quick potatoes au gratin.**

SADDLE OF LAMB OR MUTTON

In meat cutters' parlance, a saddle sometimes means the entire hind half of the lamb, including the two legs and the loin. To cooks, it means the two loins joined at the backbone—just the spot where a saddle would sit. It is a spectacular and delicious cut, and no more expensive than the same number of loin chops. Have it trimmed and well tied at the butcher's, then rub the outside thoroughly with a cut clove of garlic. Roast as for the leg, and carve parallel to the backbone, in long thin slices. Serve with **Béarnaise sauce** or **tarragon butter sauce,** crisp **fried** or **roasted potatoes,** and a purée of fresh peas.

RACK OF LAMB OR MUTTON

The rack, which is the undivided rib section, is another fine cut for roasting over charcoal. Roast it rare—between 140° and 150°—

and serve it with tiny onions cooked in cream, and mushrooms grilled with **parsley butter.**

BARON OF LAMB

Only a very young lamb can be spitted this way, as the piece consists of the two legs and the saddle. It is a spectacular cut and, if it weighs 14 to 18 pounds, it will serve 18 to 24 persons. However, be sure that your spit will accommodate it. Force the spit between the two legs and through the loin, and truss the ends of the legs securely together so that they will not spread and dry out. Some people stud the flesh with garlic slivers, but as the young meat is very delicate in flavor, take it easy. Roast until pinkly rare, testing with your thermometer. It will take about 2½ hours. Catch the drippings, if possible (**see Chapter 2,** under heading "**Flaring**") and combine them with a little cream and some tarragon— this for a sauce. Serve with new potatoes browned in butter, and with tiny green beans. A bottle of Beaujolais or Gamay would be in order.

WHOLE BABY LAMB OR KID (CAPRETTO)

Don't brush off the idea of either of these sensational roasts—you'll be delighted with them, and so will your guests. Have the meat well cleaned, and reserve liver, heart, and kidneys for a garnish. Tie the front legs together and fold under the body. The back legs, also tied together, are stretched out on the spit. Truss securely and roast to a fine juicy pinkness, basting with the drippings (**see Chapter 2,** under heading "**Flaring**") mixed with melted butter and a little white wine or some broth. Sauté the liver, heart, and kidneys in butter very quickly. Slice very thin and combine with the juices that collect on the cutting board, along with ¼ cup of Madeira and ¼ cup of butter. Serve this as a sauce, and accompany with **galette,** a salad of tender young lettuces, and a Grenache rosé.

ROAST BREAST OF LAMB

This inexpensive cut of meat is most delicious when cooked over charcoal. Allow 1 pound of meat per person. Leave whole, and rub well with garlic that has been mashed with salt and rosemary.

(Prepared mustard may be used in place of the rosemary.) Spit as you do spareribs, and roast over a low fire until they are crisp and the fat is pretty well cooked out. This will take at least an hour, probably longer. Best way to test is to make a cut with a sharp knife and take a look. Serve with big fat wedges of lemon.

MARINATED BREAST OF LAMB

For 6 pounds of breast of lamb make a marinade of 1½ cups of red wine, 3 cloves of garlic, crushed, 1 large onion, chopped, 2 teaspoons of basil, 2 teaspoons of salt, and some freshly ground black pepper. Marinate 6 hours or more, then spit and roast as above, and serve with rice and **Cecily's French fried onions** or pan-fried green peppers.

BROILED LEG OF LAMB

This is a favorite picnic meal for Geiger Lookout, a heavenly spot overlooking Carson Valley below the no longer ghost town of Virginia City, Nevada.

If you do not have a spit or are going into the hinterland for an outing, have the butcher bone a leg of young lamb, leaving the shank intact (or do it yourself). Do not roll the roast or tie it. Rub the meat with salt and pepper, and stud it with slivers of garlic, if you wish. Place it in a basket grill and broil over medium coals, brushing it now and then with a little butter or oil if it needs it. The total cooking time, if not spread, should be around 1½ to 2 hours. If spread out, a small leg will take from 45 minutes to 1 hour. It should be served fairly rare, and is easy to carve; simply start at the end and slice across—there's no bone to stop you. Serve with French rolls, toasted over the charcoal, and with ruddy ripe tomatoes, thickly sliced and dressed with olive oil, salt, and orégano. Cold beer is the perfect drink to carry along for this meal.

veal

Leg, boned shoulder, and loin of veal are all roasts that may be cooked over charcoal. Because veal is inclined to be dry, it should be cooked slowly, and either basted well or both larded and barded.

(To lard is to run pencillike pieces of pork fat through the meat with a larding needle; to bard is to tie thin slices of salt pork on the outside of the meat.) Cook veal until it reaches 160° on the meat thermometer. It should coast to 165° or 170°, and it will be completely done but still juicy.

BONED SHOULDER OF VEAL WITH ANCHOVIES

Have a shoulder boned, spread out the meat, brush inside with olive oil, and lay a dozen anchovy fillets across the middle. Roll, tie, and roast slowly, basting with a mixture of olive oil and sweet vermouth, in equal parts. Serve with spinach and **fettuccine Alfredo** or **spaghetti olio e aglio**.

pork

Pork needs long slow cooking. When done over charcoal, wondrous things will happen to it. The shoulder, the leg (or fresh ham), and the loin all take well to the spit. Here is one case where we believe the meat should be very well cooked. However, as with other meats, it should be removed from the fire and allowed to "coast" when at 160° or 165°—it continues to cook after leaving the heat, until 170° has been reached, and it is done but still juicy.

DOUBLED ROAST LOIN OF PORK

This is a nice meal for a fairly large group. Have two loins of pork boned and tied together, so that the fat is all on the outside, or have one loin cut in half and tied together the same way. Rub the outside with orégano, and cook over a slow fire, catching the drippings to prevent too much flaring. Serve with **roasted apples** and **onions,** and with plenty of hot buttered **corn bread,** or **roasted corn.**

ROAST FRESH HAM

Have it boned or not, as you prefer. Spit, score the skin, and rub with orégano, thyme, or rosemary and with salt. Roast over a low fire, as above, allowing plenty of time, as a 12-pound ham will take about 4 hours. Serve with whole fried hominy, to which you've added a little cream and a generous amount of freshly ground black pepper. Serve applesauce, too, made with white wine, and a big bowl of **cole slaw.** Beer is the drink to serve with this.

BARBECUED PORK

The shoulder, leg, and loin may all be cooked in this manner. Make a basting sauce by combining 2 cups of orange juice, ½ cup of lemon juice, ½ cup of olive oil, 2 teaspoons of rosemary, and 1 teaspoon of black pepper. Brush the meat with this every 15 or 20 minutes during the roasting.

CANTON STYLE ROAST PORK

Marinate any pork roast for several hours in a mixture of ½ cup each of soy sauce and tomato catsup, ¼ cup of honey, and 2 cloves of garlic, crushed. Roast as for **barbecued pork,** using the marinade as a baste. Serve with a Canton sauce, made by combining a tablespoon of dry mustard with enough white wine or sherry to make a paste, and ¼ cup each of soy sauce, tomato sauce, and toasted sesame seeds. (Toast sesame seeds in a heavy skillet over a low fire, stirring continually.) We like **fried rice** with this, and you will too.

MONTERREY STYLE ROAST PORK

Use any pork roast and rub well with garlic and orégano. Roast as above, catching the drippings. Brown ¼ cup of the fat with ¼ cup of flour, add 2 cups of tomato juice and ½ cup of tomato purée (or use 2½ cups of canned tomatoes), and cook until thick. Season with 1 teaspoon of chili powder, ½ cup each of pine nuts, white raisins, and sliced ripe olives. Pass this sauce with the meat. Serve with **frijoles refritos,** tortillas, and beer. Wonderful!

ROAST SUCKLING PIG

This spectacular feast needn't be reserved for winter holidays—it makes fine summer fare and, as it roasts to a gorgeous crackling brown, its heavenly odor will have everyone drooling. Select a pig weighing from 12 to 18 pounds, and leave the head on. Rub the inside well with lemon juice and salt. Save the liver, heart, and kidneys. Sew up the stomach and spit the pig carefully, having the legs tied together. Brush the entire surface with a mixture of melted butter and white wine, or with heavy sweet cream. Roast over a medium fire, basting with the wine mixture or the cream. It will probably take from 2 to 3 hours to cook. Sauté the reserved innards in butter, then slice them and return to the sauté pan, with a cup of cream, salt, pepper, and a dash of cayenne. Simmer 10 minutes and serve with the pig, along with **hominy spoon bread** (made in your electric skillet if you wish), applesauce, and the giblets.

To carve the pig, first cut off the little hams, then cut down the backbone and carve off the chops from the ribs and loin. See that each person gets some of the ham, some of the chops, and plenty of the wonderful crisp skin. It's rich, so don't overeat if you can help it. Serve it with a rosé wine or some beer.

POLTRY

Poultry broiled over charcoal can be as delicious a dish as ever went from grill to table, or it can be dry and almost tasteless. The trick is to avoid overcooking.

chicken

BROILED CHICKEN

Have the broiling chickens split and the backbone removed—this to keep them flat. If large fryers are used, they may be cut in pieces. Rub the meat well with olive oil or butter, and season with salt and pepper. Start cooking with the bone, or cut side, toward the fire, and finish on the skin side long enough to brown beautifully. If the chicken seems dry, baste with butter or oil, or with a mixture of olive oil and vermouth, or melted butter and white wine. Small chickens will take about 30 minutes, larger ones closer to 50 minutes. Serve chicken with **roasted corn** and beer, or with **potato galette, broiled mushrooms,** and a Chablis, Pouilly, or Folle Blanche.

HERBED BROILED CHICKEN

Combine ¼ cup each of chives, parsley, and butter with 1 teaspoon of tarragon. Cream well together and spread under the loosened skin of two broilers. Brush outside with butter, and grill as above. This will delight all comers.

MARINATED BROILERS

Marinate split broilers in ½ cup of sweet or dry vermouth, to which ½ cup of olive oil, ½ cup of chopped onion, and ¼ cup of chopped parsley have been added. Baste with this while grilling.

BROILED CHICKEN SESAME

Marinate split or cut-up chicken in equal parts of sake or sherry, oil, and soy sauce, to which 1 clove of garlic, crushed, and 1 teaspoon of ground ginger have been added. Baste with the marinade while cooking. When almost done, dip each piece of chicken in the marinade, roll thoroughly in sesame seeds, and return to the broiling unit to brown.

DEVILED BROILERS

Cook split or cut-up chicken as above, basting with ½ cup of melted butter to which 1 tablespoon each of mustard and Worcestershire sauce and ¼ cup of vinegar have been added. When almost done, dip each piece in the marinade, then roll in fine crumbs. Return to the grill until brown. Serve with **sauce diable.**

ROAST CHICKEN

Few foods are as tremendously improved by charcoal cookery as poultry. A fine plump chicken or capon cooked over coals is a not easily forgotten treat. Select a bird weighing from 4 to 8 pounds, and spit it so that it is balanced well. This means that the spit should enter through the backbone about an inch above the pope's nose and come out through the extreme front end of the breastbone. Roast over a moderate fire, basting with a mixture of melted butter and white wine (or just butter or oil, or one from **Chapter 20**). A medium-sized chicken over a medium-sized fire should take from 45 to 60 minutes. A 5-pound one may take as long as an hour and 40 minutes. We test the doneness of chicken in two ways. One is to pull the leg; if it moves easily at the joint, it is done. Another test is the thermometer one—when, inserted in the thick part of the thigh, it reads 185°, the chicken is done. However, although this works beautifully with a capon or turkey, it's not always accurate with a small chicken. Neither do we feel that the test advised by some cooks—that colorless juice exuding from the pierced thigh is proof that the chicken is done—is an accurate one. In other words, the most accurate test for doneness is the easy moving of the joint, unless you can tell at a glance when a chicken is done enough. If you wish, the chicken may be stuffed before roasting. In this case it will take longer to cook, as the heat cannot enter the body cavity. Serve these roast chickens sliced, or give each guest a quarter of one, using poultry shears to do the job easily.

ROAST CHICKEN TARRAGON

Stuff the chicken with a handful of fresh tarragon sprigs, or soak ¼ cup of dried tarragon in white wine and use that. Also add a teaspoon of tarragon to a sauce of white wine and butter and baste the chicken with it. Serve with spinach and new potatoes.

GINGERED ROAST CHICKEN

Paint the chicken, inside and out, with a mixture of ½ cup each of soy sauce and sherry, to which ¼ cup of grated fresh ginger has been added. Combine the remaining marinade with ¼ cup of oil and use it for basting the chicken while it cooks. Serve with rice and Chinese peas.

CHICKEN CARIBBEAN

Place a couple of slices of onion in each chicken before roasting, allowing 1 chicken for each 3 or 4 persons. Roast as above. When the chickens are done—in approximately 1 hour—remove them to a deep flameproof platter, pour over them 4 ounces (½ cup) of dark rum, and ignite it carefully—it will flare up suddenly—then allow the flames to die out. In another pan put the chicken drippings if you manage to salvage any, and ¾ cup of rich chicken stock made from the neck and the gizzard of the chicken. Let simmer 5 minutes, then add 1 cup of heavy cream to which 1½ teaspoons of arrowroot has been added (or thicken with 1 tablespoon each of butter and flour, kneaded together). Season with salt and pepper, and cook until thickened. Serve separately from the chickens, which have been quartered. With this dish have green beans which have been cooked until barely tender, then sautéed in butter to which chopped parsley and chives have been added. Rice, too, and a hearty red wine.

CHARCOAL-BROILED CHICKEN BREASTS

Allow 1 chicken breast for each person to be served. Marinate for 3 hours in ¼ cup each of melted butter, soy sauce, and white wine, to which 1 teaspoon each of tarragon and dry mustard have been added. Broil over charcoal for 10 minutes, or until tender but still juicy, basting them with the sauce. Serve with fresh asparagus and rye-bread-and-butter sandwiches. The wine could be a fine bottle of Pouilly Fuissé.

STUFFED BROILED CHICKEN BREASTS

Make small pockets in the breasts, using a thin-bladed sharp knife. Make a paste with ⅛ pound of butter, ¼ cup each of chopped parsley and chives or green onions, and 1 teaspoon of dried basil. Stuff the chicken breasts with this mixture and secure the opening with a toothpick. Brush the breasts with butter and broil for 10 to 12 minutes, starting on the bone side and finishing skin side down. Just before they are finished, brush them with heavy cream and sprinkle with salt and pepper. Serve with tiny new potatoes that have been dressed with crumbled bacon and garlic-flavored bacon fat. **Roasted corn** and a bottle of chilled rosé would be nice too.

CHOPPED CHICKEN CAKES

Mr. A. C. Dolder, who for many years spread good will for Switzerland and its great cheeses, is responsible for this fine recipe. Bone 3 chicken breasts or half a large turkey breast, and put on a chopping board. Using two heavy French knives, one in each hand, chop the meat in small bits. When it is well hashed, add as much cream as it will absorb and still be firm enough to mold. Add salt and pepper, form the meat into one large or several individual cakes, brush well with butter, and broil over charcoal, turning once, until delicately brown. This will take 12 to 14 minutes over a medium fire. Serve with **parsley butter, mushroom sauce, or hollandaise sauce,** or just with a wedge of lemon and a great piece of butter melting on each cake. These cakes, by the way, may be sautéed in butter instead of broiled over coals. The meat may also be chopped with one knife—it will take longer and won't be as spectacular, but it will do the job nicely. Besides, everyone doesn't *have* two heavy French knives!

Ducks

CHINESE BROILED DUCKLING

Allow 1 Long Island duckling for each 2 or 4 persons, depending on the size of the bird and the appetites of the *convives*. Split or quarter the duckling and rub with a mixture made with 2 egg yolks, ⅓ cup of soy sauce, and ¼ cup of honey. Broil, cut side down, for about 45 to 60 minutes, over a low fire, turning a few times. Toward the end of the cooking, raise the fire in order to crisp the skin. Serve with **charcoal-broiled pineapple,** rice, and a fine white wine—maybe Chardonnay or a Pinot Blanc.

CURRY BROILED DUCKLING

Combine ¼ cup each of honey and lemon juice with 1 tablespoon of curry powder, and rub into the skin. Proceed as above. Serve with rice, chutney, chopped preserved ginger, and white raisins that have been plumped (soaked) in Cognac. Drink a vin rosé or, better yet, beer.

OLIVE SAUCE FOR BROILED DUCK

Broil split Long Island ducklings and serve with a sauce made by sautéing 3 tablespoons of chopped shallots or green onions in 2 tablespoons each of butter and olive oil. Add ½ cup of tomato purée, 1 cup of white wine, 1 tablespoon of meat extract or 2 bouillon cubes, 1½ cups of sliced green olives, and salt and pepper to taste. Simmer for 5 minutes.

PEKING DUCK

This recipe, developed by Mabel Stegner for those delectable Long Island ducklings, is quite a production, but more than worth it. We serve it as an appetizer before a Chinese dinner, or with the dinner, but it would be just as sensational if it preceded a meal in any other language. Actually, only the heavenly crisp and flavorsome duck skin is used, so the duckling itself may be saved for other purposes. With it serve the **Chinese doilies** (recipe below)— flat little cakes which are close kin, in fact identical twins, to the Mexican wheat tortilla. The crisp skin is put on a doily, a few shreds of green onion are added, and some of the spicy sauce, then all is rolled together to make as delectable a tidbit as ever passed your lips.

✔ PEKING ROAST DUCK. Stuff a Long Island duckling, weighing not over 5 pounds, with paper towels, and allow to stand, uncovered, in the refrigerator for at least 2 days, changing the towels on the second day. Object: dryness. Remove towels and, if possible, put in front of an electric fan for 3 hours. Object: further dryness. Rub the duck inside and outside with **heung new fun spices** (recipe below), and spit the duck in the usual manner. Have a very hot charcoal fire ready and roast for approximately 1½ hours, or until the skin is a rich mahogany and irresistibly crisp. Slice off the skin with a sharp knife, allowing little or no meat to cling to it. Cut the skin into neat pieces with a sharp knife or scissors, and roll a piece, with some green onion shreds and **red bean sauce,** in the pancakes **(doilies).** Eat with fingers!

✔ HEUNG NEW FUN SPICES. Blend together 1 tablespoon each of ground cinnamon and cloves, 1 teaspoon of ground black pepper, and ½ teaspoon each of ground anise and fennel seeds.

✔ RED BEAN SAUCE. Put a can of red kidney beans in a blender or food processor and purée until smooth. Add 1 tablespoon of chili powder, 1½ teaspoons of the **heung new fun spices,** and ½ teaspoon of salt. In the meantime, cook together 1 cup of plum jam, ⅓ cup of water, and 1 clove of garlic, finely minced or pressed.

Boil for 5 minutes, stirring. Combine with the bean mixture and cook another 10 minutes.

✔ CHINESE DOILIES. Cut 1 tablespoon of shortening into 2 cups of flour that has been sifted with 1 teaspoon of salt. Add ⅔ cup of water, or enough to make a stiff dough. Knead lightly on a floured board and divide into 24 portions. Roll each piece into a circle about 1/16 inch thick and cook on one side only on a lightly greased griddle, for about 2 minutes. When ready to serve, brush the white sides of the doilies with melted butter, and heat slightly in the oven.

goose

In this country, goose is not so popular as it should be, which is a pity, for it has a personality and richness unequaled by any other poultry. It takes beautifully to charcoal cooking, for the fat renders out and the skin becomes magnificently mahogany-colored and crispy.

ROAST GOOSE

Rub a 12- to 14-pound goose well with salt and some thyme seasoning powder, and rub the inside with a cut half of a lemon. Spit the goose and roast over a medium fire, having a dripping pan placed to catch the fat, which should be saved for baking and other cooking. Pricking the skin with a sharp fork will help the fat to flow. Cook until the leg moves easily in its joint, or about 2½ hours. Serve with sauerkraut that has been cooked for 3 hours in red wine and seasoned with a few juniper berries or caraway seeds. Fried potatoes, cooked in some of the goose fat, would be good too. Drink a fine Pinot Noir with this—a memorable meal.

GARLICKED GOOSE

Stuff the goose with 2 cups of garlic cloves which have been slightly crushed. It is not necessary to peel them, as they are not eaten. Sew up the opening and roast as above. Yes, we said 2 *cups!*

squab

Although squab is usually associated with formal dinners, we feel it is much more suited to informal dining because it can be eaten as it should be—with the fingers.

ROASTED SQUAB

Allow 1 good-sized squab for each person. Secure the birds—4 to 8 of them—on the spit, and roast over a moderate fire, basting with melted butter and wine if you wish. It will take about 1 hour. Serve with fried corn meal mush, and with peas cooked with chopped ham and green onion. If desired, a sauce may be made by adding the cooked giblets, chopped, ½ cup of chopped sautéed onion, and 1 cup of white wine to 1 can of beef gravy. Just before serving, 1 cup of pitted green olives, a large pat of butter, and 1 tablespoon of lemon juice are added to the sauce.

BROILED SQUAB

Broil squabs either whole or split or, if you wish, split and flattened with a cleaver. The latter trick crushes the rib cage. Still another way to broil a squab is to do it *crapaudine*. This means "toadlike," for that's the way they look when they are split down the back and opened out in one piece. In any case, butter the birds well and broil them over a moderate fire. If whole, they will take about 45 to 60 minutes; if split, 20 to 40.

SQUAB IN THE COALS

Wrap each prepared squab in a slice of bacon and then, if available, in grape leaves. Cover with a double layer of aluminum foil and bury the birds in the coals. Let them cook for 15 to 18 minutes, then poke with a knowing fork, right through the foil. If they feel tender, they are done. Serve with canned shoestring potatoes, peas smothered in butter, and a Beaujolais or Gamay wine.

turkey

Either large or small turkeys may be cooked over charcoal. Turkeys weighing from 4 to 9 pounds are good either broiled or roasted; the larger birds are best roasted on the spit. Large turkeys may also be boned, rolled, and tied before roasting.

BROILED TURKEY

Have a small turkey split and the spine cut out. Brush with butter and broil, cut side down, over a moderate fire. After 15 minutes, turn and continue cooking until the leg moves easily when pulled, or until it is fork-tender. (If you wish, test with a meat thermometer; it should be removed from the fire at 175° to 180°.) A 5-pound broiling turkey will take from 40 to 60 minutes to cook. Any **baste for broiled chicken** may be used. Serve with a purée of broccoli, dressed with butter and cream, and with little new potatoes rolled in crisp crumbled bacon and bread crumbs.

ROAST TURKEY

The ideal size turkey for roasting seems to be from 15 to 18 pounds, eviscerated weight. The turkey may be stuffed or not, as you wish. Truss the turkey, having the legs and wings tied close to the body so that they won't dry out, and making sure that the neck skin is securely fastened at the back with a skewer, and that the cord does not pass over the breast to mar it. A good way is to insert one long or two short skewers through the body at the second joint, and use the ends of the skewer, the ends of the legs and wings, and the tail piece as fastening posts for the twine. The center of gravity of a stuffed turkey is different from that of an unstuffed one, so they are spitted differently. With an unstuffed turkey, insert the point of the spit at the back or spine, just in front of the tail. Have the spit come out about an inch from the front end of the breastbone. You'll have to use a hammer or mallet to drive the spit. Now fasten the holding forks securely and balance. If the turkey is stuffed in the body cavity only, the spit is inserted in just about the same way, but if the front cavity is full of stuffing, the point of the spit must emerge farther forward in order to compensate for the added off-center weight. As there is no bone there for the spit to penetrate, the holding forks should be firmly anchored on either side of the wishbone. Until it sets in the cooking, it is difficult to balance a stuffed turkey perfectly, as it can't be stuffed so full that it is rigid. Therefore, the stuffing shifts a little at each turn. Don't worry, however—this won't last long. Baste the turkey or not, as it roasts. We have found that it isn't really necessary, though butter, olive oil, or any **baste recommended for chicken** may be used.

A turkey of about 14 to 16 pounds, eviscerated weight, will take about 3 hours to cook (spit temperature about 250°) and 30 minutes of coasting. (A stuffed turkey will take longer to cook.) We find that if the thermometer, inserted in the thickest part of the breast, reads 175° to 178° when coasting starts, it will reach 180° or so, and the turkey will be juicily, perfectly done. Another test is to grasp the end of a drumstick and push it toward the body. If it responds readily, moving without resistance, the bird is done.

Turkey cooked on the spit will be, in most climates, a summer dish, so we see no need to treat it as a holiday meal and have the usual "fixings," unless, of course, you have a charcoal grill in your kitchen. Cranberry sauce is good with it, but so, too, are **broiled peaches** or **pineapple.** Creamed onions have an affinity for turkey, but **foil-roasted onions** have that same quality. **Roasted corn** is good, as are **yams** or **sweet potatoes,** roasted in the ashes. As for stuffing, that might just as well be different, too. Here's one we found delicious.

✔ TURKEY STUFFING. Allow about 1 cup of stuffing for each pound, dressed weight. For a 15-pound turkey, combine 3 quarts of dried or toasted bread crumbs, 3 bunches of green onions, chopped and cooked until wilted in 1 cup of butter, 1 green pepper, chopped, 1 cup of chopped celery, 3 tablespoons of tarragon soaked in ¼ cup of white wine, and the cooked chopped giblets of the turkey. Add enough stock from the giblets barely to moisten, and season to taste with salt and pepper.

✔ GIBLET SAUCE. If you don't stuff your turkey, you may want some sauce made from the giblets and the drippings. Place a long narrow pan beneath the spit, having it toward the front to catch the drippings. (We have found that two of the old-fashioned 10-cube ice trays, fastened together, are just right.) Cook the heart, neck, wing tips (if you've removed them), and gizzard in salted water to cover. When they are almost done, add the liver. When it is done but still pinkly juicy, chop all the giblets and return to the stock. Take ¼ cup of the drippings from your roast, and in it cook 4 or 5 chopped shallots or green onions until wilted. Add ¼ cup of flour, the chopped giblets, and the stock, season with a little soy sauce or Kitchen Bouquet, and add salt and pepper to taste. If desired, some thick cream may be added. Just before serving, stir in a jigger of brandy.

ROAST TURKEY IN THE MANNER OF D'ARTAGNAN

D'Artagnan was a Gascon, and all Gascons are notoriously good eaters and lovers of fine food. Here is a variation from Gascony on that most beloved of native American foods.

This is especially good for young turkeys roasted on the spit. Before spitting the bird, stuff it with a 6-inch hunk of dry French bread which has been rubbed with garlic to saturate it, and then rolled in freshly ground black pepper. This combination of flavors makes for a particularly heady seasoning, while the turkey is roasted according to the directions given above.

ROAST TURKEY ROLL

Skin the turkey, keeping the skin whole, and remove the meat from the bones. Lay skin out flat on a table, inside up, and on it lay the body meat and the boned legs and wings. Sprinkle with salt and pepper and, if you wish, with some herbs. Roll in a tight log-shaped piece and tie firmly with twine in several places. Fasten on the spit (this will be easy to balance), and cook as for the whole turkey. When it reaches 175° let it coast for another 5 degrees. This rolled turkey will not be so dramatic a sight to watch while it's cooking, but it will be very easy to carve.

SPITTED BREAST OF TURKEY

This is for those of you who actually prefer the white meat. Purchase a whole breast—it will probably weigh from 5 to 8 pounds. Rub well with butter and tie in a compact form, spitting it through the center. Roast over a moderate fire, basting with olive oil and vermouth, or butter and white wine. A 6-pound breast will take from 1½ to 2½ hours. Do be careful not to overcook it. Try it served with **hollandaise sauce,** fresh asparagus, toasted rye bread, and, for dessert, a deep-dish fresh peach pie with rum ice cream. For the latter, simply beat ¼ cup of Jamaica rum into a quart of soft ice cream.

DEVILED TURKEY BREAST

Use thick slices of **broiled** or **roast turkey** for this. Dip them in melted butter and then in **sauce diable,** and roll in fine bread crumbs, pressing them in well. Broil very quickly over a moderate fire until brown on both sides. Serve with more **sauce diable.** This, served with **broiled pineapple** slices and **pilaff,** is a delightful day-after version of turkey.

BROILED TURKEY LEGS

Allow about ¾ to 1 pound of turkey legs for each serving. Spread them with softened butter and put on the grill, skin side up. Cook over a medium fire for about 1½ hours, turning occasionally and basting with white wine and melted butter, to which dill, tarragon, curry, or rosemary has been added. The meat is done when it is fork-tender. If you can't tell that way, why not make a slit with a sharp knife and peek? Serve with a casserole of mashed potatoes and mushrooms, and with a salad of finely sliced celery with French dressing.

BROILED TURKEY THIGHS

If from a large bird, thighs will weigh about 1½ pounds each. Remove bone, lard thigh with strips of salt pork, then roll and tie in a compact form. Spit and roast, basting or not while cooking. It will take from 1½ to 2 hours.

TURKEY STEAKS

When these are good they are very, very good, but they have been known to disappoint us, and we really don't know why. Anyway, they're fun, and nice for a change. A frozen turkey must be used, in order to get even pieces. The bird is cut by the butcher on the electric meat saw in crosswise slices (at right angles to the breastbone) from where the wings start to where the drumsticks begin (the pieces at either end can be cooked and used for other things). The slices should be from ¾ to 1 inch thick, and here is one time when we think the white meat is better than the dark. Most of the steaks will have both kinds of meat in them. Brush them well with any marinade (we like white wine and butter, or soy, sherry, and oil), and cook over a medium fire. The 1-inch ones will take about an hour, and they should be basted while cooking. Serve them with spoon bread and with **charcoal-broiled peaches** or **pineapple**.

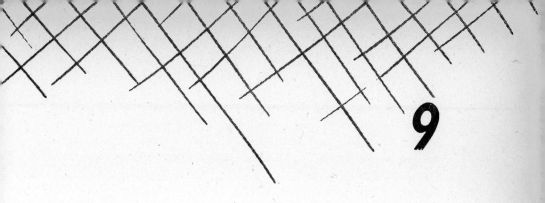

FISH
AND SHELLFISH

Confirmed fans of outdoor cooking use fish at every opportunity. It gains charm from charcoal, is less expensive than many meats, and is delicious and nutritious. We don't know of a fish or shellfish that can't be cooked in this manner. It, like many other foods, should *not* be overcooked. Also, because it's delicate, it should be handled carefully; always have the grill hot and well-greased—a hinged one is very helpful for turning all fish.

NOTE: Remember, the Canadian system of timing fish cooking is just about foolproof—10 minutes per inch of thickness.

grilled whole fish

This category can cover anything from a fresh sardine or smelt to as large a salmon as your grill will accommodate. If the fish has a substantial skin that is rich in fat, basting will not be necessary, though it does no harm. For large fish, have a more moderate fire than for smaller fish. Sprinkle the inside of the fish with salt or with pepper and lemon juice before broiling. It may be split or not, depending on its size. Put on a well-greased grill, or in a greased hinged broiler, and brown carefully on both sides, basting if you wish with equal parts of melted butter and white wine, or with melted butter flavored with lemon juice and tarragon or thyme, or with a mixture of soy, sherry, and oil. A fish weighing about 5 or 6 pounds will take anywhere from 20 to 45 minutes. It will be done when the internal temperature is 150°, or when the flesh flakes easily with a fork or toothpick. Small whole fish will cook in 15 minutes. When serving, remove bones, if you wish, but do give each guest some crisp charcoal-flavored skin. Serve with lemon, quartered the long way, and with **parsley butter,** or the sauce of your choice.

GRILLED FISH WITH HERBS

Remove the fish, cooked as above but basted simply with butter, to a hot platter on which you have heaped dried sprigs of fennel, parsley, and thyme. Sprinkle more of the same herbs on top of the fish, and pour over all 2 or 3 ounces of Cognac or brandy. Light the alcoholic herbs and allow the flames to die down before serving. The herbs will impact a delicious flavor to the fish.

NOTE: Another way to add the flavor of herbs to the fish is to toss some dried ones on the charcoal toward the end of the cooking. Bay, thyme, fennel, dill, and marjoram are all good choices.

WHOLE ROASTED SALMON

The Indians who live in the Northwest, and probably those in other parts of the country as well, used to roast whole salmon in several ingenious manners—ways which are well adapted to cooking on the beach today. Remove the head, tail, and fins of a salmon, and also remove the backbone from the inside, being careful not to cut through the skin. Now split a long sweet-tasting sapling, having the split longer than the fish. Insert the fish in the split, having the stick in the center, where the backbone was, and extending beyond the fish at both ends. Tie the split end securely, then put 4 or 5 or 6 cross pieces of wood through the split, first on one side of the fish and then on the other, and piercing the belly sides of the fish to hold it open. This kitelike affair is propped up in front of a bed of coals by sticking the unsplit end of the stick in the ground. It is turned when browned on the skin side, and finished cooking to a lovely amber. Serve with **roasted potatoes, roasted corn,** and sliced tomatoes.

PLANK-ROASTED SALMON

You will need a hardwood board about 1½ or 2 inches thick, and a little wider and longer than the split fish. If you wish, cover the plank with foil. Nail the fish, skin side down, to the plank. Salt and pepper it, and spread it with butter, then prop the board at a slight angle near enough to the fire so that the fish will cook slowly. Brush it with oil or butter from time to time. When the fish flakes easily it is done. Serve with the same vegetables as above, and with lemon and copious quantities of butter.

FOIL-ROASTED FISH

A whole fish, any size, may be successfully roasted by wrapping it in a double thickness of oiled aluminum foil and cooking right on the coals, without benefit of grill.

SPITTED WHOLE FISH

Salmon, sturgeon, bass, haddock, tuna, or any large, firm-fleshed fish may be spitted whole and roasted over coals. The fish should be tied securely to the spit with heavy twine, or wrapped in chicken wire. Baste the fish in the same manner that you would for broiling. Spit attachments for holding whole fish are available in fine cookware shops. They do away with the need for tying.

SPITTED WHOLE ALBACORE

In California, when the albacore flags are flying, everyone wants to roast his prize. A 15-pound albacore, head and tail removed, takes about 1 hour to cook to perfection. It should be tied to the spit in several places or wrapped in chicken wire before it's spitted. Foil may be used, too, but unless it's pretty thoroughly punched the baste won't reach the fish. We like white wine, butter, and lemon juice for albacore, though any fish baste may be used. Albacore, when cooked this way, will divide into four fillets and come easily from the bone.

TROUT AND OTHER SMALL FISH

These fish may all be broiled in the same manner as a **fish steak** or **fillet,** but we really prefer them pan-fried, because of the rich crispy skin that is so wonderful. This can be done over a campfire or at your charcoal grill, as well as in the kitchen. Roll fish in flour or corn meal, and cook quickly in either butter or bacon fat until brown on both sides. Serve with bacon and fried potatoes. **Cucumber salad** would be good too.

SPITTED SMALL FISH

This method of cookery is well adapted to camping. Run green twigs or skewers through the fish from mouth to tail, and hold over hot coals until done, rather as a child roasts a marshmallow. If desired, a piece of bacon may be inserted in the fish or wrapped around it before it's cooked. If the fish are very small 3 or 4 may be cooked on two twigs, having one pierced near the heads, the other near the tails.

FOILED SMALL FISH

Like large whole fish, the small ones may be wrapped in a double thickness of aluminum foil and roasted in or on the coals. It will take a very short time, say 15 or 20 minutes. If you wish, you may add sliced onions, mushrooms, sliced green peppers, tomatoes, or bacon to the fish before roasting. It's also good when roasted with a thick slice of lemon and a big chunk of butter.

BLUE TROUT (TRUITE AU BLEU)

This famous dish is usually to be found only in restaurants specializing in Continental cuisine. However, since the fish must be live, we think that the bank of the stream in which they were caught is the perfect place to cook them. Have ready 1 quart of boiling water to which 1 cup of vinegar and 1 tablespoon of salt have been added. Keep the fish alive until cooking time, then clean quickly and plunge at once into the boiling liquid. Remove pan from hot part of the fire and allow to simmer for 8 or 9 minutes, or until the fish are *just* done. The skin will turn blue—hence the name. Serve with butter, lemon juice, and boiled potatoes, and do have a pepper mill or some whole pepper that you can crush for this classic dish of fish.

fish steaks and fillets

Fish steaks and fillets broil beautifully over coals. The only trick is to have both fish and grill well oiled, so that there will be no sticking. If the fish is thick it will take a more moderate fire and a little longer time than if it is thin. However, no such fish takes very long. A fish steak 1½ inches thick takes about 15 minutes; one an inch thick takes 10 minutes; one 2 inches thick about 20 minutes (see chart). Test with a fork for easy flaking. Fillets will cook in 7 minutes for fairly large ones, 5 for smaller ones. In any case, brush them well with softened butter or oil, heat your broiler (a hinged one is almost a must), and grease it too. Brush while cooking with melted butter to which lemon juice or herbs have been added. Season well with salt and freshly ground pepper, and serve with plenty of lemon. Also good with charcoal-broiled fish are lemon butter, **parsley** or **tarragon butter, Béarnaise** or **hollandaise sauce,** or **salsa fria.**

VARIATIONS ON FISH STEAKS AND FILLETS

1. Marinate the fish in a good French dressing flavored with curry, dill, ginger, or tarragon. Broil as above.

2. Dip the fish in a mixture of soy, oil, and sherry, to which garlic may be added. Roll in sesame seeds, and cook over a moderate fire until the fish flakes easily and the seeds are brown.

3. Combine fish in foil with onion, tomato, mushrooms, and green pepper, add a lump of butter, wrap in foil, and cook 7 or 8 minutes near the coals, turning halfway through the cooking.

GRILLED FINNAN HADDIE

This is a perfect dish for an outdoor breakfast or lunch. If the finnan haddie is very salty, soak it in water or milk for an hour or two.

Drain and spread with soft butter. Broil until nicely browned and serve with melted butter and parsley, and with small boiled potatoes.

BROILED FROGS' LEGS

Select small frogs' legs if possible—they are tenderer and sweeter than the large ones. Tie the ends of the legs together and soak them in garlic-flavored melted butter for a few minutes, then chill so that the butter will adhere. Put in a hinged broiler and cook over moderate heat until nicely browned. Serve with lemon.

shellfish

GRILLED ABALONE

Slice abalone thin and pound it very gently until it feels tender. (Very often this is done for you at the fish market.) Brush well with butter, pass through sifted crumbs, and grill very quickly—about 1 minute to a side. Serve with the all-important lemon.

GRILLED CLAMS

Some clams, such as the mud clams of the Pacific Coast, are wonderful grilled. Remove from the shell, split through the neck, dip in melted butter and then in crumbs, and grill quickly over moderately hot coals.

CRABS

The Dungeness crab of the Pacific Northwest, the King crab of Alaska, and the soft-shelled crab of the East Coast all lend themselves graciously to the coals. They are all three available in the frozen state in many parts of the country, though of course they are better when fresh.

BROILED DUNGENESS CRAB

If possible use live ones, if not, the boiled ones are still well worth while. Clean them, crack the claws, and place them over the coals bottom shell down (the top shell is removed in the cleaning). While broiling, baste with a sauce made by combining ½ cup each of melted butter and white wine. (If you wish, add 2 tablespoons each of soy sauce and tomato catsup, 1 clove of garlic, crushed, and some marjoram seasoning powder.) Turn the crab once during the cooking, and serve when thoroughly hot. Huge bibs, plenty of lemon and melted butter, and some crisp French bread are all in order to complete the feast.

NOTE: Cracked cold Dungeness crab, served with mayonnaise and lemon juice, is a wonderful dish for outdoor eating.

BROILED KING CRAB LEGS

King crab is the Gargantuan member of the family, caught in the icy waters of Alaska. The center section of the leg is most prized for broiling. Cut a cross-shaped slit in the soft underneath part of the shell. Put on the grill, split side up, and baste with melted butter and lemon juice, until the crab is hot, the shell brown. Serve with crisp French fried potatoes, and shredded cucumbers smothered in mayonnaise and scented with dill and onions. Choose a chilled white wine—a Chablis or a White Pinot.

SOFT SHELLED CRABS

For broiling—and, for that matter, for any purpose—the small crabs are by far the best. Have them cleaned, dip in a mixture of melted butter and lemon juice seasoned with a whisper of cayenne, and broil quickly on both sides. Serve with **tartar sauce,** and with freshly made potato chips and a big bowl of **cole slaw.**

BROILED WHOLE LOBSTERS

Practically everyone's idea of the ultimate in gastronomical indulgence is a fine broiled lobster served with tubs of melted butter. A lobster should be a good-sized one—1¼ pounds minimum weight. Try broiling it whole, split it when it is done (in about 12 to 14 minutes), remove stomach, and fill with melted butter. In this way you husband all the juices and get the full benefit of the charcoal cookery.

BROILED SPLIT LOBSTERS

For those who prefer the conventional way, split live Eastern lobsters and remove intestinal vein and stomach. Brush the meat well with melted butter and cook for a couple of minutes, flesh side down, then turn, baste lavishly with more butter, and finish broiling with the shell to the fire. This will take 15 minutes or so, depending on the size of the lobster. After cooking, the empty part of the shell may be filled with toasted buttered crumbs. Serve with melted butter (each guest having his own dish of it) and halves of lemon. Beer is in order too. If live lobsters are unavailable, use boiled ones, and cook only long enough to heat, basting generously with butter.

BROILED LOBSTER SLICES

Very large lobsters are delicious this way. Cut right across the tail, in 1-inch slices, shell and all. Also crack the large claws, and the small ones if they have enough meat to make this worthwhile. Dip in melted butter and broil in a basket grill, basting with more butter.

ROCK LOBSTER TAILS

These are now available frozen in most parts of the country. Cut out the soft part of the shell and broil the meat in the remainder of the shell, basting with butter.

FIREPLACE OYSTERS

Any shell oyster may be roasted over or on the coals—any except, perhaps, the tiny Olympias of the Northwest. The large Pacific oysters are ideal, and so are the medium-sized ones from the East. Wrap them well in aluminum foil if you are going to do them on the coals, otherwise put them deep-shell side down on the grate. If they are iced, and they almost certainly will be, they will take 6 or 7 minutes for the largest ones—anyway, you'll know when they are done because they will open their shells. If large, leave them on another minute or so to be sure they are hot. If they are Eastern oysters, don't let them cook too long—they will toughen. The Pacific oysters have a strange and wonderful trait—they stay tender even though they are given extra heat. Break off the top shells and serve in the deep bottom one, with lemon wedges and grated horseradish, or with **Béarnaise sauce, tarragon butter sauce,** or **Mornay sauce.**

BROILED SCALLOPS

Scallops, perhaps more than any other shellfish, must be cooked very lightly. Dip them in butter, roll them in fine crumbs, and cook quickly in a hinged broiler over moderate coals. Cook for not more than 4 or 5 minutes. Serve with lemon and garlic-flavored mayonnaise.

BROILED SHRIMPS, CHINESE STYLE

There's nothing much better than a broiled shrimp if it's a large one and isn't cooked too much. (You will find more recipes for them in **Chapter 13,** for they are a favorite before-dinner snack.) This is one of our favorite ways. Select raw jumbo shrimps (they call them prawns in some parts of the country), and remove shells, or if you prefer, split them down the back with scissors. In either case, remove the black sand veins. Marinate the shrimps for a couple of hours in equal parts of soy sauce, sherry, and oil, seasoned if you wish with garlic and/or fresh grated ginger. Broil over a medium fire for 3 or 4 minutes (perhaps a minute longer if the shells are on), and serve at once. If unshelled, finger bowls, large paper napkins, or hot towels are in order. Serve with **fried rice** and everyone will be happy.

BROILED SHRIMPS, TARRAGON

These are done exactly as those above, but the marinade is 1 cup of white wine, in which 2 tablespoons of tarragon have been soaked, and ½ cup of oil or melted butter. Tiny roasted potatoes and asparagus would round out this meal to perfection.

BROILED SHRIMPS, DILL

These are also done the same way, but ½ cup of chopped fresh dill is substituted for the tarragon, and 2 tablespoons of lemon juice are added.

BROILED SHRIMPS, ITALIAN
(SCAMPI STYLE)

In Italy they'd probably use *scampi* (close kin to the shrimps) for this heavenly dish. Crush 4 cloves of garlic in 1 tablespoon of salt, add 1 cup of olive oil, ¼ cup of minced parsley, and 1 tablespoon of lemon juice. Marinate unpeeled shrimps (the shells may be split and the shrimps cleaned, however) for a couple of hours in this flavorsome mixture, then broil as above. Serve with **fettuccine Alfredo** and **broiled eggplant,** and be sure to allow twice as much as you think you need.

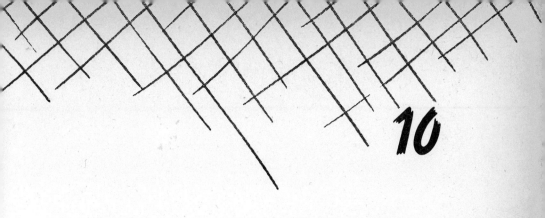

10

SKEWER COOKERY

Call it cooking on skewers, kebab cookery, cooking *en brochette,* or just plain cooking on a stick—it's all the same and has been ever since Adam. Your skewers may be green twigs, wires, metal skewers, split bamboo skewers, or even copies of elaborately wrought silver *hâtelets,* or of swords, such as are sometimes used in chichi restaurants. Your fire may be a campfire, fireplace, inside or outside grill, or an inside range or rotisserie. Your foods may be almost anything: meat, game, fish, poultry, fruit, or vegetables, alone or in combination of two or a dozen of them, strung on skewers and broiled. Sometimes these foods are marinated, sometimes merely brushed with oil or sauce. We give you many combinations—you will doubtless dream up others of your own.

meats on skewers

SHISH KEBAB

Probably the best-known of all the skewered dishes is that of the Near East, shish kebab. In its native land this is made, almost invariably, of lamb or mutton, but Americans have found it delicious if beef or veal is used, and even fish and fruits on skewers we have dubbed "kebabs."

A basic Near Eastern shish kebab is made with boneless meat, cut in 1½- or 2-inch cubes. With lamb, mutton, or veal, use the shoulder or leg; with beef, the round, chuck, or rump. Allow ½ to ¾ pound per person. String the cubes on your skewers, having them pushed close together if you want your meat rare and juicy, farther apart if all-around crispness is the system for you. The classic way was to tip each skewer with a cube of bread to keep the meat from falling into the flames. The meat may be simply brushed with lemon juice and with olive oil, or marinated for from 2 hours to 2 days in this mixture: Combine 1 part of lemon juice with 3 parts of olive oil, and season with 1 clove of garlic, crushed, salt and pepper to taste, and, if you wish, some thyme, orégano, bay, cumin, or what you will. The meat may be strung before or after marinating. The broiling, which is done as for **steaks** and **chops,** will take from 10 to 16 minutes, depending on how well done you want it. Shish kebab is usually served with **pilaff** or with **kasha** or rice. But suit yourself.

SHISH KEBAB, GREEK FASHION

String marinated meat on skewers, alternating with slices of onion or small whole ones (parboiled), and squares of green pepper. (If the onion is sliced from stem to root, in sections, it will be easier to skewer.) Season the marinade with mint or orégano.

SHISH KEBAB, TURKISH FASHION

Alternate marinated lamb with pieces of parboiled sweetbread, onion, and either quartered tomatoes or whole cherry tomatoes. Season marinade with bay leaves. This is perfectly delightful and a bit surprising.

SHISH KEBAB, LEBANESE FASHION

Marinate meat in olive oil, salt, and pepper, and string on skewers with green pepper squares, onion, and tomatoes. Season with thyme, if desired.

SHISH KEBAB, RUMANIAN FASHION

Alternate meat cubes with unpeeled eggplant cubes, wedges of tomato, and squares of green pepper. Brush with a mixture of ½ cup of olive oil, ½ cup of lemon juice, 1 teaspoon of orégano, and 1 clove of garlic, crushed.

SHISH KEBAB, DODECANESE FASHION

Marinate meat in 1 cup of olive oil, 2 teaspoons of orégano, 1 clove of garlic, crushed, 1 teaspoon of dry mustard, ¼ cup of lemon juice, salt and pepper. String with squares of green pepper and small whole potatoes, either parboiled or canned.

ORIENTAL KEBABS

Marinate the meat cubes in 1 cup of canned pineapple juice, 3 tablespoons of soy sauce, and 1 clove of garlic, crushed. Alternate with cubes of pineapple, and brush skewered meat with oil or melted butter while broiling.

IRANIAN KEBABS

Combine 2 pounds of ground lamb with 2 teaspoons of salt, 1 clove of garlic, crushed, ½ cup of pine nuts, ¼ cup of chopped parsley, ½ teaspoon of coarsely ground pepper, 2 eggs, and ¼ cup of dry bread crumbs. Mold around the skewers or make into meat balls and skewer. Brush with melted butter and grill. Serve with broiled eggplant, or alternate cubes of eggplants on skewers with the meat balls.

SHASLIK

This is the Caucasian or Russian version of shish kebab. It is variously spelled shashlik or shasslick, and variously composed. The classic version is a cube of mutton alternating with a cube of mutton fat. The marinade varies, though it is usually made with oil, vinegar, red wine, and spices. The latter may be bay, or sometimes parsley or dill, sometimes cloves or allspice. Here's a simple one: 1 cup of red wine, 1 cup of salad oil, 2 tablespoons of red wine vinegar, 1 clove of garlic, crushed, salt, freshly ground pepper, and a bay leaf. Sometimes the juice of a ripe pomegranate is used for a marinade, and that is very good indeed. So, too, is just plain lemon juice. Like shish kebab, shaslik may be varied by stringing with tomatoes, onions, green pepper, mushrooms, eggplant, and such.

other skewer combinations

BEEF

1. Cubes of beef strung with mushroom caps, tiny parboiled or canned onions. Brush with butter or melted beef suet.

2. Cubes of beef marinated in red wine, chopped onion, and rosemary. Baste with marinade and butter while broiling.

3. Cubes of beef alternating with bacon-wrapped oysters.

4. Meatballs, small parboiled or canned onions, and cherry tomatoes.

CHICKEN

1. Squares of raw chicken, with cubes of ham and squares of green pepper.

2. Squares of raw chicken with pineapple chunks; soy and oil marinade.

3. Squares of chicken with pineapple chunks, ham, and green pepper squares.

4. Small cubes of raw chicken, pitted ripe olives.

5. Chicken livers, bacon-wrapped, and pineapple chunks; soy-sherry baste.

DUCK

1. Cubes of cooked duck, and green olives; brushed with orange juice and butter.

2. Cubes of raw duck, basted with melted butter and dill.

HAM

1. Cubes of ham, pineapple chunks, green peppers; soy and pineapple juice baste.

2. Sliced cooked ham, wrapped around cubes of Swiss or Cheddar cheese.

3. Cubes of ham and veal; soy and sherry baste.

LAMB AND MUTTON

1. Lamb or mutton cubes, quartered apple, small parboiled onions, seasoned with curry or ginger. Brush with oil before grilling.

2. Lamb or mutton cubes, pineapple chunks, stuffed green olives.

3. Lamb kidneys, cut in half, with squares of bacon.

4. Lamb kidneys and mushroom caps; baste with **tarragon butter sauce** while broiling.

LIVER

1. Cubes of liver (calf, beef, or lamb), alternating with squares of bacon.

2. Thin strips of liver and slices of bacon, woven on skewers, with stuffed green olives.

3. Cubes of liver, parboiled onions, and Canadian bacon.

PORK

1. Pork cubes, pineapple chunks and green pepper squares. Baste with pineapple juice and soy sauce.

2. Pork cubes and apple quarters, with cubes of parboiled sweet potatoes. Baste with pork fat.

3. Thick slices of pork tenderloin, apple quarters, and parboiled or canned onions. Baste with melted butter and white wine.

SAUSAGES

1. Cubes of canned luncheon meat, with sections of banana, well buttered.

2. Frankfurters, cut in thirds, with cherry tomatoes and small parboiled onions.

3. Knackwurst, cut in 1-inch slices, with parboiled potatoes and onions.

SWEETBREADS

1. Pieces of parboiled sweetbreads, cubes of ham, mushroom caps. Brush with butter.

2. Chunks of parboiled sweetbreads, rolls of partially cooked bacon, parboiled onions. Baste with butter.

TURKEY

1. Cubes of raw turkey, alternating with oysters wrapped in bacon.

2. Cubes of raw turkey breast, pineapple chunks, and ripe olives; butter baste.

3. Cubes of cooked turkey, sprinkled with curry powder, wrapped in bacon, and alternating with ripe olives and cherry tomatoes.

VEAL

1. Thin squares of veal and ham, threaded on skewers, and basted with butter and white wine.

2. Squares of veal and Swiss cheese, wrapped in bacon.

fish on skewers

ANY WHITE FISH

1. Cubes of any white fish, alternating with quartered tomatoes and quartered onions; soy, sherry, and oil baste.

2. Cubes of any white fish, alternating with pineapple chunks and green pepper squares; soy, oil, and white wine baste, ginger-flavored.

3. Cubes of any white fish, alternating with oysters. Brush with melted butter to which a little lemon juice and some chopped parsley have been added.

SALMON

1. Cubes of salmon, ripe olives, and green pepper. Add dill seeds to melted butter baste.

2. Cubes of salmon with tomatoes, onion, and green pepper; soy and oil baste.

3. Cubes of salmon and mushroom caps; white wine, oil, and tarragon baste.

4. Cubes of salmon with pineapple chunks and stuffed green olives; melted butter and pineapple juice baste.

FINNAN HADDIE

1. Cubes of finnan haddie (soaked if salty) and mushroom caps. Baste with melted butter.

2. Cubes of finnan haddie, green and red pepper squares; baste with melted butter.

SCALLOPS

1. Dip in melted butter to which lemon juice has been added; broil quickly.

2. Dip in melted butter and olive oil, to which chopped parsley and crushed garlic have been added.

3. Roll scallops in partially cooked bacon, and alternate with stuffed green olives.

4. Alternate with mushroom caps, and baste with melted butter.

5. Alternate with shrimps and/or oysters. Marinate in olive oil flavored with garlic and soy. After broiling, sprinkle with copious amounts of minced parsley.

SHRIMPS

1. Roll raw cleaned shrimps in bacon, and alternate with ripe olives.

2. Marinate raw shrimps in melted butter, olive oil, chopped garlic, and curry powder. Alternate with squares of green pepper, and broil.

3. Marinate raw shrimps in equal parts of soy and sherry. Roll in sesame seeds and broil.

4. Marinate shrimps in equal parts of oil, sherry, and soy sauce, flavored with garlic and grated ginger; broil.

5. Raw peeled shrimps, pineapple, brown-and-serve sausage.

LOBSTER

1. Alternate chunks of cooked lobster meat with mushrooms, brush with butter; broil.

2. Alternate chunks of raw lobster with cherry tomatoes and green pepper. Brush with garlic-flavored olive oil; broil.

3. Marinate chunks of raw lobster in **tarragon butter sauce** and white wine; broil.

4. Marinate lobster chunks in curry-flavored tomato sauce. Alternate with pineapple chunks; broil.

OYSTERS

1. Dip raw oysters in melted butter, then in crumbs; string on skewers; broil.

2. Dip raw oysters in melted butter, roll in a mixture of half crumbs and half Parmesan cheese; broil.

3. Dip small raw oysters in butter, put each in a mushroom cap, string on skewers, and broil.

4. Roll oysters in partially cooked bacon slices, skewer, and broil.

5. Sprinkle bacon with chopped shallots or green onions, and roll around raw oysters. Skewer and broil.

6. Dip raw oysters in melted butter; alternate with ham squares; broil.

vegetables on skewers

1. Eggplant cubes, small onions, cherry tomatoes; marinated in olive oil seasoned with salt, pepper, garlic, and orégano.

2. Eggplant cubes, wrapped in bacon, alternating with pieces of green pepper and onions.

3. Mushroom caps and small whole tomatoes, brushed with butter or olive oil.

4. Mushroom caps, bacon, and small parboiled onions.

5. Small parboiled or canned onions, with small parboiled potatoes, cherry tomatoes, and green pepper squares.

6. Chunks of yam or sweet potato, parboiled, and brushed with melted butter.

7. Thick slices of green tomato, onion, and green pepper, brushed with garlic-flavored olive oil.

8. Green tomato dipped in oil flavored with ground ginger.

9. Zucchini or cucumbers, cut in chunks, tomatoes, onions, and green pepper, marinated in garlic-flavored olive oil.

fruit on skewers

1. Apple quarters, rolled in melted butter, and sprinkled with sugar.

2. Apple quarters, alternating with bacon squares.

3. Apricots, dipped in melted butter, and broiled. They may be flamed with brandy before serving.

4. Bananas, cut in quarters, dipped in butter, and broiled; then rolled in chopped peanuts.

5. Banana chunks, alternating with bacon squares.

6. Orange sections, dipped in butter, and alternating with green pepper squares.

7. Pineapple chunks, dipped in the juice from preserved ginger, and served with grated coconut.

8. Pineapple chunks, dipped in butter, broiled, and rolled in macaroon crumbs. These may be blazed with rum.

9. Pineapple chunks, alternating with banana sections and bacon squares.

teriyaki

The crave for teriyaki was certainly Japanese-inspired, though many natives of Japan don't know it by that name. It was first popularized in the Hawaiian Islands, but now it has invaded the mainland. Though some seem to believe that the word means "meat strung on sticks and broiled," this isn't necessarily so. It means "glaze-broiled"—*teri* means "sunshine" or "shiny," and *yaki* means, in most cases, "broiled" or "roasted." Anything may be teriyaki: steak, fish, "little birds," pork, or any meat for that matter. The only resemblance one teriyaki may have to another is that all the marinades seem to include shoyu or soy sauce. Here we give you several versions—some as authentic as they come, some adaptations by an imaginative cook. These dishes are served as entrees, usually with rice. One word before we start cooking: if using bamboo skewers, it is well to soak them in water lest they burn; or have the bare part of the sticks (the handle that's not strung with meat) hanging over the edge of the grill. For the sticks, split the inexpensive bamboo chopsticks in four or five pieces, lengthwise.

Just to confuse the teriyaki issue, *yakimono* also means "charcoal-broiled" meat or fowl, but without the shiny glaze. *Kushiyaki* is meat strung on skewers and grilled. *Maruyaki* is whole meat, roasted—or roasted whole.

PORK TERIYAKI

Either cut boneless pork into 1½- to 2-inch cubes, or have a rather thin (½ inch) slice of leg cut in strips 1 x 6 inches. In either case, marinate for several hours in ½ cup of shoyu or soy sauce, 1 clove of garlic, crushed, 1 teaspoon or more of sugar (and that's optional —the Japanese love it, but most Occidentals don't), and ¼ cup of sherry or sake. String the cubes, 3 or 4 to each skewer, or weave the strips of pork on them. Broil slowly over charcoal until done but not dry, basting during the process with the marinade. The cubes will take longer than the strips.

CHICKEN TERIYAKI

This one is not strung on skewers, but there is no reason why it can't be done that way with boned chicken. So . . . Have a fryer cut in the usual pieces and bone or not, as you prefer. Marinate in ½ cup of shoyu, 2 tablespoons of slivered fresh or crystallized ginger, and 3 tablespoons of whiskey or sherry, for 3 or 4 hours. Broil, basting with the marinade. If you use skewers, we think it advisable to put 2 parallel ones through each piece of chicken.

STEAK TERIYAKI

Use sirloin steak cut about ½ inch thick (some like it thinner), and cut in strips 1 inch wide and 6 inches long. Weave a strip on each bamboo skewer, leaving the end as a handle, soak in the **pork teriyaki** marinade for only an hour and grill. The other technique is to have 2-inch cubes of the steak and proceed as for **pork teriyaki**. This latter way makes rare steak possible.

A friend who lives in San Mateo, California, has developed a fascinating recipe for teriyaki. It is used for fish, chicken, or pork slices, and we found it also good for beef:

TERIYAKI

"Three tablespoons shoyu or soy sauce; add 3 tablespoons of water, 2 tablespoons of sugar, 2 teaspoons of tarragon vinegar, 2 split cloves of garlic, and 1 split medium-sized shallot. Simmer to cook the garlic and shallots, and then remove them. Add 3 tablespoons of sake, sherry, or whiskey, and ½ teaspoon of crushed sesame seeds. Marinate the fish, chicken, or pork slices for an hour or more, turning frequently. Broil or barbecue, interrupting 5 or 6 times to dip into the sauce, turning to cover well. When completely done, sprinkle with powdered ginger and serve."

MAINLAND TERIYAKI

Another teriyaki that's definitely an adaptation has, nevertheless, great charm. Two pounds of sirloin are sliced thin (¾ inch), then cut in 1½-inch squares. These are marinated in 1 cup of canned pineapple juice to which ½ cup of shoyu has been added, along with 1 clove of garlic, crushed, and 2 teaspoons of chopped ginger (or 1 teaspoon of powdered ginger). After an hour, string the meat squares on skewers, alternating with canned pineapple chunks and stuffed green olives. Broil over charcoal, using the marinade as a baste. Serve as an appetizer to 10 to 12 persons, or as an entree with rice to 4 or 6.

DUCK TERIYAKI

Do this exactly as for the **chicken teriyaki,** but have the duck split in half when broiling. Cut into serving pieces later with poultry shears.

SQUAB TERIYAKI

Have squab split down the back and flattened out with a cleaver. Put on 2 strong skewers, preferably steel, having one go through the body at the wings, the other at the second joints. Proceed as for **chicken teriyaki.**

FISH TERIYAKI

You'll need small fish for this—smelts, fresh sardines, or whatever little fish you may be able to find. Marinate them as for **pork teriyaki,** but add 1 tablespoon of lemon juice to the marinade. String 3 or 4 fish for each serving, using 2 parallel skewers about 1½ inches apart—one through the front and one through the rear part of the fish. Marinate 1 hour and broil, painting with marinade during the brief cooking. These are called *wakasagi.* Small birds are done the same way, 2 or 3 to a skewer, or use single fish or birds spitted from stem to stern.

VENISON TERIYAKI

This is done exactly as is the **steak teriyaki.**

KABAYAKI (GRILLED EEL)

Don't discount this; it is a Japanese favorite, and rightly so. What's more, if you don't like the shape of an eel it doesn't matter, as they are split and opened up flat, the bone removed, then skewered with 2 skewers to stay that way. The marinade is the same old soy and sake—or use equal parts of soy and sherry. The Japanese would add sugar too. Broil and marvel!

sasaties

Sasaties, from South Africa, must be kitchen kin to the Malayan *satés*. The sasaties are cubes of veal, mutton, or pork, spiced—often with curry powder—and sometimes marinated in vinegar or fruit juices, then broiled over charcoal. That vagueness gives an imaginative cook plenty of opportunity.

PORK OR LAMB SASATIES

Stew a cup of dried apricots until soft, and put through a food mill. Add water to make 2½ cups, ¼ cup of vinegar, 2 tablespoons of curry powder, 2 cups of onion, chopped and cooked clear in ¼ cup of butter, and salt to taste. If not hot enough, add a dash of Tabasco or cayenne. Marinate 1- to 1½-inch cubes of pork or lamb or mutton in this for 12 hours, then broil. Use marinade for basting and sauce.

satés

In Malaya satés are morsels of this and that, strung on sticks and roasted over charcoal. They are naturals for the charcoal grill.

PORK SATÉS

Combine ½ cup of shoyu or soy sauce with 1 tablespoon of honey, ¼ cup of oil, ¼ cup of lemon juice, 1 tablespoon each of curry and chili powder, and 1 cup of finely chopped onion. A crushed clove of garlic may also be added. Marinate large cubes of pork (or use lamb, mutton, veal, or beef) for 1 hour, then thread on bamboo sticks (3 or 4 to a stick) and broil slowly over a clear fire. If used as appetizers, the cubes may be much smaller, or the larger ones may be 1 to a stick.

KOON-KO-KI (KOREAN SKEWERED STEAK)

Dip 2 pounds of thinly sliced, 1-inch-wide strips of sirloin steak in a marinade made by combining 1 clove of garlic, crushed with ½ cup of shoyu or soy sauce, ¼ cup of sesame or other oil, and ¼ cup of minced green onions. Now dip in crushed toasted sesame seeds to cover the meat completely, and return to the marinade for an hour. Weave on bamboo sticks and broil quickly, or, if you prefer, fry quickly in a little oil. The sesame seeds are toasted by cooking slowly in a heavy skillet, until brown. They are then crushed in a mortar or heavy bowl, with salt. The mixture should not be smooth.

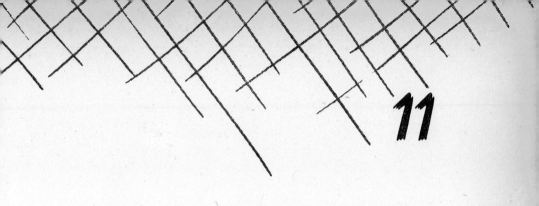

OTHER GRILLED MEATS, INCLUDING INNARDS

Steaks, chops, and roasts are not, by any means, the only cuts that can be cooked to perfection over charcoal. We, in our experimenting, have tried them all, and have found most of them superlative. Here they are—those we liked best.

pork

GRILLED PIGS' FEET

Allow 1 foot per person, and if possible get them cut long, as they do in Chinese markets. Clean the feet and bandage each one well with muslin strips. Fasten and cook in 6 quarts of water to which 1 onion, 4 cloves, 2 carrots, a bay leaf, 1 tablespoon of salt, and ¼ cup of vinegar have been added. When tender—in 3 or 4 hours— cool in the liquid and remove the wrappings. Roll in oil and heat well over charcoal, then again dip in oil and roll in buttered crumbs. Return to the grill and broil until prettily browned. Serve with **sauce diable** or with wedges of lemon.

SPLIT PIGS' FEET

Sometimes the cooked feet are split, dipped in egg and crumbs, and then grilled.

SPARERIBS

The popularity of spareribs keeps their price in the luxury class. They are delectable charcoal-broiled, and prepared in any of these many ways. Because of their high fat content they must be cooked very slowly and turned constantly. This is most easily done when they are left in a whole strip and woven on the spit. Lacking a spit, constant turning on the grill is a necessity, for they must be crisp outside but not charred, and the meat must be tenderly, juicily done. Spareribs are finger food, so large paper napkins are in order, or finger bowls, if you prefer. Allow 1 pound per person.

HONEY-GARLIC SPARERIBS

This one has a Chinese heritage but gets along nicely with Occidental dishes. Make a marinade of ½ cup of honey, ½ cup of soy sauce, 2 cloves of garlic, crushed, 3 tablespoons of tomato catsup, and ½ cup of water. Allow a strip of ribs to stand in this for several hours, turning a few times. Weave on the spit and cook, basting occasionally, over a slow fire for 1 to 1½ hours, or until the ribs are shinily brown and tender to the fork. If you catch the drippings (**see Chapter 2,** under the heading "Flaring") you'll have less trouble. Cut the ribs apart for serving. Rice is good here, and tomatoes and green peppers in a sweet and sour sauce.

BROILED GLAZED SPARERIBS

These are done on the broiler, though of course they may be spitted. If broiled, cut 4 pounds of spareribs in sections of about 5 ribs each. Sprinkle with salt and pepper, and broil over a slow fire, brushing them frequently with a mixture of melted fruit jelly (apple, quince, orange marmalade, or plum) and 1 tablespoon each of lemon juice and Worcestershire sauce. Two teaspoons of dry mustard may be mixed with the baste. Remember to turn the ribs frequently, and douse the fire if it flares. Serve with **sauerkraut,** boiled potatoes, sliced raw onions in vinegar, and beer.

SPARERIBS WITH RED WINE

Marinate 5 pounds of spareribs in 2 cups of red wine, 3 cloves of garlic, crushed, 1 tablespoon of salt, ½ teaspoon of freshly ground black pepper, 1 teaspoon of thyme, 1 cup of tomato purée, and 2 tablespoons of wine vinegar, for 12 hours or more. Wipe dry and broil or roast until done (see above), using the marinade, which has been reduced one half, to baste the ribs. If you wish, you may sprinkle them with granulated sugar 5 minutes before removing from the fire; this will caramelize and form a glaze. Serve with sliced tomatoes dressed with olive oil, ripe olives, and garlic, and with hot French bread. Red wine and cheese go well with these.

BARBECUED SPARERIBS

Allowing a minimum of 1 pound of ribs per person, precook them in the oven for 45 minutes at 350°. Then marinate them for 12 to 24 hours in the following: Combine 2 chopped onions, 1 cup of seeded chopped tomatoes, ¼ cup of wine vinegar, 1 cup of sugar, 1 cup of red wine, 2 tablespoons of chili powder, a dash of tabasco, 1 tablespoon of Worcestershire sauce, 1 teaspoon of dry mustard, 1 tablespoon of salt, and 2 tablespoons of cocoa. Broil the ribs about 1 foot from the fire, basting with the marinade.

PINEAPPLE BROILED SPARERIBS

These are parboiled, a method many cooks prefer as it cuts down the long slow broiling time. Cover 5 pounds of spareribs with water, add 1 onion stuck with cloves, 2 cloves of garlic, 1 table-spoon of salt, 1 teaspoon of orégano, and ½ teaspoon of freshly ground black pepper. Bring to a boil and simmer 35 to 40 minutes. Remove ribs and cool the liquid, skimming it of its fat. Add 5 or 6 cloves of garlic, crushed, and 1 quart of pineapple juice to the liquid, and marinate the meat in it for 1 or 2 days. Drain, and boil as above, brushing the ribs at the last with a little honey to form a glaze. If you wish, serve with dry mustard that has been blended with kumquat syrup or orange marmalade to make a thick paste. Serve **broiled pineapple** slices and potato chips. A chilled white wine, not too dry, would be nice here.

CURRIED SPARERIBS

Marinate 4 pounds of spareribs in 1 cup of tomato catsup, 3 table-spoons of curry powder, 2 cloves of garlic, finely chopped, ½ cup of chicken or beef broth, 1 teaspoon of salt, and 1 teaspoon of freshly ground black pepper, for several hours, turning them often. Spit the ribs and roast as above. Lentils, boiled until tender and sautéed with bacon, onion, and parsley, are delicious with roasted ribs. A bowl of sliced tomatoes and sweet Italian onions, with a basil-flavored oil and vinegar dressing, is a most refreshing accompaniment.

NOTE: Breast of lamb, or lamb riblets, may be cooked in any of the above ways.

BROILED PORK TENDERLOIN

Not always easy to get, but more than worth a try. Allow 1 tenderloin per person. Salt and pepper them well, and broil over a low fire, brushing them occasionally with butter, or a mixture of soy, oil, and sherry. Serve with baked or roasted potatoes and sour cream, and with applesauce or **roasted apples**.

PORK TENDERLOIN ORIENTALE

Marinate tenderloins in ½ cup of soy sauce, 2 tablespoons of grated ginger, 1 teaspoon of dry mustard. While broiling, brush with the marinade to which 2 tablespoons of honey have been added. Serve with **fried rice** and with crisp celery and green onions.

GRILLED SAUSAGES

Any and all sausages take nicely to the grill. They are particularly adapted to the hibachi, as they are ideal for a hurried hot addition to an otherwise cold meal. Frankfurters are prime favorites and we like them best when split and brushed with a little butter before broiling. We prefer most other small sausages split, the larger ones sliced, before grilling. The first category includes Knackwurst, Vienna Wurst, chorizo, Swiss sausage, and such; the latter, Bologna, Braunschweiger, mortadella, and the like. Plain pork or breakfast sausage is best grilled unsplit, and the brown-and-serve type is very satisfactory, as it exudes less fat while broiling.

BROILED SHORT RIBS OF BEEF

Short ribs which have a good streak of lean are delicious when marinated and broiled to a crusty rareness over low coals. Do not have them cut into chunks. It is much better for broiling to have them in large pieces, which may be carved afterward.

KOREAN SHORT RIBS

Marinate 4 pounds of short ribs in ¼ cup of peanut or other bland oil, ½ cup of soy sauce, ¼ cup of crushed sesame seeds, 1 clove of garlic, finely chopped, 1 tablespoon of brown sugar, ½ cup of water, and a little freshly ground black pepper, for 24 hours, turning now and then. Broil the ribs over a moderate fire until they are crisped and browned, and done to your liking. Baste from time to time with the marinade.

MARINATED SHORT RIBS

Marinate 4 or 5 pounds of short ribs in a **game marinade** for 24 hours. Remove from the marinade, wipe dry, and broil slowly over moderate heat until crisp and brown. Serve with mustard, boiled potatoes sprinkled with parsley and chives, and **garlic loaf**.

DEVILED BEEF RIBS

This is a fine way to use the bones of a rib roast; providing you can withhold them from the begging crowd. Carve the bones completely away from the cooked roast, leaving some meat on them. Separate the ribs and dip in ¼ cup of melted butter to which you've added 2 tablespoons of tarragon vinegar. Now roll in sifted dried bread crumbs and grill over a low charcoal fire from 10 to 20 minutes, turning occasionally. The crumbs should be brown, the meat tender. Serve with **sauce diable**. Though this is often the specialty of swank restaurants, it is best eaten outdoors, for there it is accepted as finger food. Precooked short ribs, with surplus fat removed, may be cooked the same way.

MIXED GRILLS

This English menu item has become well known in other countries. It can include almost any combination of broiled foods, and its charm lies in a harmonious balance of flavor, texture, and color. In preparing a mixed grill it is obvious that the foods that take longest to cook should go on the broiler first. Here are a few combinations that never fail to please:

1. A loin lamb or mutton chop rolled around a kidney, 3 or 4 mushrooms, a slice of Canadian bacon, 2 green tomato slices, and ½ slice of eggplant.

2. A small tenderloin steak, a small thick slice of liver, 2 sausages, a thick slice of onion, and one of tomato.

3. A chicken leg and thigh, a small thick slice of ham, a green pepper half, a tomato half, and a slice of veal kidney.

4. A small thick liver steak, 2 slices of bacon, 2 slices of tomato, a small hamburg patty.

5. A lamb patty, 2 slices of apple, 2 sausages, a kidney wrapped in bacon.

innards

Call them "variety meats" if you will, we prefer the more realistic term of innards. Liver and sweetbreads are the most popular, perhaps because of their snob appeal, but they all take on new glamor when cooked over charcoal.

brains

BROILED BRAINS

A calf's brain will serve 1 or 2, a lamb's brain probably not more than 1. Soak the brains in cold water, then simmer in acidulated water (1 pint of water to 1 tablespoon of vinegar) for 15 minutes, then plunge into ice water until time to remove membrane and broil. Dip the brains in melted butter and then in crumbs, and broil slowly until hot and the outside is crisp. Serve with **beurre noir** and boiled potatoes. Another way to serve is with Greek lemon sauce. Beat 4 eggs well, combine with ¾ cup of hot chicken broth, and cook over hot water until thick, adding ¼ cup of lemon juice and salt to taste.

hearts

Hearts are delicious when charcoal-broiled. If cooked rare, they will be tender, but if you prefer them well done, it is wise to use an unseasoned tenderizer. Lamb, veal, and beef hearts are all good.

BROILED BEEF HEART

Clean a beef heart and cut it in slices about ½ inch thick. Brush with melted butter and broil quickly on both sides—about 6 to 8 minutes in all. Serve with lemon wedges.

CHOPPED BEEF HEART

Clean heart and put through a food chopper. Mix with salt and pepper, and form in patties, wrapping each in aluminum foil. Broil on the grill as you do hamburgers. Serve in the foil, with baked potatoes and lots of butter.

BROILED LAMB OR VEAL HEART

Clean and split a lamb or veal heart, and marinate in ¼ cup of soy sauce, 2 cloves of garlic, finely chopped, 1 teaspoon of rosemary or tarragon, 2 tablespoons of wine vinegar, 1 teaspoon of salt, and 1 teaspoon of coarsely ground black pepper, for an hour. Drain, brush with oil, and grill over a rather brisk fire until brown on the outside, but still rare. Serve with rice and a purée of spinach. Less tender hearts, such as pork, may be tenderized this way: 30 minutes before grilling, sprinkle with 1 teaspoon of unseasoned meat tenderizer, and "fork it in" by jabbing the surface thoroughly with a long-tined fork.

kidneys

Lamb, veal, and even pork and beef kidneys take well to charcoal cooking. If beef or pork kidney has a stronger flavor than you like, try soaking it in milk or white wine before cooking.

BROILED VEAL OR LAMB KIDNEYS

Split kidneys and remove cores, brush with melted butter, and broil on both sides, not too long. Kidneys that are overcooked will toughen, so watch them. They should be cooked in from 6 to 14 minutes, depending on their size. When done they should be tender, with a juicy pink color. To serve, slice the kidneys, and add a good piece of butter, salt, and pepper. Serve with boiled potatoes, dressed with **parsley or tarragon butter.**

A variation of this dish is to have the kidneys left in their surrounding suet, and broiled until the fat is brown and crispy. It is then removed, and the kidneys are sliced and served as above. The kidneys may also be sliced before grilling, in which case they will take about 4 or 5 minutes to cook.

KIDNEYS BOULE D'OR

This rather luxurious dish was named after the Parisian restaurant. Broil 2 veal kidneys as above. Heat ¼ cup of butter in a chafing dish or electric skillet, and in it sauté 6 mushroom caps, cut in slices. When the kidneys are cooked rare, slice them very thin, and add to the mushrooms. Season to taste, pour on 2 ounces (¼ cup) of gin, and blaze it. Add to this ⅔ cup of heavy cream or sour cream, and heat gently. Serve on rice. Serves 2 or 3.

DEVILED KIDNEYS

Broil split kidneys until almost done. Dip in melted butter to which vinegar and mustard have been added, then roll in crumbs. Grill until brown, and serve with **sauce diable.**

Liver, once described by the great chef, Escoffier, as "bourgeois food" that should appear only at breakfast, is now the favorite of both dietitian and gastronome. When cooked over charcoal, it is sheer delight.

WHOLE ROASTED LIVER

Choose a whole calf's or lamb's liver, or a 4- or 5-pound piece of beef liver. Roll and tie it, stripping it with slices of salt pork or bacon, or have it larded. (If you're feeling fancy, soak the lardoons in Cognac before using.) Spit the liver, and roast it over a moderate fire until the internal temperature is about 150° if you like your liver pink and juicy. This will take from 50 minutes to over an hour. Serve this elegant dish with **Béarnaise sauce** and crisp **potato galette**. A salad of sliced oranges and sweet onions would be pleasant too.

LIVER STEAKS

Thick liver steaks, grilled over charcoal until they are crisply brown on the outside and juicily pink in the middle, are epicurean treats. Have the liver—calf or beef—sliced about 1½ inches thick, butter the steaks well, and grill as you do a steak, testing them by making an incision with a small sharp knife—you will be able to see when it is done to your liking (**see chart, Chapter 4**). Serve with **Béarnaise sauce** and with grilled tomato and bacon, or with a great bowlful of **French fried onions**. Liver steak is also good served with butter and lemon wedges, and accompanied by spinach flavored with tarragon. A bottle of chilled California rosé wine or some beer seems particularly fitting.

sweetbreads

These tender, delicately flavored morsels don't gain as much from charcoal broiling as do other meats, but they are still delectable when simply cooked. All sweetbreads should be blanched before further cooking—this keeps them white and firm. Simmer them for 15 minutes in 1 quart of water to which 1 teaspoon of salt and the juice of ½ lemon have been added. Drain, plunge into ice water, and remove membrane and discolored portions.

NOTE: A new and wonderful way with sweetbreads is to split them with a sharp knife, sprinkle on both sides with salt and pepper, and grill over very hot coals for about 3 minutes. No boiling, no skinning—just be sure you have plenty!

BROILED SWEETBREADS

Prepare as above, dip in ½ cup of cream to which 1 beaten egg has been added, then roll in crumbs. Cook over a low fire until brown on both sides. Serve with wedges of lemon, or with **Béarnaise** or **Mousseline sauce,** or with melted butter to which capers have been added. Shoestring potatoes and a mixed vegetable salad would go well here, and so would a bottle of Sancerre.

SWEETBREADS MILANESE

Combine equal quantities of grated Parmesan cheese and buttered crumbs. Dip prepared sweetbreads in butter and then in the cheese and crumbs. Broil and serve with **broiled mushrooms** and **risotto.**

tongue

GRILLED TONGUE, TARRAGON

This delicious dish gets only its final benediction of charcoal flavor from the grill. It starts out, like all proper tongues, by being cooked tender in a pot or pressure cooker. In either case, an onion and an herb bouquet of bay, parsley, celery, and thyme are cooked with it, as well as salt. A fresh beef tongue, for such this is, will take from 2 to 4 hours to boil tender, but only 1 hour in a pressure cooker at 15 pounds pressure. When the tongue is done, remove skin and trim. Make a paste with 2 cloves of garlic, crushed, 1½ tablespoons of dried tarragon, 1 tablespoon of prepared mustard, 1 tablespoon of tarragon vinegar, and ½ tablespoon of salt. Rub half of this on the tongue. To the remainder add ½ cup of tongue broth, 3 tablespoons of butter, and 1 tablespoon of tarragon vinegar. Arrange tongue on spit from tip to root, fasten and balance, then grill at moderate heat for about 45 minutes. While roasting, baste with the sauce. The tongue should be brown and crusty on the outside, tender and juicy within. We like this with spinach *en branche,* cooked lightly in a covered pot on the back of the grill, and with **roasted potatoes,** with lots of butter and freshly ground pepper.

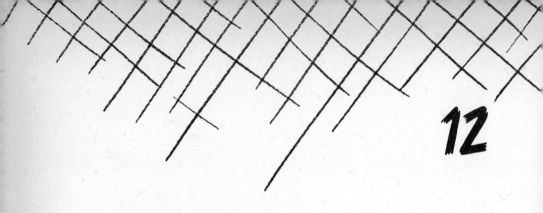

GAME

There has been no reawakened interest in cooking game over coals, because such interest never slept. Hungry hunters have always cooked at least part of the bag over the campfire, and so enjoyed it that much of the catch that was toted home was treated in the same manner. With the possible exception of a very ancient deer or bear, or a very fishy water fowl, we know of no game that isn't improved by cooking over coals.

wild ducks and geese

There is no need to bring up the old argument as to whether ducks should be cooked rare or well done. Almost everyone who has tried them rare prefers them that way, for they are tenderer, better-flavored, and naturally juicier. However, if you don't agree, don't let anyone, even us, talk you out of it—just pay no attention to our timing. Still, we must have the last word—we advise such eaters to eschew the wild duck and chew a domestic one instead.

ROAST WILD DUCK OR GOOSE

First pick your ducks or goose, or—better—make eyes at your butcher. Allow, usually, 1 duck a person. If they are very small, allow 1½, or even 2; if extra large, 1 duck might conceivably serve 2 people. As for geese, a wild one will serve from 2 to possibly 6, depending on its size. Ducks and geese are cooked in the same manner.

Clean the birds and singe them, but do not stuff. You may rub them with lemon and put in the cavity a slice of onion, or a slice of onion plus a rib of celery and a piece of apple, or perhaps a few juniper berries. Spit the ducks firmly, having one breast-up, the next breast-down. Usually 5 or 6 ducks can be put on a spit. Spit them crosswise through the center, just below the breast; then, using long skewers, fasten the ends of the birds together, and lastly fix the holding forks firmly in the two end birds. In this way the center birds are prevented from spinning on the spit.

Roast over a medium fire for 20 to 25 minutes—less if you want them bloody rare, say 12 to 15 minutes. Basting is not necessary, but do it if you wish. General Bartron, mentioned frequently in this book, allows the fire to flare at the end in order to crisp the skin. The same result may be achieved by pouring brandy over the finished ducks and flaming them.

To serve, cut ducks in halves or quarters with poultry shears. Serve with wild rice if you're feeling rich, though we like brown rice mixed with butter crumbs or chopped pecans just as well. We also think fried hominy grits, lentils cooked with bacon, or maybe just a dish of mashed turnips are fine with ducks. A salad of sliced oranges may please you, too, or one of romaine with a green olive dressing. For wine, a fine Burgundy.

DUCK WITH RED WINE AND GIN

Baste ducks, prepared as above, with equal parts of red wine and melted butter. Blaze at the end of the cooking with some heated gin.

DUCK OR GOOSE WITH OLIVE SAUCE

Roast duck or goose as above. Make a sauce by first preparing a stock with the feet, gizzard, neck and heart, cooked in water or chicken stock. Sauté 2 chopped shallots or green onions in ¼ cup of butter, and add 1 cup of sliced manzanilla olives. Add the broth, which has been reduced to ¾ cup, and season to taste. Serve with the roasted or broiled duck or goose.

BROILED WILD DUCKS

Split the ducks with carving shears and cut out the backbones. Brush with butter and broil, skin side up, for 6 to 8 minutes before turning. Broil the other side the same length of time, or until done to your liking. Blaze with gin or Cognac, if desired, before serving. Whole ducks may also be broiled, though they will take longer to cook and require more care to cook evenly.

hare or wild rabbit

There is some confusion in this country as to the difference between hare and rabbit, so we will treat them as the same. Generally speaking, a hare is larger than a rabbit, but then there are jack rabbits . . . Most of our wild rabbits come from the hunter's bag, while wild hare is imported from Canada and Australia.

MARINATED ROAST HARE OR RABBIT

Skin, clean, and remove head and feet of the animal, and marinate in a fifth of red wine, ½ cup of wine vinegar, ½ cup of olive or peanut oil, 1 large onion stuck with cloves, a bay leaf, a bouquet garni or herb bouquet (1 leek, a sprig of thyme, a rib of celery, 2 springs of parsley, and a small piece of stick cinnamon), 1 tablespoon of salt, 2 teaspoons of freshly ground black pepper, and 2 cloves of garlic. Allow to marinate for 3 or 4 days in the refrigerator, or in a cool place, turning occasionally. Before roasting, drain, wipe, and rub with oil. Truss the animal securely and tie the legs together, spitting it for perfect balance. Roast slowly until nicely browned on the outside and juicy within, basting it with a bit of the marinade while cooking (see chart, Chapter 4). Reduce the remaining strained marinade to 1½ cups. Sauté 6 shallots or green onions in 3 tablespoons of butter until melted. Add 2 teaspoons of dry mustard, a dash of tabasco, 1 teaspoon of freshly ground pepper, and simmer 5 minutes. Add ¼ cup of chopped parsley and a large dollop of butter. Stir well, correct seasoning, and thicken slightly with butter and flour kneaded together. (This is called *beurre manié*, and is the simplest way to thicken any sauce at the last minute.) Serve the hare or rabbit with the sauce, and with crisp fried potatoes and broiled tomatoes. A really good claret is ideal with this dish.

ROAST SADDLE OF HARE

Many persons prefer to use the legs and other sections of a hare or large rabbit for pâté or such, and roast only the saddle, which is the meaty section running from the haunch to the breast. This provides the finest meat. A good-sized saddle will serve 2. Brush the saddle well with oil, spit, and roast, basting with equal parts of olive oil and vermouth.

BROILED RABBIT

This is done exactly as you would do a domestic rabbit. Either cut the animal in sections and cook in a hinged broiler, or merely split it and broil as you would chicken, basting with any marinade. It is delicious with a basting of melted butter, lemon juice, and rosemary. Serve it with **hominy spoon bread,** peas cooked with green onions and cream, and a vin rosé.

partridge

ROAST PARTRIDGE

Allow 1 bird for each person, and be sure they are young—old birds are better cooked as a chartreuse, with cabbage. Pick them well and singe, then wrap a thin slice of salt pork or bacon around the breast. If you wish, put a couple of juniper berries or a sprig of thyme in each bird, and sprinkle with salt and pepper. Spit as you do squabs and roast over a moderate fire until *just* cooked, being careful that they don't become dried out. Sauté the giblets, chop them, and spread on toast as a couch for the birds. Serve French fried julienne potatoes (done in the electric fryer) and a large bowl of watercress. Champagne would be fun too.

BROILED PARTRIDGE

Spit the birds and remove the backbone. Rub with **tarragon butter,** and broil over a moderate fire, skin side up for the first 8 to 10 minutes, then 7 or 8 minutes on the other side, brushing with a little more of the tarragon butter. Test for doneness by pulling at the leg. If it wiggles easily at the joint, and if the skin is pleasantly brown and crisp, it is done. Serve with the giblets, which have been cooked in butter and flavored with a little Madeira or Cognac, as a sauce. Serve with whole hominy dressed with butter and chopped parsley, and green beans with almonds. Cold broiled or roast partridge with a **rémoulade sauce** is something pretty special.

pheasant

Pheasant can be the most delicious of the game birds, or it can be dry and dull as yesterday's toast. If it is an old bird, don't attempt to roast it. Rather, make it into a savory dish with sauerkraut and garlic sausage and white wine, cooking it long and slowly to tenderness.

ROAST PHEASANT

Cover the breast of each pheasant with a thin piece of larding pork. This is the salt pork that is without any streaks of lean. Pound it thin and tie it over the pheasants, rub the insides with butter, and put a sprig of thyme and parsley in each bird. Roast as you do a partridge, testing the same way, but remove the larding pork toward the end so that the breasts will brown. Serve with buttered fried crumbs, braised cabbage, and noodles with poppy seeds. A fine claret—maybe a Château Ausone or a Château Cheval Blanc—is a perfect partner for pheasant.

ROAST PHEASANT WITH CHERRIES

Prepare and roast a pheasant as above, but baste with a mixture of ½ cup each of melted butter and juice from a No. 2½ can of black Bing cherries, and ¼ cup each of lemon and orange juice. When half cooked, remove the larding pork from the breast and continue cooking and basting. Meanwhile, heat the cherries in the remaining juice with ¼ cup of butter. Simmer until the juice is reduced one half. When the pheasant is done, put it on a platter, pour the cherries around it, and flambé it with ¼ cup of Cognac. Serve this elaborate version of roast pheasant with a corn meal soufflé made in an electric skillet outdoors or in the oven indoors, tiny whole string beans with chopped buttered filberts, and a bottle of Rhône Valley wine, such as Châteauneuf du Pape.

There are many different types of quail in these United States, and they vary in size. The true quail is a very small bird—so small in fact that a trencherman can eat 6 or 8 at a sitting. In England, France, and many New York restaurants, and by some determined gastronomes, the quail is cooked without cleaning, and the entrails are later scooped out, chopped, and spread on toast.

Any of the following recipes may also be used for quail to be served cold for a picnic or luncheon on the terrace. Serve them with a **rémoulade** or a **Cumberland sauce**—they taste even better than when served hot.

ROAST QUAIL

Pick quail well and clean or not, as you prefer. Wrap in larding pork **(see roast pheasant)** and dust with salt, pepper, and a little thyme. Spit as for squab, and roast over a rather brisk fire for 12 to 15 minutes, basting with equal parts of melted butter and white wine. Remove the pork for the last 3 or 4 minutes of cooking, basting some more. Sprinkle the quail with some fried bread crumbs and serve on toast, with sautéed scrapple or hominy grits, and a good red wine.

QUAIL À LA FRANÇAISE

Wrap each quail in a grape leaf and then in the salt pork, and spit the birds as for squab. When they are roasted, remove the pork but leave the enveloping film of cooked grape leaves, for they impart a delicious flavor to the birds.

BROILED QUAIL

Pick the quail, clean, split, and flatten with the broad side of a cleaver. Butter them generously and broil for about 8 or 9 minutes, turning them during the process. A brisk fire is indicated, as the skin should be crisp while the flesh should remain moist. Brush well with butter, season with salt and pepper, and serve on toast. The toast is delicious if spread with the chopped giblets, which have been sautéed in butter and flavored with a little rum.

wild turkey

Considered the New World's greatest gift to the gastronomic world, wild turkey has all but disappeared from our tables. We include a recipe for it with the hope that, like the bison, its protection will eventually lead to its availability.

ROAST WILD TURKEY

This bird needs no embellishment, save, perhaps, an onion and a sprig of marjoram stuffed inside before spitting. Rub it well with butter, spit it, and roast over a moderate fire, basting with melted butter, until it is beautifully brown and the leg, when pulled, will respond readily. Serve on a platter surrounded with a wreath of small pork sausages. Have succotash made with shell beans and fresh corn, with plenty of butter. Cranberry sauce or wild grape or blackberry jelly would be good, as would a great plate of hot biscuits and fine apple cider.

venison

Venison, which is the meat of the deer, elk, antelope, and moose, is ideally suited to charcoal cooking. There are two schools of venison cookery—one believing that the only way to prepare it is to marinate the hell out of it, the other being completely happy with the unadulterated flavor of the meat itself. You know best how you prefer it.

BROILED VENISON STEAKS OR CHOPS

Have steaks or chops cut thick and brush with olive oil, then broil as you would a beef steak. Rare venison, at least for our palates, is tenderer and better than that which is cooked longer. Serve the steaks with a dollop of butter and a wedge of lemon. A **roasted potato** is a good accompaniment, if served with chopped green onions and sour cream. For a vegetable, try brussels sprouts with chestnuts. A robust red wine is very much in order.

ROAST SADDLE OF VENISON

Trim and wipe a saddle of venison, lard it well, then roll the flank under the saddle and tie securely. Spit for balance and roast over a moderate fire until the meat thermometer reads 135° to 140°. This is pinkly rare. If desired, a baste of olive oil and Italian vermouth may be used during the cooking. Serve with mashed turnips combined with an equal part of mashed potatoes, and with string beans and mushrooms.

ROAST LEG OF VENISON

This is done exactly as is the **leg of lamb** in **Chapter 7.** Serve it with red cabbage cooked with apple, onion, and red wine, and with noodles dressed with melted butter and toasted bread crumbs.

MARINATED SADDLE OF VENISON, BLACK PEPPER SAUCE

Trim a saddle of venison and prepare it for roasting by rolling the thin ends under the saddle and lacing together with heavy twine. Marinate for 2 or 3 days in the following mixture: to a fifth of red wine add 1 tablespoon of salt, 1 tablespoon of finely crushed peppercorns, 1 branch of celery, 1 teaspoon of thyme, 1 onion stuck with 2 cloves, and a bay leaf. Rub the saddle with oil and turn several times during the marinating. To roast, wipe dry and roast as above. Serve with **roasted potatoes,** and with the following sauce: sauté 6 shallots or green onions, finely chopped, in ¼ cup of butter; add 1 teaspoon of salt and 2 teaspoons of freshly ground black pepper, 1 cup of broth, and 1 cup of the marinade which has been reduced from 2 cups. To this add a dash of cayenne, 1 teaspoon of dry mustard, and small balls of flour and butter kneaded together for thickening slightly.

SPITTED LOIN OF VENISON

Rub the loin or rack with salt, pepper garlic, and orégano. Spit securely and roast rare, using olive oil if a baste is needed. Serve with **Béarnaise sauce,** fried potatoes, and turnip greens. Other sauces that are good with venison are **Cumberland, chasseur, Colbert,** and **diable.**

NOTE: Other parts of venison may also be cooked over coals. The liver is superb, either roasted or broiled, and venison hamburger is a rare treat. A fine shaslik may be prepared with the shoulder meat, as well.

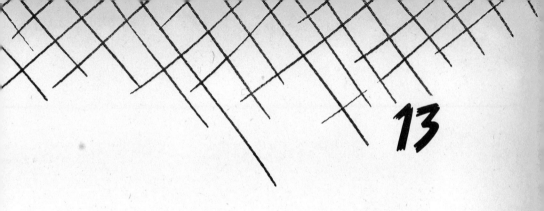

APPETIZERS,
ON AND OFF
THE GRILL

Any meat, fish, or other savory food that is cooked over coals makes a perfect appetizer when served in miniature portions, as a cocktail snack. Sometimes these are the only broiled part of the meal, in which case they are often cooked over a hibachi or other small grill, or in the indoor fireplace. At other times they precede a grilled or roasted entree, and in that case should contrast with it in kind. Little cubes of steak would be heavenly before broiled lobster, chicken livers before mutton chops, shrimps before roast pork. Here are some ideas; many others can be found in **Chapter 10.** (Incidentally, these morsels roasted on small skewers are called *hâtelettes* in France.)

✔ APPETIZER SKEWERS. For these we split inexpensive bamboo chopsticks into 4 to 6 pieces, and soak them in water 1 hour so they won't burn. Of course, metal skewers may be used if you are blessed with plenty. Or use toothpicks and cook in a hinged grill.

SKEWERED BEEF SQUARES

Impale not too small cubes of tenderloin of beef on bamboo and broil over charcoal. If you wish, use a **teriyaki** dip. Serve with

Cecily's French fried onions, or slices of raw onion, or raw onion sandwiches.

SKEWERED CHICKEN SQUARES

Cut chicken breasts in squares and marinate for 10 minutes in equal parts of soy sauce, sherry, and oil, with garlic and/or ginger, if you like the idea. Broil, one to a skewer, for 4 or 5 minutes, or until they have lost their transparent look but are brown and juicy, then dip in toasted sesame seeds. (Toast dry sesame seeds in a heavy skillet, stirring over low heat until nicely colored.) These are truly sensational!

SKEWERED FISH SQUARES

Done exactly like the **chicken squares,** above, using any firm-fleshed fish and serving on cucumber slices instead of dipping in the sesame seeds. Garlic is nice in the marinade.

SKEWERED PORK SQUARES

Make like **pork satés** and provide chopped peanuts for dunking, sliced unpeeled apple as a base.

CARNITAS

These are from Elena Zelayeta, the famous Mexican cook and author, and, like everything of hers, sheer perfection. Cut lean boneless pork in 1½-inch cubes. Sprinkle with salt and pepper, then bake at 300° for about 1½ hours, stirring and draining off fat a few times. (This may be done the day before.) Stick each nugget of meat on a bamboo skewer and finish cooking over charcoal until brown and crispy. Elena served these with *mantequilla de pobre* and *tostados,* and the combination is so good that we can't resist sketching in those recipes. The "poor man's butter" is avocado mashed with tomato and seasoned with a tart French dressing. The *tostados* are tortillas, cut in pieces and fried crisp.

CHINESE ROAST PORK

For a wonderful appetizer that can be broiled ahead of time, try this. Marinate 4 pork tenderloins or a similar amount of boneless pork in ¼ cup of soy sauce, 1 tablespoon of sugar, 1 clove of garlic, ¼ cup of whiskey, and, if you wish, 1 tablespoon of grated fresh ginger. After a couple of hours, broil at low heat for 1 hour. (These may be roasted, too, by weaving them on the spit.) Serve hot or cold, cut in thin slices. A Chinese mustard, made by mixing dry mustard with beer, is sometimes served with this.

SPARERIBS

Spareribs *have* to be eaten in the fingers, which makes them suitable for outdoor appetizers. Cook them according to the recipes in Chapter 11, separate them, and let the guests go to it. Large paper napkins are in order. Baby pork back ribs, smaller and more delicate, are even better, and they cook much more quickly.

BACON APPETIZER BROILS

Almost any little tidbit can be bacon-wrapped and broiled for a tantalizing appetizer: the familiar stuffed olives, scallops, oysters, kidneys (particularly rabbit kidneys, if you can garner enough), chicken livers, sweetbreads, shad roe, and whatever.

RUMAKI

Always a favorite. Dip halves of chicken livers in soy sauce or shoyu, and sandwich between two slices of water chestnut. Wrap in a half slice of bacon and impale on a skewer. Broil until the bacon is crisp. (To prevent too much fat dripping, and consequent fire flaring, we like to start these inside in a hot oven for 5 minutes, or until part of the fat is rendered out.)

LOBSTER-CHESTNUT APPETIZER

Make these just like **rumaki,** but use a good meaty chunk of lobster meat instead of the chicken liver.

SHRIMP-CHESTNUT APPETIZER

Substitute shelled and cleaned raw shrimp for the lobster in the recipe above.

LOBSTER-PINEAPPLE APPETIZER

Wrap a piece of lobster meat and a chunk of pineapple in ham or bacon, and broil as for **rumaki.**

LIVER-ANCHOVY APPETIZER

Wrap half a chicken liver with a fillet of anchovy, then with bacon, before broiling as for **rumaki.**

SHRIMP PIERRE

Using scissors, slit up the backs of 2 pounds of jumbo raw shrimps and remove the black veins but not the shells. Marinate in the following: 3 cloves of garlic, minced, 1 medium onion, minced, ¼ cup of minced parsley, 1 teaspoon each of basil, mustard, and salt, ½ cup of olive or peanut oil, and the juice of 1 lemon. Broil over charcoal for 4 or 5 minutes.

CELESTIAL SHRIMPS

Prepare as above, but marinate in equal parts of soy sauce, sherry, and oil, adding grated green ginger and garlic to taste. Proceed as for **shrimp Pierre.**

ANCHOVY-STUFFED SHRIMP APPETIZER

Use jumbo raw shrimp, remove shells, and split down the backs, removing the veins as you do so. Do not cut the shrimp in half. In each slit insert an anchovy strip, dip each shrimp in melted butter, and broil over charcoal until pink—first bottom side, then top. Drizzle with a little melted butter and lemon juice while broiling. This shouldn't take more than 5 minutes, as the delicious little creatures should be succulent, not dry. Serve with large paper napkins, or with small hot towels.

DATE AND CHEESE APPETIZER

Stuff a date with a piece of Cheddar cheese, wrap in bacon, and broil.

OTHER FRUIT APPETIZERS

Wrap pitted prunes, dried or fresh figs, orange sections, pieces of pineapple or apple in bacon and broil to serve as appetizers.

PEANUT BUTTER AND BACON APPETIZER

Spread slices of half-cooked bacon with peanut butter, roll, fasten, and broil crisp. If preferred, make stamp-sized peanut butter sandwiches, wrap in half slices of bacon, and broil crisp.

BACON BITS

Slice ¼ pound of bacon extra thick (from ¼ to ⅜ inch) and cut each slice in 6 or 8 pieces. Beat 2 eggs slightly with 2 teaspoons of water, ¼ teaspoon of salt, and a dash of allspice. Dip bacon pieces in the egg, then cover completely with not too fine bread crumbs. Allow to dry, and repeat the process. Again allow to dry, then broil over charcoal until crisp and brown on both sides. This may be done in a fine-meshed hinged broiler, for easy handling.

BROILED CHICKEN HEARTS

Chickenhearted? Sapid, not vapid, are these morsels. Available in most markets, a pound is a surprising number. Marinate them in equal parts of soy sauce, oil, and sherry, adding garlic and/or ginger, if you wish. String on skewers and broil for about 4 minutes on each side. They will be brown and crispy. If preferred, skip the marination and put squares of bacon between the hearts, leaving enough space so it will crisp.

MORE APPETIZER BROILS

Other little tidbits that can be broiled and served with drinks are crab legs, liver cubes (serve with a dill-flavored sour cream dunk), scallops, frankfurters (particularly the cocktail size), Polish or Vienna sausages, brown-and-serve sausages, frog's legs, shad roe, tiny meat balls, and mushrooms.

APPETIZER STICKS

Any forcemeat may be wrapped around bamboo sticks and broiled. So, of course, may hamburger, though it is well to bind each pound with a raw egg. Sausage meat made from freshly ground pork, and seasoned with salt, fresh-ground pepper, and a little grated or powdered ginger, is delicious cooked this way. It may also be rolled into balls and grilled.

MINIATURE HAMBURGERS

Very popular, these, particularly with the hamburger lovers, for that is what they are. Small long dinner rolls are sliced as if they were loaves of bread, and buttered. Proportionately small hamburg patties are broiled quickly over charcoal, seasoned, and clapped between the slices. The usual relishes may be provided: tiny round onions, sliced, miniature pickles—everything in Lilliputian size.

sandwiches

Sandwiches may be toasted over coals, cut small, and served as appetizers, too. You can't beat a cheese one, for instance, unless it's with one of the following. The bread may be varied to suit your taste, and we hope your taste runs to homemade and whole-grain breads, as well as rye, pumpernickel, **French sourdough,** and egg breads. Butter it in each case, and press firmly together, before toasting over coals until brown on both sides.

TOASTED CHEESE SANDWICHES

✔ MEXICAN. Jack or Mozzarella cheese and canned green chilis.

✔ SWISS. Switzerland cheese and sliced tongue, with a thin slice of red onion.

✔ ITALIAN. Bel Paese and salami.

✔ WESTERN. Cheddar cheese and bacon, with onion.

✔ CALIFORNIAN. Camembert or Schloss cheese, with bacon and chopped green pepper.

✔ FRENCH. Roquefort cheese mixed with Cognac and a little butter.

✔ OREGONIAN. Blue cheese with ground filberts and ripe olives.

TOASTED FISH SANDWICHES

✔ NOVA SCOTIAN. Smoked salmon with plenty of freshly ground black pepper.

✔ ITALIAN. Anchovies, chopped and mixed with grated Parmesan cheese and vermouth.

✔ SHRIMP. Broiled shrimp, split and put between bread toasted on one side only, buttered on the other.

✔ SARDINES. Just that, with a wedge of lemon on the side.

✔ TUNA. Mixed with mayonnaise and green onion before toasting.

TOASTED MEAT SANDWICHES

✔ PASTRAMI. With white or rye bread and plenty of butter —mustard too. Toast until meat is hot.

✔ HAM AND CHEESE. Sliced ham, sliced cheese, and chopped green pepper and onion.

✔ LIVERWURST. Mashed liverwurst and crisp crumbled bacon.

✔ BACON. This is best if the bacon is broiled and put between untoasted slices of bread.

✔ CORNED BEEF. Sliced, with sliced Swiss or Cheddar cheese.

✔ CHICKEN. Sliced chicken and sliced ham, with or without cheese.

✔ PÂTÉ. Any meat or fish pâté.

BEN LEVY'S TARTARE SANDWICH

This delectable morsel can also be used as a main dish for lunch or supper, or taken on a picnic for last-minute broiling on your portable grill. Thinly slice pumpernickel, rye, or any close-textured bread. Spread, clear to the edge and almost ½ inch thick, with freshly ground top round beef. Season with salt and pepper, cover with another slice of bread, and broil over charcoal until both sides of the bread are nicely toasted and the filling's just heated through, or medium raw if you prefer. Cut in small triangles or squares and serve at once. These are the best hamburgers we ever ate.

BROILED HEART SANDWICH

This is done exactly like the sandwich above, except that ground raw beef heart is used. You'll be delighted with the wonderful flavor of this one!

SEALED TOASTED SANDWICHES

These are made with a metal device that has been on the market for some years. Almost any kind of sandwich may be put in one and toasted. The result is a toasted sandwich with sealed edges, rather like a miniature pie. These are fun to do over wood or charcoal, and the children are invariably delighted with them. For appetizers, cut in pie-shaped wedges.

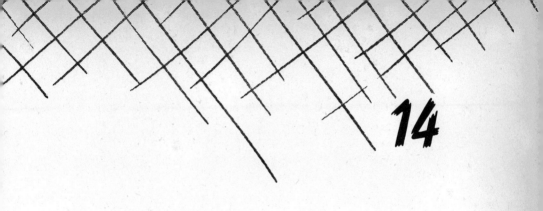

FRUITS AND VEGETABLES

Charcoal cookery need not end with meats, fish, and game. Many fruits and vegetables take on exciting new flavor when subjected to slow roasting over or in the coals. We have listed many of them in **Chapter 10.** Other fruit recipes will be found by consulting the **Index.** Vegetables are included in **Chapter 16.** The **Index** will help you here too.

charcoal-grilled fruits

Fruits, either as accompaniments to meats or as dessert, do not require much cooking, so they can usually be done after the meat has been cooked, or, if wrapped in foil, while it is broiling or roasting. There are two ways to cook fruit: the first is to broil it on the grill; the second to foil it and cook it on top of, or very close to, the coals.

ROASTED APPLES

These are best foiled. Simply wrap whole apples in heavy foil and put around the edge of the coals, turning them once or twice during the cooking. Test for doneness through the foil with a fork. They will take about 30 minutes. Serve in the foil and let each guest add sugar and butter to taste. Another way is to core them and fill with sugar, cinnamon, and butter before cooking in the same manner. Either way they're good with pork, duck, or goose.

BROILED APPLES

Cut apples in thick rings and dip in butter. Broil on both sides, using a hinged broiler. Sprinkle with sugar before serving.

ROASTED BANANAS

Wrap large unpeeled bananas, preferably red ones, in foil, and roast like the **apples**. They will take only 10 to 15 minutes. Delicious with meat, or for dessert, with a rum sauce.

BROILED BANANAS

Peel bananas and cut in half crosswise. Wrap each half in a piece of bacon and broil until crisp. You'll like them with broiled chicken or with ham.

BROILED DATES

Wrap in bacon and broil. They may first be stuffed with cheese, for an appetizer.

BROILED FIGS

Fresh figs, or even juicy dried ones, may be wrapped in bacon and broiled for an appetizer, or to serve with meat.

BROILED GRAPEFRUIT

Many people like broiled grapefruit, but they are difficult to do over charcoal. One way is to put them, cut side up, over the coals until hot, then add a lump of butter, some sugar, and some brandy or sherry to them, and broil the top by filling a hinged broiler with coals and holding it over them. We hope you have tongs or heat-proof gloves.

BROILED ORANGE SLICES

Cut oranges, peel and all, in thick slices, dip in butter, and broil quickly on both sides, using a hinged broiler. Good with broiled duck or chicken. They may also be dipped in flour after the butter dunk.

BROILED PEACHES

Use canned or fresh peaches. The latter should be peeled and halved, and the stones removed. Brush with butter and broil, cut side down, then turn, put a little butter and brown sugar—rum, too, if you like—in the cavities, and finish broiling. Good with meat such as ham or turkey, or for dessert.

BROILED PINEAPPLE

Use either canned sliced pineapple, or cut fresh ones in lengthwise sixths or eighths, cutting through leaves and all. Brush with melted butter and broil until hot and nicely browned. Fine with pork, poultry, ham, or spareribs.

vegetables

BROILED ARTICHOKES

Use just the bottoms, or *fonds,* and have them precooked. Dip in olive oil and broil until lightly browned. Serve with a mixed grill.

ROASTED BEETS

Wrap whole unpeeled beets in a double thickness of heavy foil, and put close to the coals. Roast for 1 hour, or until fork-tender. Serve with butter and a wedge of lemon. They are particularly good with veal.

BROILED CARROTS

Boil carrots, rub off skins, dip in butter, and broil until nicely browned all around. A fine vegetable to serve with broiled liver steaks.

ROASTED CORN

This, of course, is the most popular of the charcoal-cooked vegetables. Pull back the husks, remove all silk, replace husks, and tie their ends together. Soak corn in cold water for at least 30 minutes before roasting on the grill. The ears should be turned 2 or 3 times, and will take 10 or 15 minutes over a hot fire. Some people wrap bacon around the corn before replacing the husks, or brush with butter, but we like to add our butter and seasoning while we're eating.

BROILED CORN

In this case, the corn is husked and brushed with melted butter or wrapped in bacon, then broiled on the grid. It tastes better if slightly browned here and there.

FOILED CORN

Remove husks, brush with butter and, if you wish, season with salt, pepper, and maybe chili powder or orégano. Wrap in heavy or double foil and cook as for **roasted corn.**

ROASTED EGGPLANT

Roast a whole unpeeled eggplant right over the coals. When it's fork-tender the skin will peel right off. Serve with butter.

BROILED EGGPLANT

Cut unpeeled eggplant in slices or wedges, brush with olive oil, garlic-seasoned, if you wish, and broil slowly until brown and tender. More oil may have to be brushed on during the broiling. Use a hinged broiler for easy handling.

FOILED EGGPLANT

Peel eggplant and cut in wedges. Put on squares of foil, adding a slice of onion and half a tomato to each. Season with salt and pepper, and rosemary. Fold foil like an envelope, securing the edges well, and bake or broil for 20 minutes, turning.

BROILED MUSHROOMS

Select large ones (or string on skewers), brush with butter and, if done in a hinged broiler, cook cup side up with a dot of butter in each.

FOILED MUSHROOMS

Put 5 or 6 mushrooms on a square of foil, add a lump of butter, salt, pepper, and some tarragon, rubbed fine. Fold in a packet, securing the edges, and broil for about 8 minutes, turning once during the cooking. Serve with steak or with anything.

FOIL-ROASTED ONIONS

Wrap onions, either peeled or not, in foil, and bake in the coals for about 30 minutes, or until fork-tender. Serve with butter and with any meat. If desired, onions may be stuffed before foiling—try chopped apples, chicken livers, onions, and ripe olives; or nuts, onions, and cream.

BROILED PEPPERS

Cut peppers in quarters, remove seeds, dip in oil, and broil until tender. Nice with mutton or liver.

ROASTED POTATOES

Scrub baking-sized potatoes and bury in the coals for 45 minutes, or until done when pierced with a fork. The skins will be black, but the insides will be wonderfully tender and flaky. Lots of butter is in order.

FOILED POTATOES

Wrap the potatoes in foil and proceed as above. This way, the skins, too, are edible.

BAKED POTATOES

Use coffee cans with lids, and put 2 or 3 potatoes in each, covering tightly. (Or use your Dutch oven, cooking the whole batch together.) Put around the edge of the coals and "bake" until done. It will take close to 1 hour for good-sized potatoes.

BAKED POTATO BAR

Serve large Idaho or other **baked** or **roasted potatoes** with a variety of accompaniments, so that each guest may choose his own. Such garnishments might include chopped chives or green onions, minced parsley, sour cream, whipped butter, grated cheese of various kinds including blue, Cheddar, and Gruyère, cheese sauce, and mixed herbs.

SWEET POTATOES AND YAMS

Cook in exactly the same ways as suggested for white potatoes. A small red yam will take about 45 minutes with a medium fire.

BROILED TOMATOES

Cut in half or slice thick, brush with butter, and dust with flour or fine crumbs. Cook in a hinged broiler until nicely browned. A good partner for fish or chops.

ROASTED PUMPKIN, ZUCCHINI, OR OTHER SQUASH

Peel, cut in sections, and wrap in foil, along with butter and seasonings. Cook like **roasted potatoes,** until a fork stuck through the foil shows them to be tender.

SPIT-ROASTED VEGETABLES

If you are not using your spit for roasts, or if your barbecue equipment has multiple spits, you will find that spitting whole unpeeled vegetables is very satisfactory. Whole white potatoes, large ones, will take 1 hour or more over a medium fire. Yams will take the same length of time. A whole eggplant needs over an hour, if it is large, and whole green peppers will take about 20 minutes. Onions, unpeeled and of good size, need 50 minutes to cook soft, but they are good eating after 20 minutes. They may first be peeled and wrapped in foil before spitting. Acorn squash, when roasted whole, will need 1½ hours, but if cut (and this applies to banana and Hubbard squash, too) it will take only 1 hour over a medium-hot fire. But all this is a matter of convenience. Frankly, we can't see that the vegetables are any better spitted than if they had come from your kitchen oven.

SMOKING
AND SMOKE
COOKERY

When smoking food or smoke-cooking it, the coals over which it is placed are smothered with damp sawdust, or such, to produce the necessary smudge. *Smoking* is a process of curing in which meat or fish is brined or marinated, then smoked by either the hot-smoke or the cold-smoke method. The food, depending upon its nature, may or may not require further cooking. *Smoke cookery* is something else again. It is a means of cooking food partially or entirely by surrounding it with hot smoke. Recently many outdoor cooks have been smitten with the fascination of this type of cookery. We think it has its charming aspects, but we also believe this smoke business has gone too far. We can no more enthuse over a porterhouse steak, smoke-cooked, than we can about smoke-flavored salad dressing or potato chips, nor do we crave an entire meal of smoked chicken or even smoked pork. However, when it comes to smoked fish, cheese, sausages, or meat, for hors d'oeuvre, we happily acquiesce, and we are the first to admit that a slow-cured and smoked old-fashioned ham has it all over today's pumped-full-of-brine-and-smoked-salt variety.

Our greatest success has been with smoked pork loins and tenderloins, ducks, pastrami, fish, cheese, stuffed chicken necks, and sundry little tidbits, but that is only because we haven't had time to try everything. There are many devices, both commercial and homemade, that are satisfactory for the home smoking of foods. Of the commercial ones, the *Weber Kettle* is far and away the most popular, as it may be used for conventional cooking as well. It has excellent draft control—so good, in fact, that you can easily put out the fire! This can be avoided by cocking the lid a tiny bit to admit air, which will keep your smoldering coals alight but will not fan them into flames. *Weber Kettles* come in a variety of sizes and colors. For anglers, there is the compact *Swedish Smoker,* which is about the size of a shoe box, and is admirable for small fish like trout, or for fillets of larger fish, as well as for chicken breasts and the like. It comes with a supply of special fuel, a sort of fine sawdust, which is moistened before lighting. Even the ubiquitous gas barbecue may be used for smoking, by turning the fire down after the ceramic briquets are well heated, adding moist fuel to create smoke, and closing the top to keep it in.

The simplest type of homemade smoker is a barrel with its bottom knocked out. It is set over a hole in the ground which contains a fire; wires or racks near the top hold the food, or hold hooks from which the food hangs for smoking. The top of the barrel is covered, the escape of smoke being regulated by tipping it slightly. If you're in a hurry and don't have a fitted barrel handy, a large carton will do. Remove the bottom and cut holes in the box to support cross rods. The meat may be hung from them or they may support a grill. Cut a flap at the bottom for adding fuel. Simply make your fire in a shallow hole in the ground, add green wood and leaves, and when it's smoking, put the box over it. Of course, such a smoker won't last very long, but it will do in a pinch. Still another way is to use an inexpensive portable oven with the bottom removed. This may be placed on the charcoal grill, with the firebox in its lowest position. Cover the rest of the grill with heavy-duty foil to keep the smoke from escaping, and proceed.

In all these devices for smoking, the principle is the same—a charcoal fire, made in the usual manner, is smothered with damp sweet-smelling sawdust, wood chips, corn cobs, leaves, or green wood, so that a dense smoke will be produced. Any wood that is sweet-smelling or -tasting may be used—and that means steer clear of the resinous woods with the possible exception of juniper. Hickory seems to be preferred, perhaps because of a good press agent, but the wood from any fruit or nut tree is fine, as are maple, oak, alder, and grapevine trimmings. Dried herbs, or fresh ones for that matter, thrown upon the sawdust will produce a pleasant flavor. When the damp fuel dries out and starts to burn, add more; thus the fire can be kept smoking indefinitely. Do remember, however, to add enough at night so that it will burn through until morning. A fine way to get a good heavy smoke is to put the wet sawdust in a pan atop the coals, rather than sprinkling it directly on them.

The old type of smoking, and for our money still the best, is done in two ways—hot-smoking and cold-smoking. The first is not very hot, as the temperature usually doesn't get above 225° F. However, it is hot enough to preclude further cooking, if desired. Cold-smoking is more for flavor, and is done at 100° to 120°, but preferably the lower.

smoking

For the old-fashioned smoking, the meat must first be cured, either by rubbing with salt, sugar, and spices, or by soaking in brine. Both methods are described below.

✔ DRY-CURING MEAT. This should be done at from 40° to 45°. Make a salt mixture by using a formula for **pastrami,** or this one, for 10 pounds of meat: 2 cups of salt (we find the coarse kosher salt the most satisfactory), 2 cups of sugar, 1 tablespoon of saltpeter (sodium nitrate), and pepper and any spice or herb that suits your fancy—garlic, too, if you like it. Rub half this mixture on the meat, then pack it in a crock or enameled pan and cover it. (We use a large enameled baking pan which we cover with heavy aluminum foil; then we can put it in the refrigerator.) The meat should stand for 3 days, then the remaining cure is rubbed in. If the pieces of meat are about 5 pounds each and not too thick, they should be cured for 10 days. A larger thick piece, say a ham, will require 2 weeks or longer. This cure is fine for pork and mutton—the latter, "mutton ham," being a great favorite with the Scandinavians.

✔ BRINE-CURING MEAT. This is done very much the same way, but the temperature should never be above 40°. The same salt mixture is used; about ½ cup of it is rubbed into the meat, the remainder is dissolved in 2½ quarts of boiling water and cooled.

The meat is put in a crock or pan as above, weighted down, covered with brine and with a cover. On the third or fourth day, shift the meat, putting the top meat on the bottom. Repeat this in 3 more days. When the curing time is up, soak large pieces of meat in water for 2 hours, small pieces for 30 minutes; dry thoroughly, preferably under an electric fan, then scrub with a stiff brush, and smoke.

✔ SMOKING CURED MEAT. Make a smoke fire as above, and when it's smoking well, with a temperature in the smoke oven or barrel of 100° to 120°, hang the meat in the oven from hooks, or put it on the smoke racks. Open ventilators at first to allow escape of moisture, then smoke until the meat has reached the rich mahogany color that you desire. This usually takes from 1 to 3 days, at this temperature, and is called cold smoking; the meat will require further cooking. With hot smoking, the process combines cooking and smoking, and the temperature should be from 120° to 225°. In the latter case, further cooking is not needed.

✔ KIPPERED FISH. Any filleted fish may be kippered, though sturgeon, albacore, salmon, cod, herring, and other fat fish seem best. Three- or 4-inch steaks from medium-sized fish, and whole smaller fish, may also be kippered or smoked. Make a brine of 1 tablespoon of salt to 1 cup of water, add spices if you desire, and marinate overnight. Dry well, and place on the rack skin side down. Smoke at very low heat—not above 90°—for 4 hours, then raise heat to 170° for an hour, or until the fish is beautifully colored and cooked. This kippered fish, for such it is, may be kept refrigerated for about 4 weeks, frozen for a much longer time.

✔ SMOKED FISH. The difference is that the smoked fish is done with cold smoke for a much longer time than the kippered. It is also brined before smoking, at the lowest possible temperature, sometimes as long as 6 days, though most amateurs will find their patience wearing thin at the end of the first 48 hours. The fish is delicious when done this shorter time, by the way.

VIRGINIA-STYLE SMOKED HAM

The term "Virginia ham" has as many meanings as there are farms in Virginia. And that goes for the Kentucky ham and the Tennessee ham too. But in general they are of two kinds—salt-cured and sugar-cured. As to the merits of either, that is a matter of individual taste. This recipe was given us by an expert: Morton Clark.

No ham is ever better than the hog from which it is cut. For a ham will taste of whatever its parent has been predominantly fed. Apple-fed hogs tend to taste of apples. Corn-fed hogs are sweet. And swill-fed hogs follow the pattern precisely.

The best ham to smoke is a freshly killed one that has hung just long enough to remove *all* body heat. Butcher-bought hams can be cured satisfactorily but they will never be as good. And a ham that has been frozen is out of the question.

Hams, to be at their very best, should be cured in a dry cold temperature. Once in the cure, a hot day or two will not spoil them but they do not like extreme changes of any kind. Hams *may* be cured in refrigerators and walk-ins but they will never be at their best. They love 40° to 50° weather, and if you give it to them, they will reward you adequately.

For the cure, blend thoroughly 5 pounds of salt with 3 ounces of saltpeter and 2 cups of black pepper. (This runs into money but it's cheaper than buying a really good ham at the store!) Rub the ham thoroughly with the mixture, pressing it deep into any flesh cut, around and beside all the bones, and as far into the hock as you can reach.

Lay the ham, skin side down, on a slightly sloping board which has been spread thickly with the cure mixture. (This will let the brine drain off, which, for this cure, is essential.) Dust the flesh side of the ham with more of the mixture and forget it for 4 or 5 days. Then check your ham carefully—wherever you have stowed it . . . and like as not, if the temperature is right, this will be a tool shed—smelling it and probing the shinbone with a skewer. If spoilage is setting in, it will have done so already. Common sense will be your guide. In this unhappy event, you must throw the ham away. If all is going well, sprinkle your ham with more of your cure mixture. Then leave it alone, checking it at intervals with a passing sniff.

At the end of 40 days, scrub the ham with a stiff brush and let it dry. Thread a wire through the *flesh* end for smoking—so that the fat will run down through the meat—and you're ready to go.

Hams must have a cold smoke. The colder the better. Hickory or any fruitwood is best for the job but corn cobs will do if the woods are lacking. The smoke does not have to be continuous but should be given at intervals until the ham is a beautiful mahogany color and smells like the ham you have dreamed of. You may smoke it continuously, of course, but it adds nothing. And there is a school of Ham Thought which claims that a delayed smoking is far superior. Give it a few hours on smoke and several days off . . . then let it coast. Then more smoke again. Et cetera.

When your ham is as beautiful as can be, rub it with a mixture of borax, black pepper, and thyme . . . equal parts. The pepper and thyme for flavor and the borax to repel insects. Rub it well but do not press the mixture in as deeply as the cure. Wrap the ham lightly in cheesecloth or wax paper and then place it in a paper bag. Tie the open end of the bag and hang it so that it touches absolutely nothing else. Hams, to be good, believe it or not, have to breathe. And spots that cannot breathe tend to spoil.

Now forget your ham for a year if you can . . . so far as eating goes. Check it from time to time to be sure that no insects are near it. Any room temperature will do for the aging. Then, when the year is over, eat it. You will be richly rewarded for your time and trouble.

PASTRAMI

It's a big thrill to make your own pastrami and not so difficult as you might think. First the meat must be cured. Select the second cut of the brisket with the deckle out. This will weigh around 5 pounds. For 4 of them, or 20 pounds of beef, combine 2 cups of salt, ½ cup of sugar, 4 teaspoons of saltpeter (sodium nitrate, not potassium nitrate), ⅓ cup of ground ginger, ⅓ cup of cracked black pepper, 4 or 5 cloves of garlic, crushed. Sprinkle this evenly over the surface of the meat, put the meat in a flat pan, cover with foil, and weigh down. Keep in the refrigerator, at from 38° to 45°, for 20 days. (This same dry cure may be used for beef tongues too.) Dry in the air or under a fan, and smoke at 150° to 175° for 24 hours, then cover with water and simmer for 3 or 4 hours, or until tender. How everyone loves a hot pastrami sandwich! Try small ones for a superb appetizer.

SMOKED SAUSAGES

Have 10 pounds of lean pork and 2 pounds of pork fat ground together. If you prefer a finer-grained sausage, have it run through the grinder two or three times. Work into it thoroughly with your hands a mixture of ⅓ cup of salt, 2 tablespoons of freshly ground or cracked black pepper, 2 tablespoons of thyme, 2 tablespoons of orégano or marjoram, and 1 teaspoon of nutmeg. Pack into bags of unbleached muslin which can be easily basted together by hand or run up on a machine. These should be about 3 inches wide and 6 inches long. Tie the tops with a generous length of string so that you can make a loop for hanging and cold-smoke them over hickory, fruitwood, or corn cobs for 24 hours. Finish the cooking with a hot smoke or form the sausage into patties or balls and cook over charcoal. The cakes may also be steamed with **sauerkraut**. And tiny ones are perfect with cocktails.

If you like a heavily smoked sausage, cold-smoke the bags at intervals over several days. The bags may then be dipped in hot melted paraffin and, if completely coated, will keep very well at a cold temperature for several weeks and possibly longer.

SMOKED GOOSE

Have goose disjointed, and use the legs, thighs, and breast. Chop the remaining meat very fine, season it, and stuff it in the neck skin, tying both ends. Combine 1 teaspoon of saltpeter, 1 cup of salt, 1 clove of garlic, crushed, 1 teaspoon of allspice, and 1 tablespoon of sugar. Put goose in a crock, sprinkle each layer with the mixture, and weight down—a brine will form. Keep in a cool place and turn after 4 days, leaving it in the brine a week in all. Cold-smoke for 24 hours, or until beautifully browned. Serve cold, as an appetizer, sliced paper-thin.

SMOKED DUCKLING
AND OTHER POULTRY

This same method may be applied to goose breast, squab, turkey, chicken, and other fowl. Make a brine with 2 cups each of white wine, water, and soy sauce, 3 tablespoons of brown sugar, 1 teaspoon of black pepper, crushed, a bay leaf, and 1 teaspoon of marjoram. Have the fowl cut in pieces, with backbone, neck, and wing tips removed. Marinate large birds for 3 days, smaller ones for 1 or 2, then dry well with an electric fan or in a well-ventilated spot. Smoke at 200° for several hours, brushing the bird (especially if it's duck) with honey diluted with an equal amount of hot water a few times during the cooking, or until it is a deep rich bronze in color.

SMOKED STUFFED
CHICKEN NECKS

When you buy chicken necks for stock, remove the skin of the necks, being careful not to tear them. For about 12 necks, prepare the following stuffing: boil 6 to 8 chicken gizzards until tender in water to which has been added 1 onion stuck with 2 cloves, a bay leaf, and a sprig of thyme. When the gizzards are tender (in about 1 hour), add ½ pound of chicken livers and cook for only 3 or 4 minutes. Chop or grind the giblets rather coarsely, adding 1 small onion or 2 shallots, 1 teaspoon of salt, 1 teaspoon of tarragon, a few grindings of black pepper, and ½ cup of bread crumbs. Bind with 1 egg and a little Cognac or Madeira. Correct the seasoning and add ¼ cup of chopped parsley. Tie a string around one end of each of the neck skins. Stuff well with the mixture and secure the other end with string—so that you have the equivalent of puffy little sausages. Cold-smoke the necks in the smoke oven for 4 hours. Finish cooking at hot-smoke heat for about 2 hours, or until tender and deliciously brown. An excellent hors d'oeuvre or lunch or dinner dish.

SMOKED SALMON

Select a salmon of about 6 or 7 pounds, and fillet it. Slash the skin in a few places and rub with a mixture of 1 cup of coarse salt, 1 teaspoon of saltpeter, 2 teaspoons of coarsely ground pepper, and 1 or 2 tablespoons of sugar. Refrigerate overnight, then rinse, dry, and smoke at a temperature not over 100° for 2 or 3 hours. This is as close as we have been able to come to the lox found in good delicatessens. However, it's wonderful, so we make no apologies.

KIPPERED SALMON

Prepare as above, but smoke at about 150° for 4 hours, or until the flesh separates into flakes. This is delicious as is, or steamed and served for breakfast, with a dill-flavored cream sauce.

SMOKED CHEESE

Any kind of cheese may be smoked, though we found a rich, well-aged Cheddar, a Jack, a Swiss, and an Edam the most satisfactory. Arrange the cheese, either cut in cubes or in larger shapes and chunks, on aluminum foil punched with holes, and cold-smoke—under 100°, if possible—until it is colored and flavored to your taste. If done in cubes, which are later impaled on wooden picks, you have a close to perfect appetizer to serve with a dry sherry, before dinner.

smoke cookery

In smoke cookery, food is either cooked and smoked at the same time, using a hotter fire, 250° to 300°, or it is first cooked as usual over charcoal, then finished in the smoke oven. Sometimes, also, that procedure is reversed, and the food is first given its dose of smoke and then finished over the coals. The first method of smoke cookery, however, is the most popular one, and everything from turkeys to spareribs to rib roasts is cooked that way. That last, and the smoking of fine sirloin steaks and such, gives us the vapors. We can't see how smoke can improve the flavor of fine beef. Advocates of smoke cookery disagree; they say there is no charred, bitter, and acid taste to the meat, but *we* claim that neither is there when it is cooked over charcoal, when done *properly*.

In smoke cookery meat and fish may be marinated or not, as you wish. Any of the **bastes** in this book may be used, though the simplest ones are the best. We like soy sauce, diluted with water, and sometimes with garlic added. For a shiny glaze, some brown sugar or honey may also be used: equal parts of honey and soy, and twice as much water. Timing and temperatures for smoke cookery are given in the individual recipes.

SMOKE-COOKED HAMBURGERS

These require a hot smoke so they will stay juicy. Make large ones for dinner or tiny ones for appetizers—we prefer the latter. Season well and brown quickly over charcoal, then finish by smoking for 10 minutes or so, or until done to your liking.

SMOKE-COOKED CHICKEN LIVERS

We find these easier to handle if they are strung on skewers or put in a wire basket grill. Dip them in soy sauce or white wine flavored with tarragon, and smoke-cook at 350° for about 6 minutes.

SMOKE-COOKED CHICKEN SQUARES

Prepare as for **skewered chicken squares** but do not broil. Instead, smoke at 150° until they have lost their transparent look and acquired a brownish hue. Very nice tidbits, these.

SMOKE-COOKED DUCKLING
AND OTHER POULTRY

Prepare as for **smoked duckling,** but cook at a temperature of 300° to 350°, and smoke from 1 to 5 hours, depending on the size of the bird.

SMOKE-COOKED FISH

This is different from **kippered** or **smoked fish,** for it is brined a short time only, and hot-smoked for immediate eating. Fish fillets are best. Make a brine with ¼ cup of salt, 1 tablespoon of sugar, 1 teaspoon of mixed herbs, and 2 quarts of water, and allow the fish to stand in it for 3 hours—small fish require less time. Dry thoroughly, then smoke-cook at 250° until nicely colored and well done. If to be served as a main dish, pour on a very hot thin cream sauce, and serve at once. Cold, as an hors d'oeuvre, it is delicious when served with lemon wedges and buttered pumpernickel bread. Haddock fillets, by the way, become finnan haddie when so smoked, so you see . . .

SMOKE-COOKED SHRIMPS OR LOBSTER

There are two ways of smoking shrimps. One is to precook them for 4 minutes in a well-seasoned court bouillon, then dry them well under an electric fan, and cold-smoke them for an hour. The other method, and the one we like best, is to leave them raw and hot-smoke them for 1 to 3 hours. In either case the shrimps may be shelled or not. Lobster is done exactly the same way, either removing the meat from the shells and cutting it in good-sized chunks, or cutting through shell and all.

SMOKE-COOKED OYSTERS, CLAMS, AND SCALLOPS

These bivalves should be removed from their shells, dipped in soy sauce, and arranged on a greased piece of wire screening, or on a piece of foil well punched with holes. Cold-smoke for about 30 minutes.

PARTNERS
FOR GRILLED
FOODS

What goes with grilled meats and fishes? Lots of dishes, though first choice is pretty apt to be a hearty one that can come hot from an indoor or outdoor oven, or can be made on the patio in an electric cooker. It is usually a casserole of starchy character, often featuring rice, legumes, pasta, or corn. If it is plenty hot when it comes from the oven and is snugly wrapped in many layers of newspaper, or popped into an insulated bag, it will stay that way for a long time. Here are some of our favorite dishes of this kind. They are mostly simple ones, and therein, we think, lies their charm. **Unless otherwise indicated, they serve 6.**

rice

Rice is nice with many outdoor meals, particularly those of a Near or Far Eastern ancestry, or with meals in which chicken or sea food plays the lead. We recommend the long-grained Carolina rice, or a Patna. Converted rices are also quick and easy, and instant rices are a great boon to cooks in a hurry. We suggest that, when making plain boiled or steamed rice, you follow the directions on the package, or use your own favorite method. It is tops with many highly seasoned dishes. One cup of cooked rice will take a tablespoon or so of melted butter, if it is to be served that way. Allow ½ to ¾ cup of cooked rice per serving.

RICE WITH CHEESE

Combine 4 cups of hot cooked rice with ¼ cup of melted butter and 3 tablespoons each of grated parmesan and Gruyère or Swiss cheese, salt to taste, and a dash of cayenne. A fine companion for **hamburgers** or **liver steaks**.

RICE WITH BUTTERED CRUMBS

This is a nice substitute for the more—lots more—expensive wild rice. Combine 4 cups of hot cooked rice with 1 cup of dried bread crumbs which have been browned in ½ cup of melted butter. Salt and pepper to taste.

RICE WITH NUTS

Combine 4 cups of hot cooked rice with ¼ cup of melted butter, and anywhere from ½ cup to 2 cups of chopped pecans, walnuts, filberts, almonds, or what you wish. Good, this, particularly with **poultry**.

GREEN RICE

Combine 4 cups of hot cooked rice with ¼ cup of melted butter and ½ cup each of finely minced parsley and watercress, with salt to taste. Other green herbs, such as chives or green onions, and tarragon, marjoram, or basil may also be added. Try this savory rice with **lamb** or **mutton,** or with **kidneys.**

GARLIC RICE

This is just plain buttered rice, except that a large clove of garlic, well crushed, has been added to the butter while it melts. It is later discarded. If desired, minced parsley may also be mixed in, and so may grated cheese or little snips of anchovies. A fine companion for **fish.**

PILAFF

1 cup raw long-grained rice	Salt and pepper
1 small onion	Thyme or orégano
¼ cup butter	Butter
2 cups bouillon or stock	

Wash and dry rice—use a towel for the drying. Chop onion quite fine and brown it lightly in the butter, then add the rice and stir it until it begins to color. Add boiling bouillon or stock, salt and pepper to taste, and a pinch of thyme or orégano. Cover and put in a 350° oven for about 15 minutes, or until the liquid is absorbed and the rice tender. Add a goodly dollop of butter just before serving. This is classic with **shish kebabs** and **shaslik**.

PILAFF MOGHUL

Puff raisins by cooking in a little stock or wine, then draining. Add them, along with toasted slivered almonds and/or peanuts, to a **pilaff** that has been lightly flavored by adding a pinch of saffron to the bouillon in which the rice was cooked. Arrange rice on a platter, sprinkle with more nuts and raisins, and surround with crisp French fried onions. Use 1 cup of raisins and ½ cup of nuts, in all. Delicious with a simple **broiled chicken** that has been basted with curry-flavored butter.

RISOTTO

This is close kin to pilaff, and goes best with Italian dishes, as it hails from that country. However, it is made on top of the stove, and the liquid is stirred in ½ cup at a time, allowing the rice to absorb nearly all the liquid between additions, until it is tender but still bity and has a creamy texture.

RISOTTO MILANESE

Make as above, but add a pinch of saffron to the bouillon. Also, at that time, add ½ cup of raw button mushrooms and 1 seeded and peeled tomato, chopped. Sautéed chopped chicken livers and/or tiny shreds of ham are also sometimes added. We like this version with **broiled shrimps** or **scampi**.

GREEK RICE

Make like the **risotto,** but add 2 cups of cooked green peas, some small bits of garlic sausage, and some chopped green or red pepper, after the rice is cooked. **Roast mutton** likes this rice dish.

FRIED RICE

4 cups boiled rice	¼ cup sliced cooked
3 tablespoons oil	mushrooms
3 tablespoons shredded green	2 eggs
onions	1 tablespoon soy sauce
	Optional additions

Let's not forget this delectable Chinese dish, so perfect with **spareribs, chicken,** and many other grilled foods. Cook rice in bland-flavored oil for 4 or 5 minutes, stirring lightly but constantly. Add green onions and mushrooms. (Also add ½ cup of shredded cooked pork, ham, or shrimps, if you wish, though this isn't necessary for a side dish.) Cook a couple of minutes, then stir in eggs, which have been well mixed with soy sauce. Cook until the eggs are set, and serve sprinkled with more minced green onions or with slivered toasted almonds.

MEXICAN RICE

3 green onions, chopped	1 cup tomato juice
1 green pepper, chopped	1 cup water
½ cup olive oil	1 teaspoon salt
1 cup raw rice	Orégano or chili powder
1 cup canned tomatoes	

This is very much like the famous Spanish **paella,** a dish not included here as it is a meal in its own right, being completely independent of grilled or any other kind of meat. Mexican rice is made by cooking green onions and green pepper in olive oil for 3 minutes, then adding rice. This is cooked until it colors, when tomatoes, tomato juice, and water are added. It is seasoned with salt and a little orégano or chili powder, then covered and cooked until the rice is tender, the liquid absorbed. It may be necessary to add more water during the cooking. Chicken livers, minced clams, mushrooms, olives, bits of ham, or whatever may be added to this dish, but in that case it might turn out to be an entree instead of an auxiliary dish.

ELENA'S RICE WITH
GREEN CHILIS AND SOUR CREAM

¾ cup raw rice	1 7-ounce can peeled green
2 cups sour cream	chili peppers
Salt	Butter
½ pound Jack cheese	½ cup grated cheese (optional)

This, to our way of thinking, is a dish that everyone should know. Serve with grilled meat, fish, or fowl—it's perfection. A fascinating combination of robust and delicate flavors, it is the creation of San Francisco's famous blind cook, Elena Zelayeta.

Cook rice in your usual manner (quick-cooking rice may be used). Combine it with sour cream and season to taste with salt. Arrange half of the mixture in the bottom of a casserole, and on it place domino-sized pieces of Jack cheese which have been wrapped in strips of chili peppers. Top with the remaining rice and dot with butter. (If desired, more Jack cheese may be grated over all.) Come almost serving time, heat for about 30 minutes in a 350° oven, and rush to the outside dining room. This is superb with **roast pork,** grilled **hamburgers, London broil,** spit-roasted **rabbit,** or broiled **swordfish.**

OLIVE-RICE CASSEROLE

1½ cups raw rice	5 cups tomato juice
2 tablespoons olive oil	2 teaspoons chili powder
2 tablespoons butter	2 teaspoons salt
2 cloves garlic, crushed	½ to 1 teaspoon dill seeds,
2 small cans sliced ripe olives	crushed

Brown rice in olive oil and butter, along with garlic. When amber-colored, discard the garlic, add olives, tomato juice, chili powder, salt, and dill seeds. Bake in a greased covered casserole at 350° for 1 hour, or until the liquid is absorbed and the rice tender. Serves 6 to 8.

WILD RICE CASSEROLE

1 cup wild rice	¼ cup butter
6 green onions, chopped	2 cups **Béchamel sauce**
½ pound mushrooms, sliced	

Cook rice until tender but not mushy. Sauté green onions and mushrooms in butter, and combine with the rice. Mix with **Béchamel sauce** and put in a casserole. Reheat in the oven before serving.

beans

Beans have always been right with outdoor meals, whether they come from a bean hole, a can, or a well-equipped nearby kitchen. They are, besides, the most American of the legumes. From scores of our favorite bean recipes we give you these.

FRIJOLES

1 pound pinto beans	Salt
Water	½ cup lard or bacon fat

Dear to the hearts and bellies of all Mexicans and those of us who adore Mexican food, they are delicious with roast pork, steaks, hamburgers, and many other grilled foods. Use Mexican pink or red beans, or pinto beans, cover them with warm water, and cook them at a simmer until very tender, adding salt to taste toward the end of the cooking. Melt lard or bacon fat (for the true Mexican flavor) in an earthenware casserole or *cazuela,* or a large and heavy skillet. Mash a few beans in the fat, then add some liquid and more beans, mashing as you go, until all the beans are used. Cook, stirring a bit, until the beans are the consistency you desire—they should be not too dry nor yet too soupy. Mexican food cries for these.

FRIJOLES REFRITOS

Melt more lard—½ cup for each 3 cups of **frijoles** cooked as above —and add the beans, cooking and stirring until the beans are very hot and the lard is absorbed, and there are lovely little crispy bits around the edge. *Frijoles refritos* can become an addiction.

FRIJOLES CON QUESO

To either hot **frijoles** or **frijoles refritos,** add small cubes of Jack or Cheddar cheese, allowing just enough time for them to melt before serving. These are exceptionally exceptional!

COGNAC BEANS

1 pound dried white beans	1 small onion, chopped
Water	¼ cup butter
1 clove garlic	2 cups tomato purée
1 onion	¼ cup minced parsley
2 cloves	2 teaspoons salt
Bay leaf	⅓ cup Cognac
Thyme	

Superb with lamb or mutton, or with almost any grilled meat you mention. Soak beans in water to cover. Add garlic, the onion stuck with the cloves, bay leaf, and a sprig or pinch of thyme. Simmer until the beans are tender, drain and reserve the liquid. Sauté the small onion in butter until colored, add tomato purée, parsley, salt, Cognac, and 1 cup of the bean liquid. Simmer this mixture 30 minutes, mix with the beans, correct seasoning, and reheat in a casserole before serving. Serves 8 or more.

TIPSY BLACK BEANS

2 pounds black beans	A ham bone or ¼ cup diced
Water	salt pork or ¼ cup olive oil
1 onion, sliced	or bacon fat
1 bay leaf	Salt
Sprig of thyme	Dash of Tabasco
2 stalks celery	**Beurre manié**
Parsley	½ cup Jamaica rum
	Sour cream

While we are on an alcoholic jaunt, let's not forget black beans and rum. Soak them overnight. Next day add more water to cover, the onion, the bay leaf, a sprig of thyme, the celery, and some parsley. If you have a ham bone, add it, too, otherwise use salt pork, olive oil, or bacon fat. Cook until the beans are tender, add salt to taste and a dash of Tabasco. Drain the beans and thicken the liquid with a **beurre manié.** Put the beans in a casserole, discarding the seasonings and vegetables. Add rum to the liquid and pour over the beans, then bake in a 350° oven until well heated. Serve with cold sour cream. This is heavenly with charcoal-grilled **ham steak** or with grilled **sausages.** The dish may be varied by topping with grated cheese and strips of bacon. Serves 12 to 16.

WHITE BEANS, COUNTRY STYLE (COLD)

1 pound pea beans	2 tomatoes, peeled and seeded
2 cloves garlic	¼ cup chopped parsley
2 teaspoons salt	⅓ cup olive oil
½ teaspoon pepper	2 tablespoons wine vinegar
3 large onions, chopped	Salt and pepper
1 green pepper, chopped	Minced green onions
¼ pound butter	

Simmer beans with garlic, salt, and freshly ground black pepper until tender. Sauté onions and green pepper in butter. Add tomatoes and parsley. Drain the beans and combine with the vegetables. Chill. Just before serving, mix with olive oil blended with wine vinegar, and salt and pepper if needed. Sprinkle the top lavishly with minced green onions.

NEVADA CHILI BEANS

1 pound Mexican pink beans	½ teaspoon orégano
Water	Pinch of ground cumin
¼ pound salt pork	2 cups tomato purée
3 cloves garlic, chopped fine	3 tablespoons chili powder
2 cups chopped onions	Salt and pepper

Cook beans in water to cover until they are not quite cooked—just a bit bity. Cut salt pork in small pieces and try out until crisp in a large skillet or Dutch oven. Add garlic and onions and brown well. When the onions are soft, add orégano, a healthy pinch of ground cumin, tomato purée, and chili powder. Salt and pepper to taste and bring to a boil. Add the beans, reduce the heat, and simmer for 1½ hours. Taste for seasoning—you may want it hotter or saltier. Old-fashioned soda crackers or tortillas and beer with this, please. (Add 1 pound each of diced cooked pork and beef to this, and you have *chili con carne con frijoles*.)

BAKED GARBANZOS

1 quart cooked garbanzos (chick-peas)	1 large onion, chopped
	1 clove garlic, minced
Salt and pepper	1 teaspoon rosemary
3 large tomatoes, chopped	½ cup olive oil

Put garbanzos (canned ones do nicely) in a baking dish and season with salt and pepper. Top with a mixture made by combining tomatoes with onion, garlic, rosemary, and olive oil. Bake at 375° for 45 to 60 minutes. A good dish.

GARLIC GARBANZOS

Soak 1 pound of garbanzos (chick-peas) overnight, then cook in salted water until just tender. Drain. Crush 3 cloves of garlic and heat in ¼ pound of butter. Remove what's left of the garlic and add the drained garbanzos, cooking very slowly until they have attained a wonderful nutlike flavor of browned butter. They themselves should be nicely colored and crisply tender. Season with salt and, if you wish, some chili or curry powder, and make twice as much as you think you need.

CHEESE AND BEAN CAZUELA

3 cans kidney beans	½ cup minced onions
1 cup canned tomatoes	2 tablespoons bacon fat
1 tablespoon chili powder	2 cups finely diced Jack or
1 teaspoon salt	Cheddar cheese

Combine kidney beans, tomatoes, chili powder, salt, and minced onions which have been cooked in the bacon fat. Cook slowly on the back of the grill while the meat is broiling—anywhere from 20 to 40 minutes. About 2 minutes before show time, stir in cheese. Serve as soon as the cheese is melted, with grilled **steak, ground beef patties,** or **roast pork**. **Tortillas** are in order too. Serves 8 or more.

KIDNEY BEAN CASSEROLE

1 clove garlic, crushed	½ cup red table wine
3 tablespoons olive oil	2 tablespoons minced parsley
2 cans kidney beans	½ cup stuffed green olives

Cook garlic in the olive oil for a minute or so, then add beans, wine, parsley, and green olives, cut in halves through their equators. Heat and serve with anything from the grill.

ANOTHER SPEEDY BEAN DISH

2 cans kidney beans	1 tablespoon lemon juice
2 tablespoons butter	Salt and pepper
¼ cup minced parsley	

Combine beans with butter, parsley, lemon juice, and salt and pepper to taste. Heat on the grill or in an electric cooker or skillet, and serve with any meat, fish, or fowl, roasted or broiled.

ONION LENTILS

2 cups lentils	Curry powder (optional)
Salted water	Chopped parsley
3 cups chopped onions	Chopped hard-boiled egg
¼ pound butter	

Soak lentils overnight. Next morning cook until tender in salted water to cover. Drain. Cook onions in butter until lightly browned, mix with the lentils, and cook until the lentils are dry. (If desired, curry powder to taste may be added to the onions while they are cooking in the butter.) Serve with the top sprinkled thickly with chopped parsley and/or chopped hard-boiled egg. Watch this disappear!

LIMA BEANS PAPRIKA

1 pound dried lima beans	2 tablespoons paprika
Salted water	1 tablespoon flour
2 large onions, chopped	3 cups sour cream
¼ cup butter	Salt
½ pound mushrooms, sliced	Minced parsley

Soak beans overnight, then cook in salted water until tender. Sauté onions in butter until wilted. Add mushrooms, cook 4 minutes, then stir in paprika and flour. Cook 2 minutes more, before adding the drained beans, sour cream, and salt to taste. Heat and serve, sprinkled with minced parsley. Serves 8 or more.

CALIFORNIA LIMA BEAN CASSEROLE

1 pound dried lima beans	Thyme
Salted water	1 cup white table wine
2 carrots, chopped	1 cup bread crumbs
1 onion, chopped	¼ cup melted butter
¼ pound salt pork, diced	½ cup minced parsley
Salt and pepper	1 clove garlic, pressed

Soak beans overnight, then simmer in salted water for 15 minutes. Cook carrots and onion with salt pork until the pork is crisp, the vegetables lightly browned. Combined with the drained beans, season to taste with salt, pepper, and thyme, put in a casserole, and add the wine and enough water to come almost to the top of the beans. Cover and cook in 300° oven until the beans are tender. Combine bread crumbs, melted butter, parsley, and garlic, sprinkle on top, and return to the oven to brown. What a wonderful way to help feed a hungry crowd!

casseroles of grain

BARLEY AND MUSHROOM CASSEROLE

½ pound mushrooms, sliced	¼ pound butter
3 tablespoons butter	1½ cups pearl barley
2 medium onions, coarsely chopped	3 cups chicken stock (or more)
	Salt

Mildred Oakes, of Seattle, makes such a wonderful barley casserole that it earned her the title of "The Best Cook in Our Town" from *McCall's*. Her recipe may be varied in several ways, but all of them call for oodles of butter, so if you are feeling parsimonious or poor, skip this masterpiece.

Cook mushrooms in 3 tablespoons of butter for 4 minutes. Set aside. Now cook onions in ¼ pound of butter until they are wilted, then add barley. Stir over heat until the barley gets beautifully brown—this is important. Put in a casserole or electric skillet, and add the mushrooms and 1½ cups of chicken stock. Cover and cook in a 350° oven for 30 minutes. Add another 1½ cups of chicken stock and cook 30 minutes longer, adding salt if necessary, and a little more chicken stock if the mixture seems too dry. The dish is ready when the barley is tender but *not* mushy.

BAKED HOMINY

2 cups hominy grits	Salt and pepper
¼ cup butter (and more)	1 cup grated cheese (optional)
3 eggs, well beaten	

Cook hominy grits according to the directions on the box. Cool slightly, and add ¼ cup of butter and the eggs. Season with salt and pepper and pour into a very well-buttered casserole, dotting the top with more butter. Before eating, heat in a 400° oven until the top is brown and crispy. If desired, grated cheese may be mixed with the cereal before it's put in the casserole. Serves 8 to 12.

HOMINY SPOON BREAD

1 tablespoon butter	2 teaspoons baking powder
2 cups cooked hominy	½ teaspoon salt
3 eggs, separated	Milk
½ cup white cornmeal	

Combine butter and hominy. Add the egg yolks, well beaten, cornmeal, baking powder, and salt. Pour in just enough milk to make a thin, custardy consistency. Fold in the beaten egg whites, stiff but not dry, and turn into a buttered baking dish. Bake about 1 hour at 350°.

KASHA (BUCKWHEAT GROATS)

1 cup dried brown buckwheat groats	2 cups boiling water or stock
	Salt
1 egg	¼ cup butter or chicken fat

Put buckwheat groats in a heated frying pan or an automatic skillet. Add egg and stir vigorously over high heat. When each grain is separate, add water or stock and salt to taste, cover, and lower heat. Steam for 30 minutes, stirring in butter or chicken fat at the last.

POLENTA

There are numerous ways of fixing this, but the simplest is the best with grilled meats. Just make a thick cornmeal mush (see directions on package), spread it about ¾ inch thick and allow to cool, then cut in shapes—diamonds, squares, crescents, anything that fancy calls for—and arrange on a well-greased baking dish. Brush lavishly with melted butter, sprinkle with grated Parmesan, and put into the oven to heat and brown. If desired, the hot mush may be spooned out in servings, and the melted butter and grated cheese passed separately. It may also be laved with a rich tomato or **mushroom sauce**.

POLENTA PIE

Make cornmeal mush according to directions on the package and pour it into a well-buttered round deep dish. When thoroughly cold, turn out and slice crosswise into 3 or 4 layers. Put back in the rebuttered casserole, a layer at a time, dotting each layer with lots of butter and sprinkling with cheese. Do the same to the top, and bake at 350° for about 45 minutes. This may be varied by putting between the layers **mushroom sauce,** or a thick layer of Mozzarella cheese, or a layer of grated cheese and chopped green chilis. Cut the "pie" in wedges, as if it *were* one.

vegetable casseroles

SIMPLE CORN CASSEROLE

Combine 6 cups of grated raw corn, 2 cups of cream, ¼ cup of melted butter, and salt and pepper to taste. Bake in a casserole at 350° for 1 hour, or cook in an electric cooker or skillet for the same length of time.

CORN PUDDING

4 cups corn (about 8 large ears)	3 cups milk
3 tablespoons butter	Salt and pepper
2 tablespoons flour	4 eggs, separated

This is a good hearty dish to carry to the outside area for eating with ham or pork, chicken, duck, game, or sausages.

Scrape corn from the cobs. Prepare a cream sauce with the butter combined with the flour in a saucepan, and the milk stirred in. Stir until the mixture thickens slightly, then combine with the corn. Add salt and freshly ground black pepper to taste, and remove from the fire. Add the lightly beaten egg yolks and blend with the corn mixture. Cool slightly and fold in the stiffly beaten egg whites. Pour into a well-buttered soufflé dish or baking dish, and bake in a pan of hot water at 325° until the custard is just set—about 1 hour is usually sufficient time. Serves 8 or more.

CORN AND CHILI PUDDING

Combine 2 cups of grated raw corn, 2 eggs, slightly beaten, 2 tablespoons of melted butter, ½ cup of diced canned green chilies, 1 cup of cream, and 1 teaspoon of salt. Set in a pan of hot water and bake at 325° until firm—about 45 minutes. You'll go for this if you're serving chicken or turkey.

GREEN CORN TAMALE PIE

2½ cups fresh masa or 2 cups tortilla flour	2 cups diced Cheddar cheese
¼ cup lard	1 can green chili peppers
2 teaspoons salt	Salt and pepper
4 cups grated raw corn (about 12 medium ears)	Melted butter
	Ripe olives (optional)

Tamale pie has always been one of our favorite dislikes, probably because what was once a fine dish has been hammed up until it is a mess. It wasn't until we ran out of corn husks, when making green corn tamales, that we made this pie to use up our filling and masa —*tamal en cazuela,* we guess you'd call it. Don't attempt it unless you can buy fresh masa or tortilla flour.

Cream lard and add, along with salt, to masa. (If using tortilla flour, mix it with 1 cup or a little more of warm water, enough to make it like putty—this is masa.) Line a 2-quart baking dish with two thirds of the mixture; reserve the rest. Grate corn and mix with cheese and chili peppers that have been cut up. Season to taste with salt and pepper. Put in the casserole, adding 1 cup of pitted ripe olives, if desired. Cover with the remaining masa, which you've rolled out on a damp cloth. Seal as you would a pie. When almost eating time comes, brush top with melted butter and bake at 350° for 40 minutes, or until hot and brown. Serves 8 or more.

BAKED CHILIS RELLENOS

Here is a simple way to get all the wonderful flavor of *chilis rellenos* without the tedious deep fat frying. What's more, the dish can be made in an electric skillet right near the charcoal grill. Cut ½ pound of Jack or Mozzarella cheese (or a processed Swiss, if you can't get either of these) into pieces the size of dominoes. Wrap each piece with a strip of canned green chili—the strip should be from one third to half a chili. Beat the yolks of 4 eggs until very light, then fold in ¼ cup of flour and ¾ teaspoon of salt. Beat the egg whites stiff and combine with the yolks. Have a casserole or electric skillet well buttered, and pour in half the batter. Add the cheese, top with the remaining batter, and bake at 400° (or hot) until set and nicely browned. (In the electric skillet it will have to be cooked with the top on and won't brown, but it will taste just as good.) Serve at once, with **hamburgers** and **frijoles refritos**. What a meal!

EGGPLANT CASSEROLE
OR RATATOUILLE

1 large eggplant	¼ cup olive oil
4 large tomatoes	Salt and pepper
2 large onions	1 pound zucchini
2 green peppers	(optional)
2 cloves garlic (or more)	

Peel the eggplant and cut it in slices. Slice tomatoes, onions, and peppers. Crush garlic cloves and add to olive oil. Brush a casserole with this oil mixture, then arrange the vegetables in it, in alternating layers, sprinkling each layer with salt and pepper and some of the garlic oil. Cook over a very low fire (such as the back of the grill, or the electric cooker, turned low) or in a 325° oven for about 45 minutes, or until the vegetables are tender. (Sometimes zucchini is added to this dish.) This is delightful with a **roasted leg of lamb.**

GREEN ONION PIE

9-inch pastry shell
1 egg yolk, beaten
3 cups chopped green onions
¼ cup butter
2 cups thin cream

4 eggs, slightly beaten
Salt
Pepper
Basil

Line pie pan with rich pastry, fluting the edges prettily. Brush with beaten egg yolk and bake at 450° for 5 minutes, then place an empty pie pan inside the pastry one, reduce heat to 300°, and bake until slightly brown. Cook green onions (some of the green part, please) in butter until wilted. Put over the bottom of the baked shell and pour over them the thin cream, scalded and mixed with the slightly beaten eggs, and salt, pepper, and basil to taste. Bake at 350° until set and the top handsomely browned. Serves 8.

SOUR CREAM ONION TART

1½ cups biscuit dough
2 cups sliced onions
4 tablespoons butter
Salt

Orégano
3 eggs, slightly beaten
1½ cups sour cream
Pepper

Rich and delicious, this is best with steak or chops. Make biscuit dough with a mix or with your favorite recipe, using 1½ cups of it. Press it into a well-greased large pie pan and flute the edges. Cover with sliced onions that have been wilted in the butter and seasoned with salt and orégano. Combine eggs with sour cream, and salt and pepper to taste. Pour over the onions and bake at 400° until nicely browned and the crust is done.

POTATO AND EGG CASSEROLE

Arrange fairly thick slices of cooked potatoes and hard-boiled eggs in alternate layers in a casserole. Pour over a thin cream sauce, well seasoned with salt, pepper, and crushed dill seeds. Cover with buttered crumbs and bake until hot and well browned. This is pleasant with fish, lamb, or chicken. If you wish, make it the quick way with canned potatoes and ditto cream sauce—the latter thinned with cream.

TURNIP AND POTATO CASSEROLE

Surprisingly delicious, this simple dish. Combine equal parts of .mashed potatoes and mashed turnips, mix with sour cream, salt, pepper, and, if desired, some crisply sautéed chopped onions, or some of **Cecily's French fried onions,** crumbled in bits. Top with buttered crumbs, or with more crumbled onion, and bake until hot and the top brown. Serve with duck or goose, or with grilled **mutton chops.**

CHEESE POTATOES

Just the dish to serve with broiled fish, or with kidneys, lamb, or liver. Boil 2 pounds of peeled potatoes with 1 clove of garlic. Mash, add 3 tablespoons of butter, salt and pepper to taste, and 3 well-beaten eggs. Butter a baking dish well and sprinkle with crumbs. Spread half of the potatoes on the bottom, sprinkle with ½ pound of grated Jack cheese, and top with the remaining potatoes. Brush with melted butter, sprinkle with more crumbs, and bake at 350° for 1 hour, or until brown and crispy on top.

BAKED POTATO CASSEROLE

This casserole couldn't be simpler, couldn't be better. Try it with any meat from the grill. Bake potatoes, scoop from skins, and mash with salt, pepper, and enough sour cream to make fluffy. Beat well, pile in a casserole, brush the top with melted butter, sprinkle with sesame seeds, and bake at 350° until nicely browned.

POTATO CAKE

Maybe this should be called *kugel,* but whatever its name, it's a honey! Peel and grate 3 pounds of potatoes and 1 large onion. Cook 6 slices of bacon until crisp, crumble, and mix with the potatoes and onion, along with the bacon fat, 3 eggs, 2 tablespoons of flour, 1 teaspoon of salt, and a few grindings of black pepper. Put in a bacon-greased shallow baking dish and bake at 325° for 1 hour, or until brown and the potatoes tender. Serves 8 or more.

MUSHROOM AND POTATO PIE

What a dish! Mash potatoes and season them well with butter, salt, and pepper. Add as many sautéed mushrooms as you wish, pile in a baking dish, cover with a pastry (or simply with buttered crumbs), and bake until the top is well browned. A bottom crust may be used if the pie is made in a shallow pie tin.

SPINACH CASSEROLE

2 pounds spinach	½ cup grated cheese plus 2
1 ½ cups cream sauce	tablespoons
4 hard-boiled eggs, chopped	Ground cumin
1 teaspoon salt	

Cook spinach until wilted but still bright green. Drain, chop, and combine with cream sauce, eggs, salt, ½ cup of cheese, and a very small amount of ground cumin—just a pinch. Put in a baking dish, sprinkle the top with 2 tablespoons of grated cheese, and reheat in a 350° oven. You'll like this with **roast veal** or **broiled ham steaks.**

CHEESE TOMATO PIE

For the perfect accompaniment to **roast veal** or **liver,** we suggest this. Line a pie pan with 1 ½ cups of biscuit dough. Cover completely with 2 or 3 layers of thickly sliced peeled tomatoes, seasoning between the layers with salt, pepper, and fresh or dried basil. Combine 1 cup of grated cheese—Cheddar, Gruyère, or Jack—with 1 ½ cups of mayonnaise, and spread over the tomatoes. Bake at 400° for 35 minutes, or until the crust is done, the top a beautiful brown.

FETTUCCINE ALFREDO

1 pound homemade or
   commercial fettuccine
Salted water
6 tablespoons butter
⅓ cup grated Swiss cheese

⅓ cup grated Parmesan cheese
Salt
Pepper
Nutmeg
½ cup heavy cream

Make your own fettuccine, or purchase the best egg noodles available. Boil them in salted water until just tender. Drain, and lift with a fork so that the steam escapes. Add butter, which has been well creamed, and the cheeses. Toss lightly, adding salt, freshly ground pepper, and a dash of freshly grated nutmeg. At the very last, mix in hot cream. Serve pronto, passing more cheese. You'll have to taste this before you know how delectable it is. We like it with broiled **turkey**.

FETTUCCINE BARINESE

To the cooked **fettuccine** (narrow noodles), add 1 clove of garlic, pressed, 1 tablespoon each of minced parsley and basil, ½ cup of grated Parmesan cheese, and ¼ cup of melted butter. Salt to taste and mix thoroughly.

LASAGNA AL PESTO

½ pound lasagna (broad
   noodles)
¼ cup olive oil
½ recipe **pesto** (see below)
½ pound Mozzarella or Jack
   cheese, sliced

¾ pound Ricotta or cottage
   cheese
½ cup buttered crumbs
¼ cup grated Parmesan cheese

Boil lasagna until just tender. Dip in olive oil and line a baking dish with it, having it come up the sides. Add a layer of **pesto**, then a layer of Mozzarella or Jack cheese; next add a layer of Ricotta or cottage cheese, and a layer of lasagna, having it go in the opposite direction from the first one. Salt each layer and repeat until ingredients are used. Top with buttered crumbs mixed with grated Parmesan cheese, and bake in a 375° oven for 20 minutes, or until brown.

PESTO

3 cloves garlic, peeled	2 teaspoons salt
1 cup fresh basil	1 teaspoon peppercorns
1 cup parsley leaves	½ cup pine nuts
½ cup olive oil	½ cup spinach leaves

Pound all ingredients together in a mortar until they are a smooth paste, or blend in an electric blender or food processor.

NOODLE KUGEL

We think noodle kugel particularly good with **broiled fish,** though it's also fine with any roast. Cook 3 cups of broad noodles in salted water until just tender, drain, and combine with ¾ cup of rendered chicken or goose fat or butter. Fold in 4 well-beaten eggs and season to taste with salt and pepper. Pour into a well-greased casserole and bake at 375° until well browned.

NOODLE AND WALNUT CASSEROLE

Here's a dish with a Hungarian heritage. It's wonderfully good with **chicken** or **rabbit,** and with roast veal. Cook the desired amount of noodles in salted water and arrange in layers in a casserole, alternating with chopped walnuts, cottage cheese, and butter-browned crumbs. Season each layer with salt and pepper. Have top layer crumbs. Bake at 350° until heated and brown—about 35 minutes.

SPAGHETTI AL BURRO

1 pound spaghetti	½ cup minced olives
¼ pound melted butter	(optional)
½ cup finely minced parsley	Grated Parmesan cheese

Cook spaghetti in boiling salted water from 7 to 10 minutes, or until it's tender but still slightly resistant to the teeth—*al dente,* that is. Drain the spaghetti and mix with butter and parsley. This may be varied by mixing in minced ripe or green olives. Serve with grated Parmesan cheese. A favorite with true spaghetti lovers.

SPAGHETTI OLIO E AGLIO

1 pound spaghetti　　　　　¼ cup butter
4 cloves garlic　　　　　　Grated Parmesan cheese
¼ cup olive oil

So right with any charcoal-broiled meat or fowl. Crush garlic cloves and cook them in olive oil for 3 or 4 minutes. Discard garlic and add butter. Heat and pour over cooked spaghetti. Pass the cheese too.

FRILLS
FOR THE GRILL

Here are some little niceties that are always welcome with meals cooked over charcoal. To cook some of them outdoors may seem farfetched, but as the electric spit needs electricity, it is reasonable to suppose that the same outlet can serve the electric chafing dish and skillet, cooker and deep fryer. Again, if your spit must be turned manually, without benefit of electricity (the hard way), these frills for the grill may be cooked in a skillet or saucepan over the coals. Even deep fat frying is not impossible—didn't our grand-mothers do it in a big iron pot over the kitchen coals?

CECILY'S FRENCH FRIED ONIONS

Famed food columnist Cecily Brownstone gave us her recipe for superb French fried onions. Crisp and brittle, they may be cooked in an electric deep fryer on the patio, or a fine old-fashioned black iron pot, filled with deep fat, may grace the charcoal grill. Perfect with steaks, perfect with broiled liver, perfect as an appetizer with preprandial drinks. Slice large onions about ¼ inch thick, separate them into rings, and soak them in ice water for a couple of hours. Drain, dry thoroughly, and dip in a batter made by beating 1 egg, adding 1 cup of buttermilk, and 1 cup of flour sifted with ½ teaspoon each of salt and baking soda. Fry in deep fat at 375° until brown. Drain well on paper, then put in a moderate oven for added crispness. (Outdoors, put in a warm place near the charcoal grill.)

SAUERKRAUT

Here is a dish that may be done in the oven or may simmer at the back of the grill in a heavy covered pot. Again, it may be cooked in one of today's electric cookers or deep skillets. It's just right with roast goose, duck, spareribs, pork, and grilled sausages. Line a casserole or pot with thin slices of salt pork, and add to this 5 pounds of sauerkraut which has been rinsed in cold water. Add plenty of freshly ground pepper, 1 or 2 juniper berries if you have them, and a fifth of white wine or a quart of beer. Cover and simmer very slowly for 5 or 6 hours, adding more wine or beer if necessary. Serves 18 to 20, unless there are kraut fans about, in which case it may do for 10.

GERMAN FRIED POTATOES

As right for the terrace as for the camp—they taste wonderful when eaten under the sky. Peel and slice raw potatoes ⅛ inch thick, allowing 1 medium-large potato to a person. Heat ¼ cup of butter, goose or bacon fat, or lard for each 4 potatoes, and cook them in a skillet over a brisk fire, turning so that they brown crisp and are tender. Season with salt and pepper.

SUET-FRIED POTATOES

Chop suet and cook until the fat is rendered out. Fry potatoes as above—the little bits of crispy fat taste wonderful. The same thing can be done with bacon or with chicken fat. In the latter case, add some chicken skin, too, for extra charm.

POTATO GALETTE

A bit fancier than plain fried potatoes, this French potato cake is a fitting partner for **broiled tenderloins.** Peel and slice 3 large baking potatoes. Melt ¼ cup of butter or beef fat in a heavy skillet and arrange potatoes in a spiral layer in the bottom of the pan, starting from the center and building out around the edges, so the potatoes overlap. Repeat in layers, dotting each one with fat and seasoning with salt and pepper. Cover and cook slowly until the potatoes are soft and the bottom and sides crisply brown. Invert on a heated chop dish. This is a pretty and a tasty dish.

SWISS POTATOES

Grate 4 good-sized raw potatoes, season, and sauté in ¼ cup of fat until the bottom is brown. Turn like a pancake to brown the other side. A real treat when served with grilled **sausages.**

POTATOES BOULANGÈRE

Prepare as for **potato galette,** above, but cover with bouillon and cook until the liquid is all absorbed. This is nice with any grilled meat.

POTATOES PARISIENNE

Small new potatoes have their skins scraped off and are literally steamed in butter. Melt enough butter to cover the bottom of a skillet ¼ inch deep. Roll the spuds around in it, then cover and steam for 20 to 25 minutes, or until the potatoes are just tender. Remove cover and shake over the fire until they are brown. Salt and pepper, of course, and do try them with **broiled lobster.**

POTATOES LANDAISE

Make **potato galette,** and after turning out on the dish, sprinkle heavily with 1½ cups of minced parsley mixed with 3 or 4 cloves of garlic, finely minced. Robust, and fine for outdoor fare—especially with **game.**

SAVOY POTATOES

These originated in the cheese country and are particularly good with grilled fish or poultry. Butter a baking dish or skillet well. Slice 6 medium potatoes, and have 1½ cups of grated Switzerland Gruyère or Swiss and ½ cup of grated Parmesan cheese combined. Arrange alternate layers of potatoes and cheese, seasoning each layer and dotting with butter. Cover and cook at low temperature until the potatoes are tender and the cheese thoroughly melted. This may be varied by adding layers of grated celery root and ½ cup of bouillon. Serves 8. We like these with **roast beef.**

HASHED-IN-CREAM POTATOES

Peel cooked potatoes and chop or dice them. For each 4 potatoes, use ¼ cup of butter or chicken fat, and sauté until lightly browned. Sprinkle very lightly with flour—not more than 1 teaspoonful for 4 potatoes—and pour on enough heavy cream to show. Season with salt and pepper, and simmer until the heavy cream has cooked down and the bottom has formed a heavenly crust. Fold like an omelette and serve quickly. These are extra wonderful if some toasted sesame seeds or chopped toasted filberts are added toward the last—and they are served with **mutton chops.**

LYONNAISE POTATOES

An old favorite with **beefsteak.** Sauté a large sliced onion in ⅓ cup of butter until lightly colored. Add 5 or 6 sliced raw potatoes and cook until brown and tender, then sprinkle with ½ cup of coarsely chopped parsley, and salt and pepper to taste. Serves 8.

O'BRIEN POTATOES

Made like **Lyonnaise potatoes,** but ¼ cup each of minced green pepper and pimiento are added with the parsley, or instead of it. A quarter cup of heavy cream may also be added for the last few minutes of cooking. Try them with **chicken livers** or **calf's liver,** *en brochette.*

BROILED MARROW BONES

These may be served with broiled or roasted meat, or as an appetizer. We particularly like them as a side dish with **steak,** accompanied by a **Bordelaise sauce.** Have the marrow bones split, sprinkle them with salt, and broil, cut side up, for about 8 to 10 minutes, or until the marrow becomes brown and bubbly-looking. Serve in the bones.

foil cookery

Cooking with aluminum foil is an adaptation of a very old method —that of wrapping food in wet leaves, husks, seaweed, or even wet clay before cooking. This method keeps the juices in but allows the food to cook evenly. It must be remembered, however, that just as it keeps the juices in, so does it keep the charcoal flavor out. This matters little in many instances. We particularly like foil cookery for many fruits and vegetables (see Chapter 14) and for camping (see Chapter 22), but it is also useful for certain dishes cooked on the patio—dishes that you don't want broiled or roasted.

FOILED FROZEN VEGETABLES

Almost any frozen vegetable, such as peas or limas, may be dabbed with butter, wrapped in a packet of aluminum foil, and cooked on the grill. They will be done in 10 to 15 minutes.

FOILED POTATOES

As stated in Chapter 14, whole potatoes may be foiled and baked in the ashes or on the grill. They may also be peeled and sliced, seasoned with salt, pepper, and butter, wrapped in a little package of foil, and cooked the same way.

FOILED SWEET POTATOES OR YAMS

Prepare as above, but add a little brown sugar to the potatoes.

FOILED CARROTS

Punch holes in washed carrots, season, brush with butter, wrap in foil, and cook about 45 minutes.

ASSORTED VEGETABLES, FOILED

Sliced tomatoes, onions, and potatoes may be seasoned, buttered, wrapped in foil, and cooked about 20 minutes. Other combinations might include carrots, eggplant, cut corn, string beans, or whatever is at hand.

ONIONS SMOTHERED IN FOIL

For each good sized onion have a large square of foil. Slice the onions onto the foil, add a good big hunk of butter and salt and pepper to taste. Wrap in a flat package, double-folding the edges. Cook on the grill for about 30 minutes, and serve a packet to each guest.

ROAST CHESTNUTS

Make a slit in each chestnut, wrap them in foil, having a dozen or so in each package, and put right on the coals. They will take about 25 minutes. These are fine to serve for dessert.

ROAST WALNUTS

Crack walnuts but don't remove shells. Wrap in foil as for **roast chestnuts**. Heat over charcoal for about 10 minutes, and serve with apples and cheese for dessert.

BREAD

Bread, in one form or another, is usually included in the outdoor meal, whether it's served on the patio or at a faraway camping spot. The breads served close to home are pretty apt to be ready-baked, or baker's bread, reheated at the charcoal grill; those we deal with in this chapter. Breads actually made in outdoor ovens will be found in **Chapter 22.**

TOAST

This may surprise you, but it is a natural for the charcoal grill. If your childhood holds memories of homemade bread toasted over the campfire or the wood range in Grandmother's kitchen, you will understand. If it doesn't, you will still understand the first time you smell it toasting. The bread must be good to begin with. It may be white or wheat, rye, oatmeal, pumpernickel, or sourdough, but none of this bleached, artificially preserved and softened stuff for us. Simply use a fork or a hinged grill and toast it, first on one side, then the other, until a gorgeous, salubrious brown. Have butter softened for easy spreading.

HEATED BREAD

This must, like the toast, be good bread to begin with. We prefer homemade, of course. Simply slice it and wrap it in foil, either the whole loaf or a couple of pieces to a package, and heat it well on or near the fire.

FRENCH BREAD

First choice, probably, with ninety per cent of the meal planners. Have long loaves, either sweet or sourdough, and split them lengthwise. Spread with any of the fillings listed just below, and then wrap in a double fold of aluminum foil and put on a not too hot part of the grill until heated through. If preferred, individual foil packets may be made so each guest can unwrap his own. Rye bread can be treated in exactly the same ways.

✔ GARLIC LOAF. Mash 3 cloves of garlic or use a garlic press, and combine with ½ pound of butter.

✔ ONION LOAF. Chop a bunch of green onions, including some of the tops, and mix with ½ pound of butter.

✔ POPPY SEED LOAF. Toast ½ cup of poppy seeds and mix with garlic butter, as for **garlic loaf.**

✔ SESAME SEED LOAF. Toast ½ cup of sesame seeds, and mix with onion butter, as for **onion loaf.**

✔ CHEESE AND PARSLEY LOAF. Combine ½ pound of butter with ½ cup each of grated Swiss or Cheddar cheese and parsley.

✔ MIXED HERB LOAF. Combine ½ pound of butter, 1 cup of chopped parsley, ¼ cup of chopped green onions, ¼ cup of chopped chives, and 2 cloves of garlic, crushed. This may be varied by adding fresh basil, mint, marjoram, or what have you.

✔ HERB LOAF. This is ½ pound of butter combined with ¼ cup of any fresh herb—say rosemary, tarragon, or basil. If desired, a little chopped onion may also be added.

✔ FINES HERBES LOAF. Here the classic herbs—fresh tarragon, chives, and parsley—are combined with butter—¼ cup of each to ½ pound of butter.

✔ CHEESE AND HERB LOAF. Combine ½ pound of grated aged Cheddar cheese and ¼ pound of butter, with ¼ cup each of minced parsley and green onions.

ROLLS

Any kind of roll or bun may be heated in the same ways as the bread. That is, either split and toasted, merely heated, or spread with a filling before heating.

ONION AND CHEESE BREAD

Cut a loaf of French bread in fairly thick slices, but don't cut through the bottom crust. In each cut insert a slice of Swiss, Jack, Mozzarella, or Cheddar cheese, and a slice of onion. Wrap in foil and heat over the coals.

CHEESE AND CHILI BREAD

This is made like that above, except that a slice of canned green chili pepper is used instead of, or along with, the onion.

STUFFED ROLLS

What these are stuffed with is anybody's business. Cut a slice from the top of any-shaped roll and scoop out the insides. Mix 2 cups of the innards with 1 cup of grated cheese, ½ cup each of chopped green pepper, onion, and minced ripe olives, and enough evaporated milk or cream to make the mixture moist but not soupy. Put back in the scooped-out rolls, slap the tops on, wrap in foil, and heat on the grill before serving.

SOUFFLÉ BREAD

This may be in a skillet on the grill or in one of the electric skillets. It's light and feathery, and a delicious accompaniment to almost any meat, fish, or game. Serve with plenty of butter. Beat the yolks of 4 eggs until thick and lemon-colored. Add 2 tablespoons of melted butter and 4 tablespoons of sifted flour, in which you have mixed 1 teaspoon of baking powder and ¼ teaspoon each of salt and sugar. Add just enough milk to make as thick as cake batter.

Fold in the stiffly beaten whites of 4 eggs, and pour in a hot skillet in which you have melted 1 tablespoon of butter. Cover and place on the fire over medium heat, or in the electric skillet heated to a little more than medium (about 375°). It should take about 20 or 25 minutes to cook, and should rise like an omelette soufflé. If you have an oven handy you may brown the top in it. (The old-time recipe, which was, no doubt, cooked in a "spider," suggested carefully turning this bread for browning.) Serve from the skillet with oodles of butter.

SPIDER BREAD

This, another "skillet" bread, is a favorite with campers, but it's also fun when done in a heavy iron skillet at the charcoal grill. Combine 2 cups of bread flour, ⅓ cup of butter, lard, or bacon fat, 4 teaspoons of baking powder, and 1 teaspoon of salt. Make as you would biscuits, adding enough water to make a soft dough. Roll to fit the bottom of your skillet (or spider!), which should be hot and well greased. Cook 10 minutes on each side, and serve at once, while still plenty hot. Butter goes with this in a big way.

ONION BREAD

This has to be made indoors, but reheats nicely over the grill when foil-wrapped. Make white bread according to your usual rule. After first rising, roll enough for each loaf into an oblong, and spread with softened butter, then sprinkle with 1½ cups of chopped dried or green onions which have been sautéed lightly in 3 tablespoons of butter. Now sprinkle with salt, and with poppy seeds if desired, roll, and put in bread pans. More sautéed onions and poppy seeds may be sprinkled on top, if desired. Allow to rise until double in bulk, then bake at 400° for 50 or 60 minutes, or until the bread shrinks from the sides of the pan and slides out easily. It should be nicely browned.

CHEESE BREAD

This is made in exactly the same way as the **onion bread,** above, except that the rolled dough is sprinkled with 1½ cups of grated Cheddar cheese.

GRAHAM BREAD

This recipe is from a noted Oregon hostess who kept her friends and family happy by providing this superb homemade bread. She combined a large can of evaporated milk with an equal amount of hot water. To this, she added ¼ cup of melted shortening, ⅓ cup of sugar, 1 tablespoon of salt, and, when cooled to lukewarm, 1 yeast cake dissolved in ½ cup of warm water. Three cups of coarse graham flour are then beaten in, then enough white flour (about 6 cups) to make a stiff dough. Let rise until light, form into 2 large, 3 medium, or 4 small loaves, and again let rise, but *not* until light. This last is the secret, we think, of this delightfully moist bread. Bake at 375° for 1 hour, or until it gives out a hollow sound when thumped and shrinks slightly from the sides of the pan. This is wonderful when toasted over charcoal or simply heated in foil.

CORN BREAD

Corn bread, made with a mix or with your own favorite recipe, is wonderful when split and toasted over charcoal, then buttered generously. Try this simple recipe: Combine 1 cup of corn meal, 2 cups of scalded milk or boiling water, 2 teaspoons of salt, and 2 tablespoons of melted butter. Spread ½ inch deep in a shallow, well-buttered pan and bake at 350° until brown. Cool, split, and toast over charcoal.

ONION BISCUITS

Make baking powder biscuits or use the packaged unbaked kind, and roll into small pancake-sized pieces. Put a dab of sautéed onions on one side of each biscuit, fold over like a turnover, and seal edges with water. Bake at 450° for about 12 minutes, or until brown. These, too, may be reheated in foil at the grill.

19

SALADS

Whether or not we are having a little private rebellion of our own when it comes to salads, we are not entirely sure. We do know, however, that we are both ever so weary of the ubiquitous—the almost inevitable—mixed (or even worse, "tossed") green salad. Of course, a great bowl of lovely tender leaves, their shades varying from the deepest of green to the palest of yellow, their textures from the crispness of romaine to the buttery softness of bibb, can be lovely to look at, lovelier to eat. Lovelier, that is, when it's perfectly dressed with the finest of olive oil, and with the finesse of an expert. That we grant, but why, oh, why, need it be as certain as thirst and taxes? We think it needn't, so we here include dozens of other ideas for salads that taste good when served outside—all of them as accompaniments to foods from the grill.

APPLE AND CHESTNUT SALAD

Combine diced unpeeled red apples with diced cooked chestnuts. Dress with mayonnaise and serve with **roast goose.**

GRATED APPLE AND CRESS SALAD

Grate unpeeled red apples and combine with shredded celery. Dress with French dressing, surrounded with cress, and serve, *at once*, with **pheasant.**

APPLE AND GREEN PEPPER SALAD

Slices of unpeeled apple and rings of green pepper; French dressing and chicory. What could be better with pork chops?

ARTICHOKE SALAD

Artichoke bottoms, cut in strips, and combined with strips of celery; French dressing. Beautiful with **broiled sweetbreads.**

ARTICHOKE AND CELERY SALAD

Cut artichoke bottoms in julienne (matchlike) pieces and combine with celery cut in a similar fashion. French dressing, with truffles or ripe olives as a garnish.

ASPARAGUS SALAD I

Top cold cooked asparagus with chopped hard-boiled eggs and crumbled bacon. Pour over a hot mixture of 3 parts of bacon fat to 1 of vinegar. Serve at once, with any steak, chop, or roast.

ASPARAGUS SALAD II

Cold cooked asparagus, dressed with **vinaigrette sauce.**

BACON AND EGG SALAD

For 2 heads of romaine or leaf lettuce, or 1 of lettuce and 1 bunch of cress, hard-boil, shell, and chop 4 eggs, and crumble 8 slices (½ pound) of crisply cooked bacon. Sprinkle eggs and bacon on top of the lettuce, which has been put in a large salad bowl. Add a few green onions, chopped. Now season with salt (about 1 teaspoon) and freshly ground black pepper, pour on 3 tablespoons of vinegar and ½ cup of the bacon fat. Mix tenderly but well, and serve with grilled **chicken** and **hominy spoon bread.**

BEAN AND DILL SALAD

Green beans, cooked tender-crisp, and dressed with French dressing, well laced with chopped fresh dill or crushed dill seeds. Chill and serve with or without romaine. Serve with grilled **salmon.**

GREEN AND WHITE BEAN SALAD

Pile **white beans, country style** in the middle of a round dish and surround with whole tender green beans. Dress with **vinaigrette sauce.**

KIDNEY BEAN SALAD

Combine 1 can of drained kidney beans with a large cucumber, diced, 3 large tomatoes, diced and drained, ½ cup each of diced celery, onion, and green pepper. Dress with mayonnaise flavored with chili powder, and sprinkle top with crumbled crisp bacon. Serve on crisp romaine, with grilled **liver** or **lamb.**

LIMA BEAN SALAD

Tiny cooked lima beans are dressed with 1 cup of mayonnaise to which ¼ cup of prepared mustard and 1 teaspoon of minced fresh tarragon have been added.

STRING BEAN SALAD

Cooked string beans, sliced, with chopped onion and chopped parsley, and French dressing. A salad that goes with any meat.

BEAN SPROUT SALAD I

Dress fresh or canned bean sprouts with dressing made by combining 1 part each of soy sauce, sherry, and lime juice with 5 parts of oil. Add also shredded green ginger and green onion to taste. Nice with **roast pork.**

BEAN SPROUT SALAD II

Combine bean sprouts with shredded onion, celery, and green pepper. Dress with mayonnaise flavored with soy sauce and curry powder, sprinkle salad with chopped toasted almonds. Try this with **broiled turkey.**

BEET SALAD

Tiny cooked beets mixed with their tender uncooked leaves and dressed with French dressing which has been well laced with chopped hard-boiled eggs. This is delightful with grilled **tongue** or **roast veal.**

BEET AND OLIVE SALAD

Beets, ripe olives, and chicory; garlic-flavored French dressing. Extra special with **roast liver.**

BEET AND ONION SALAD

Sliced beets with sliced onions; dressed with cream, lemon juice, salt, pepper, and French mustard. Serve with any **fish.**

BEET AND TONGUE SALAD

Equal parts of each, cut julienne. Dress with mayonnaise, on lettuce, and serve with **fish steaks.**

BROCCOLI SALAD

Dress lightly cooked tender green buds of broccoli with 1 cup of mayonnaise and ⅓ cup of grated Parmesan cheese, plus a dash of chili powder.

CABBAGE SALAD

Cabbage, shredded, with sliced apples or oranges, and raisins that have been plumped in Cognac. We like this with **duck.**

RED CABBAGE SALAD

Chopped red cabbage and celery, in equal parts, are combined with half as much sliced cooked shrimp, and French dressing.

CARROT SALAD

Raw shredded carrots, dressed with half sour cream and half mayonnaise, seasoned with tarragon. Good with almost anything.

COLE SLAW WITH CAPERS

Chop cabbage, add capers; cream dressing, hard-boiled-egg garnish. Serve from a scooped-out cabbage. Nice with **liver steaks.**

COLE SLAW WITH CHICKEN

Combine diced chicken, chopped cabbage, and chopped hard-boiled eggs. Dress with mustard-flavored mayonnaise, thinned with cream. **Broiled shrimps** with this.

CELERIAC SALAD

Celeriac, cut julienne, and dressed with mayonnaise mixed with curry and chili sauce. Surprisingly good with **squab.**

CELERY VICTOR

Simmer split celery hearts in chicken stock until tender, or use canned ones. Dress with French dressing and crisscross with anchovy fillets and pimiento strips. A good partner for roasts.

CHERRY SALAD

Pit large cherries, or use canned ones, and combine with slivered almonds and French dressing. Sprinkle with chervil or parsley, and serve on chicory.

CUCUMBER SALAD

Cucumbers, sliced thin, combined with salt and grated onion, dressed with a small amount of mayonnaise, and allowed to chill for several hours before serving. Always right with fish.

CUCUMBER SALAD, CHINESE STYLE

Slice unpeeled cucumbers very thin and dress with equal parts of soy sauce, vinegar, and salad oil. Good with **broiled chicken breast**.

EGG AND ANCHOVY SALAD

Slice hard-boiled egg arranged on shredded lettuce and stripped with anchovy fillets. Dressing: Mayonnaise thinned with cream and lemon juice, and flavored with anchovy paste. Serve with **broiled fish fillets**.

FARMER'S SALAD

Diced hoop cheese, cucumbers, radishes, sweet onion, and green pepper are combined with sour cream, seasoned with salt, pepper, and dill, and served with pumpernickel bread, and with **broiled lobster**.

GRAPEFRUIT AND PEACH SALAD

Segments and slices, dressed with French dressing, garnished with slivered toasted almonds, and served on watercress.

JAPANESE SALAD

This is fun, too, especially when served with **chicken teriyaki**. Combine 3 cucumbers, sliced thin, with 1 cup or more of crab meat, and dress with ½ cup each of soy sauce and vinegar, and 1 tablespoon of minced green or crystallized ginger.

MELON SALAD I

Cubes or balls of ripe melon, assorted, if desired, dressed with French dressing, lime-flavored, and garnished with crisp lettuce.

MELON SALAD II

Slices of cantaloupe on Boston lettuce, lightly sprinkled with grated crystallized ginger and with French dressing.

ONION SALAD

Slice onions thin and heap in a bowl. Top with shelled soft-boiled eggs. Season with salt, pepper, and lemon juice. Mix well before serving. Try this one with **kidneys.**

ONION AND PARSLEY SALAD

Combine green onions and chopped parsley in equal parts. Dress with French dressing and serve in lettuce cups.

ONION RELISH-SALAD

Slice sweet red onions thin, cover with 4 parts of water to 1 of vinegar, and season with salt, pepper, and orégano. Will keep in refrigerator in closed jar for weeks. Just the thing for **steaks.**

ORANGE SALAD

Sliced oranges, sprinkled cautiously with cardamom, and dressed with French dressing.

ORANGE AND APPLE SALAD

Slice oranges and unpeeled apples. Arrange on Boston lettuce; French dressing with a touch of coriander.

ORANGE AND CUCUMBER SALAD

Arrange alternate slices of oranges and cucumbers on a bed of escarole (chicory). Slice green pepper and onions transparently thin and arrange on top. French dressing, here.

PARSLEY AND GREEN PEPPER SALAD

Chop both very fine, mix with French dressing, and put in lettuce cups. **Roast pork** and this like each other.

PASTA SALAD

Cook elbow macaroni, macaroni shells, or other pasta in stock or water, and dress with sour cream and fresh dill, or dill seeds. Mayonnaise may be combined with the sour cream in equal parts.

PINEAPPLE SALAD

Combine equal parts of shredded pineapple and celery, dress with French dressing flavored with rosemary, and put on lettuce-lined plates. Fine with **spareribs.**

POTATO SALAD

Dice or slice potatoes while still warm, and dress with 2 parts of white wine and 1 part of melted butter. Combine ½ cup of ripe olives and ½ cup of minced green onions with salt and pepper, and mix in lightly. Let stand several hours before serving, with the traditional **broiled ham.**

RADICCIO

Shred 2 cups each of dandelion greens, chicory, and lettuce, and combine with 1 can of grated tuna, 6 chopped anchovy fillets, 12 sliced stuffed olives, ¼ cup each of minced parsley, green pepper, and green onion, and, if you wish, chopped hard-boiled egg, salami, radishes, or anything else that is good in antipasto as this is a sort of antipasto mélange—and a good one, too. Fine with **veal.**

RADISH SALAD

Sliced radishes and celery, dressed with sour cream. We like this with **roast beef.**

RICE SALAD I

4 cups of cold cooked rice, 1 sweet red pepper, and 1 sweet red onion, sliced very thin, and 6 tomatoes, diced, and their juice and seeds discarded, are mixed with French dressing and sprinkled with minced parsley. Chops taste good with this salad.

RICE SALAD II

Cooked rice, grated fresh or candied ginger, chopped green onion and green pepper; mayonnaise flavored with curry powder and lemon juice. **Rabbit** for this one.

SAUERKRAUT SALAD

Sauerkraut cooked with garlic and pepper is chilled, dressed with French dressing, and sprinked with minced onions or with caraway.

RAW SAUERKRAUT SALAD

Rinse sauerkraut and serve with mayonnaise. Chopped or grated apple may be added.

TANGERINE SALAD

Slice tangerines and marinate in port wine. Serve with French dressing on leaves of Boston lettuce, with **roast junior goose.**

TOMATO SALAD OR APPETIZER

Large ripe tomatoes, peeled and sliced thick, are delightful when salted, then dressed with olive oil and but a suspicion of vinegar. Sprinkle minced fresh basil on top, or, lacking that, some dried orégano, and serve. These tomato slices may be arranged, one large one to a serving, crossed with anchovy fillets, and garnished with cress—that for a nice first course.

TOMATO SALAD I

Sliced tomato and sliced sweet onion; orégano-flavored French dressing. Fine with all **game.**

TOMATO SALAD II

Sprinkle sliced tomatoes with fresh chopped basil and dress with 1 part brandy to 3 parts oil. Salt and pepper for seasoning. Serve with grilled **fish.**

TOMATO AND CHEESE SALAD

Dice firm ripe tomatoes and discard seeds and juice. Combine with half as much diced Cheddar cheese and dress with French dressing, flavored with chili powder and orégano. Serve with **broiled hamburgers.**

TOMATO AND MUSHROOM SALAD

Sliced tomatoes are heaped high with mushrooms that have been chopped and sautéed lightly in olive oil, with garlic. A perfect partner for **steak.**

WHITE SALAD

Sliced cauliflower, chopped celery, white onion, the white part of cucumber are all dressed with sour cream and seasoned with salt and white pepper. A nice change from a green salad.

A "YAM" OR SIAMESE SALAD

This salad is a little unusual, but not too exotic to serve anyone. Combine 3 cups of shredded cucumbers with ¼ cup of minced green onion, 1 teaspoon of chili powder, 1 tablespoon of anchovy paste, and ¼ cup of lemon juice. Add salt to taste, and serve very cold. A good salad for dieters.

salad dressings

VINAIGRETTE SAUCE

4 parts or more olive oil to 1 part good wine vinegar; add salt and pepper, and any or all of the following: chopped chives, capers, shallots, parsley, hard-boiled eggs, olives (green or ripe), or dill pickles.

GREEN GODDESS DRESSING

1 cup of mayonnaise, ½ cup of vinaigrette sauce, 2 tablespoons of minced green onion, 1 tablespoon each of minced fresh tarragon and chives, 4 anchovy fillets, chopped.

CALIFORNIA WINE DRESSING

Soak 1 teaspoon of dried tarragon in ¼ cup of California Sauterne; add 1 cup of mayonnaise, 1 tablespoon each of capers, anchovy paste, and minced onion, 2 tablespoons each of cream and minced parsley, and salt and pepper to taste. This is the Wine Institute's version of **Green Goddess,** and it's very nice indeed. Try it especially with sea food or chicken salad, or with green beans, artichokes, or sliced tomatoes.

SOUR CREAM DRESSING

Combine the yolks of 4 hard-boiled eggs, sieved, 2 cups of sour cream, ¼ cup of lemon juice, salt, pepper, and a little basil to taste.

BASIC FRENCH DRESSING

Combine 1 cup of olive oil with ¼ cup of wine vinegar, lemon juice, or a combination of the two. Season to taste with salt and freshly ground pepper. Garlic, mustard, paprika, or herbs may be added to taste.

20

MARINADES,
BASTES,
AND SAUCES

In our years of experimenting with cooking over coals, we have found that some foods need marinating, some basting, some neither. Gone are the days when all charcoal cookery meant much dousing with so-called "barbecue" sauces—sauces which succeeded in doing nothing but ruin the fine flavor of the meat. However, there is no question that many sauces do complement the yield of the grill. We give some of them in this chapter, others are included in the various recipes.

marinades and bastes

A *marinade* is a thin sauce in which food is marinated, or soaked, before it is cooked. A *baste* is the sauce that is brushed or sprinkled on the food while it is cooking. They are often one and the same, though marinades are designed to add seasonings that will more or less penetrate the flesh and also tenderize it, while bastes are used to give the food a distinctive flavor on the outside, and to lubricate it to prevent dryness. Therefore the marinade is apt to be thinner, highly seasoned, and to contain some tenderizer such as wine or lemon juice, while the baste usually includes oil. Bastes are brushed on with a long-handled pastry brush or a bunch of parsley, celery leaves, or other herbs. Here are a few of our favorites:

RED WINE MARINADE

(For rabbit, game, and less tender cuts of beef and mutton.) Combine 2 cups of red wine, ¼ cup of vinegar or lemon juice, 1 onion, sliced, ¼ cup each of chopped onion and carrot, a few peppercorns, and an herb bouquet consisting of bay, parsley, and thyme. To use for basting, add 1 cup of oil.

WHITE WINE MARINADE

(For poultry, some game birds, veal, and rabbit.) Make as above, but substitute white wine for red, and use marjoram instead of thyme.

SOY SAUCE MARINADE AND BASTE

(For almost any poultry or shellfish, and for pork, veal, and beef.) Combine equal parts of soy sauce or shoyu, sherry or whiskey (or sake), and oil, such as sesame, peanut, or corn. This may also have garlic and/or grated ginger added.

VERMOUTH MARINADE AND BASTE

(An all-purpose one, for any meat, game, or poultry.) Combine equal parts of Italian or French vermouth and olive oil.

BARBECUE MARINADE AND BASTE

(For those who like a highly seasoned sauce for meat and poultry.) Combine 1 8-ounce can of tomato sauce, 1 teaspoon each of dry mustard, sugar, and salt, 1 tablespoon each of Worcestershire sauce and vinegar, ½ cup of red wine, 1 clove of garlic, pressed or grated, and Tabasco to taste. Simmer 10 minutes and strain. For a baste, add ½ cup of oil.

PEPPER BARBECUE MARINADE AND BASTE

(For hamburgers, steaks, and chops.) Combine 1 8-ounce can of tomato juice with ¼ cup each of olive oil, chopped green pepper, and chopped green onion. Add 3 cloves of garlic, pressed, and 1 tablespoon (or more) of chili powder, and salt to taste. Finish as in preceding recipe.

brown sauces

These classic sauces are usually made with sauce Espagnole as a base. Espagnole takes long hours of simmering and blending and skimming. We have found that a can of beef gravy, available in any market, will serve the purpose beautifully. The gravy usually comes in a 10¾-ounce can.

BORDELAISE SAUCE

(Serve with steaks and roast beef.) Cook 2 tablespoons of minced shallots or green onions in 2 tablespoons of butter. Add ¾ cup of red wine and simmer until reduced one half. Combine with 1 can of beef gravy, 2 tablespoons each of lemon juice and minced parsley, and salt and cayenne to taste. Heat, add sliced poached beef marrow, if desired, and serve. (Marrow is poached in a little salted water, until set.)

CHAMPAGNE SAUCE

(For ham or sweetbreads.) Cook a cup of champagne or white wine with half a bay leaf, 2 cloves, and 2 peppercorns. When reduced one half, strain and combine with a can of beef gravy. Heat and serve.

SAUCE CHARCUTIÈRE

(For all pork and for grilled sausages.) Brown ½ cup of chopped onion in 3 tablespoons of butter; add ¼ cup of white wine, 2 tablespoons of wine vinegar, 1 can of beef gravy, 1 teaspoon of dry mustard. Heat, and add ¼ cup of shredded sour gherkins before serving.

SAUCE CHASSEUR

(For game, mutton, poultry.) Cook 2 tablespoons of minced shallots or green onions in ¼ cup of butter. When transparent, combine with 1 can of beef gravy, ½ cup of canned tomato sauce, 2 tablespoons of lemon juice, 1 tablespoon of minced parsley, and a few sliced mushrooms. Add a dash of Tabasco, and salt if needed. Heat and serve.

CHÂTEAUBRIAND SAUCE

(For steaks and other grilled meats.) Cook together 1 cup of brown gravy and 1 cup of white wine, until very thick. Add ¼ pound of butter, 3 tablespoons of lemon juice, 1 tablespoon of minced parsley, salt and pepper to taste. Beat well, and serve when the butter is melted.

SAUCE COLBERT

(For mutton, lamb, kidneys, and game; and with broiled fillet of sole.) Combine 1 can of beef gravy with the juice of 1 lemon, ½ cup of melted butter, a dash of nutmeg and cayenne, 1 tablespoon of minced parsley, and, if you wish, ¼ cup of Madeira or sherry.

SAUCE DIABLE

(For all deviled dishes.) Cook 3 tablespoons of minced shallots or green onions in 3 tablespoons of butter until wilted. Add ¼ cup of lemon juice or vinegar, 2 teaspoons each of Worcestershire sauce and prepared mustard, a dash of Tabasco, and 1 can of beef gravy.

SAUCE MARCHANDS DE VIN

Chop 6 shallots or green onions; sauté in ¼ cup of butter until wilted. Add ¾ cup of claret or Cabernet, and reduce to ⅓ cup. Combine with 1 can of brown gravy and heat, adding 2 tablespoons of butter and 2 tablespoons of lemon juice at the end.

SAUCE ORIENTALE

(Serve with mutton, game, lobster, ham, chicken, and tongue.) Combine 1 can of beef gravy, 1 tablespoon each of currant jelly, grated horseradish, soy sauce, and raisins, and ¼ cup of port wine. Simmer and serve.

SAUCE PIQUANT

(For broiled pork and veal chops and steaks, and venison.) Cook 3 tablespoons of minced onion in 2 tablespoons of butter. Add 1 can of beef gravy, ⅓ cup of tarragon vinegar, 1 tablespoon of capers, salt and pepper. Simmer 5 minutes, add 1 tablespoon of minced parsley, and serve.

SAUCE POIVRADE

(Serve with any grilled meat or poultry.) Cook 6 shallots or green onions, chopped, 1 carrot, chopped, and 1 tablespoon of minced parsley in ½ cup of white wine. Add 1 can of beef gravy, 1 teaspoon of white pepper, ¼ cup of butter, and ¼ cup of vinegar. Heat, strain, and serve.

SAUCE ROBERT

(For all grilled meats or poultry, especially pork, goose, and turkey.) Brown ¾ cup of chopped onion in ¼ cup of butter. Combine with 1 can of beef gravy, 1 tablespoon of vinegar, ½ cup of white wine, 1 tablespoon of prepared mustard, and salt and pepper to taste. Heat and serve.

miscellaneous hot sauces

HOLLANDAISE SAUCE

This is a lovely sauce for broiled fish, and its variations are right with many meats. The whole trick of making a perfect hollandaise is low temperature. Never let the water under the bowl actually boil.

Place a heavy crockery bowl over the bottom of a double broiler containing hot, not boiling, water. In it put 1 tablespoon of lemon juice, a dash each of cayenne and salt, and 3 egg yolks. Mix well, then add ¼ pound of butter, cut in pieces. As the butter melts, add more until it's all used. Keep the water under the boil, and beat with a wire whisk until the sauce thickens. It won't curdle if you follow directions, but if it does, beat in a little heavy cream. This will keep and may be reheated over not very hot water.

BÉARNAISE SAUCE

This is marvelous when served with roast lamb or mutton, or with steaks, chops, liver, or hamburgers. It's good with sea food, too. Cook ½ cup of tarragon vinegar with 4 shallots or green onions, chopped, and 1 teaspoon of tarragon until the liquid is all but absorbed. Add to **hollandaise sauce,** made as above. A little mustard may also be added.

CALIFORNIA SAUCE

(For fish.) Add ¼ cup of tomato purée to 1 cup of **Béarnaise sauce.**

SAUCE MALTA

(For shellfish.) Add ¼ cup of lime juice or sour orange juice to 1 cup of **hollandaise sauce.**

SAUCE MOUSSELINE

(For sweetbreads and chicken breasts.) Combine equal parts of **hollandaise sauce** and whipped cream.

BASIC BÉCHAMEL SAUCE

2 tablespoons butter	A grating of nutmeg
2 tablespoons flour	¼ teaspoon black pepper
½ teaspoon salt	1 cup milk, broth or cream

Melt the butter in a pan or in the upper part of a double boiler. Add the flour, blend thoroughly, and let the mixture cook for a few minutes before adding the seasonings. Gradually stir in the liquid and continue stirring until the sauce is smooth and thickened. Let it simmer for a few minutes after thickening. Correct the seasoning.

MORNAY SAUCE

Add 1 slightly beaten egg yolk and ½ cup of grated Cheddar or Gruyère cheese and a few grains of cayenne to **basic Béchamel sauce.**

SAUCE BIGARADE

(For spit-roasted ducks and geese.) First catch your juices and skim them of fat. Combine ½ cup of them with ¼ cup of orange juice, 1 tablespoon of lemon juice, 1 tablespoon each of grated orange and lemon peel. Heat, season with salt and cayenne, and serve.

CUMBERLAND SAUCE

(For venison and other game.) This sauce is also good with duck and mutton. It should be used with grilled or roasted meats that are not marinated. Cut the outside skin, or "zest," of an orange into bits the size of pine needles, and cook with 1 cup of Madeira or port. Simmer until reduced two thirds. Add the juice of 1 orange, 1 tablespoon of lemon juice, ½ cup of currant jelly, and a dash of cayenne or ginger. Serve when the jelly is melted.

EPICUREAN SAUCE

(For broiled chicken or turkey.) Sauté 4 or 5 shallots or green onions, chopped, in ¼ cup of butter. Add ¼ pound of turkey or chicken livers and cook lightly. Put in the blender with 1½ cups of heavy cream and 2 raw egg yolks. When smooth, cook until slightly thickened, and season to taste with salt, pepper, and Madeira or sherry.

GARLIC-LEMON STEAK SAUCE

Cook 2 cups of red wine, 1 onion, chopped, and 2 cloves of garlic, minced, until the wine is reduced one half. Add 2 tablespoons each of butter, olive oil, and lemon juice, and 1 tablespoon of minced parsley. Salt and pepper to taste.

WINE-SHALLOT STEAK SAUCE

Sauté 1 cup of chopped shallots or green onions in ¼ cup of butter until melted. Add 1 cup of white wine, 2 tablespoons of wine vinegar, 1 teaspoon of salt, and ½ teaspoon of black pepper, and cook 5 minutes, then cut in ¼ pound of butter and cook until melted.

butters and cold sauces

BEURRE NOIR

Cook ¼ pound of butter until it turns a deep brown, but not, in spite of its name, black. Add 2 tablespoons each of minced parsley, tarragon vinegar, and capers. Heat and serve.

COLBERT BUTTER

(Serve with grilled meats and fish.) Cream ½ pound of butter and add 1 tablespoon each of lemon juice, Worcestershire sauce, and minced parsley, and 1 teaspoon each of freshly ground black pepper, beef extract, minced tarragon, and minced chives. Serve without heating.

GARLIC AND GINGER BUTTER

(For roast pork, grilled shrimps, steak, and chicken.) Cream ¼ pound of butter with 1 clove of garlic, pressed. Add 2 teaspoons of grated fresh ginger. Serve without melting.

MAÎTRE D'HÔTEL BUTTER

(For steaks and chops.) Cream ¼ pound of butter and add 2 tablespoons of minced parsley, 1 tablespoon of lemon juice, ½ teaspoon of freshly ground black pepper, and a dash of Worcestershire sauce. Serve without heating.

MUSTARD SAUCE

(For fish, ham, kidneys, and grilled sausages.) Combine 1 cup each of sour cream and mayonnaise, 3 tablespoons each of dry mustard and chopped green onions, ½ teaspoon of salt, and 1 tablespoon of vinegar. Tarragon may also be added, if desired.

SNAIL BUTTER

(With grilled vegetables, especially mushrooms, and with steaks.) Cream ½ pound of butter, add 4 cloves of garlic, 4 shallots or green onions, and ¼ cup of chopped parsley, which have been macerated in a mortar. Serve without heating.

TARRAGON BUTTER SAUCE

(For poultry and lamb.) Crush 2 tablespoons each of tarragon, parsley, and chives in a mortar, and combine with 1 cup of hot melted butter, 1 tablespoon of lemon juice, and ½ cup of toasted crumbs. This may be made in a blender, too. **Parsley butter sauce** and **rosemary butter sauce** are prepared in the same way, substituting these herbs for the tarragon. In **tarragon, parsley,** or **rosemary butter** the butter is not melted.

CUCUMBER SAUCE

(For fish, especially salmon steaks, halibut, and whole roasted fish.) Remove seeds from a cucumber, chop, and combine with 1 cup of mayonnaise, 1 tablespoon of minced green onions, salt, pepper, and lemon juice to taste.

TARTAR SAUCE

(For fish, especially swordfish and fillets, and for shellfish.) Everyone's favorite with sea food of all kinds. Combine 1 cup of mayonnaise, 3 tablespoons each of minced green onions and chopped sour pickles, 1 tablespoon each of minced fresh dill, capers and/or chopped green olives. Season with salt and freshly ground pepper and a little lemon juice. If fresh dill is unavailable, use a few crushed dill seeds instead. Or Spice Islands dill weed.

MEXICAN SALSA FRIA

(With steaks, hamburgers, and other broiled meats and fish.) This, sometimes simply called *salsa*, is, as its name implies, cold sauce. It is very popular in the West and Southwest.

2 pounds peeled ripe
   tomatoes, chopped
1 cup chopped sweet onions
4 or 5 canned green chilis,
   chopped
1 can Mexican tomatillas,
   chopped, or 3 small green
   tomatoes, chopped

3 tablespoons olive oil
3 tablespoons wine vinegar
Salt, freshly ground pepper,
   and coriander to taste

Combine all ingredients and serve very cold. The coriander, some-times known as *cilantro*, or Chinese parsley, should be fresh; if not available, substitute orégano.

RÉMOULADE SAUCE

(For sea food.) Especially good for shrimp or lobster that has been broiled with a simple oil and lemon juice baste. Combine 1 cup of mayonnaise, 1 tablespoon each of prepared mustard, chopped pars-ley, pickles, and tarragon, 1 clove of garlic, crushed, and 1 teaspoon of anchovy paste.

PICNICS
AND COOK-OUTS

A picnic can be an elegant meal of wines and galantines, served by a well-trained staff from a lavishly stocked station wagon, or it can be tired peanut butter sandwiches doled out by a grimy paw from a crumpled paper sack. The latter is often more fun. But there's an in-between picnic that everyone enjoys. It's a cook-out—when food is carried afield and cooked under the sky. The latter may take place in a public picnic ground, equipped with grills for wood or charcoal, or it may be held far from everywhere, and the food cooked over a campfire, portable grill, or hibachi. As this book is teeming with ways to cook over coals, we'll not go into *that* again, except to suggest a few little extras that are nice to take on a picnic. Aside from them, the grilled meats can be served with the same breads and the same salads that we suggest for meals that are eaten closer to home.

WARNING: Do remember to keep hot foods hot and cold foods cold —this not only for flavor but to eliminate any danger of food poisoning.

✔ BEVERAGES. Today's modern insulated bags and buckets and portable iceboxes make this problem as easy a one for cold beverages as Thermos jugs have made the hot-beverage problem.

Frozen concentrated fruit juices can produce punch or lemonade for the kids in a hurry, or colas can be carried already chilled. Concentrated fruit powders are useful, too, for making the gallons of cold drinks that the young ones manage to consume on a picnic.

As for adults, wine or beer can and really should be a part of the meal. It, too, can be brought chilled, in insulated carriers, or perhaps cooled in a running stream. Cocktails, highballs, and iced tea and coffee are also easily managed when ice is brought along, and if you don't want to tote your hot coffee in a Thermos, you can always make it in a coffeepot over your cooking fire.

✔ SANDWICHES. We do not feel that sandwiches with elaborate fillings are in order at a cooking picnic. However, if you want them, see suggested fillings in Chapter 13, "**Outdoor Appetizers.**" Rather, we suggest that simple bread-and-butter ones be brought along—made with a fine flavorsome bread, of course, or perhaps with a variety of breads. Then, in a portable icebox or large wide-mouthed picnic jug, bring prepared vegetables. Crisp washed leaves of tender lettuce, sliced cucumbers, tomatoes ready to be sliced, sweet onions that have been sliced and marinated in French dressing or in ice water to which vinegar and orégano have been added. Sandwiches can be made on the spot. Crisp vegetable sticks are in order too—celery, green peppers, carrots, and such. Then you'll want well-chilled radishes, green onions, ripe and green olives, and pickles, as well as a dressing or two. Mayonnaise and **rémoulade sauce** would be good choices.

✔ DESSERTS. Desserts for picnics should be kept simple, at least for cook-out picnics. If you want homemade ice cream and fresh coconut layer cake, that's fine if you can manage to carry and to eat them. We think, however, you'll settle for fruits and some fine cheeses, or perhaps some rich little cookies, turnovers, or candies to nibble with your coffee.

check list

Many a picnic has been spoiled because some very important item has been left behind. This can be avoided if you write down your menu and check the food off as you pack the hampers. (Don't leave a *hamper* at home, though!) Here's another check list that may help —it is for items, other than the meal itself, that may be needed.

Ax

Bucket—for carrying water to douse fire

Can opener and bottle opener

Carving and other cutting knife, and board

Corkscrew

Cream

Cups

Folding grill or grate

Fork, long-handled

Fuel, if necessary

Ice

Icepick

Insect spray or bug bomb

Kindling

Knives, forks, and spoons

Matches

Mustard or other condiments

Napkins, paper or cloth

Plates and glasses

Pot holder

Salt and pepper

Serving spoons

Sugar

Tongs

Tablecloth, paper or cloth

Towels

Water

picnic miscellany

There are a few classic picnic dishes that we feel should be included in this book, even if they are not cooked over coals. Certainly fried chicken is one, as it's been a favorite picnic food for generations.

JOSIE'S FRIED CHICKEN

Josephine Jackson is a rather remarkable woman who hates to cook but who would rather fry chicken than do anything else—except eat the chicken she fries.

Cut the chickens into quarters and dredge them well with flour. Heat about 1½ inches of peanut oil in a skillet. When the fat is good and hot, add the chicken pieces and brown quickly on both sides, then cover the pan and let them cook until tender, turning once during the cooking period. Remove pieces to absorbent paper, season them with salt and pepper, and keep warm in a hot dish or platter while you cook the rest. The secret of this is quick cooking, good-sized pieces of chicken, and plenty of oil. Add more oil as you go along, if needed. Bacon fat is also very good for frying chicken.

BAKED HAM

This, too, is the backbone of many an outdoor meal, but is sometimes a disappointment. Not, of course, if it is a fine slow-smoked ham from Virginia or Kentucky, but if it is one of today's hams that has been cured by the inoculation method. However, as we can't all afford the celebrated Southern variety, we must make the others do. Here is one way to cook them so that they are more like the old-fashioned kind. Bake a whole ham, uncovered, in a 225° oven until the internal temperature reaches 170°. About 30 minutes before it is done (when it is at about 155° or 160°), prick it all over very thoroughly with a long-tined fork. The juices will pour out, and that's just what you want. After the ham is done, remove the skin, score the fat, and paint the ham with a mixture of honey, soy sauce, and mustard. Return to the oven to brown, basting a few times with the same mixture. If the ham is to be served at a buffet, further decorations of blanched almonds, pineapple, peaches, cherries, and prunes are effective. Arrange them in floral or conventional designs, and fasten on with toothpicks.

OLD-FASHIONED ICE CREAM

Many of us have fond memories of the ice cream freezer being taken on a picnic. It is for this reason that we include it. You'll find old-fashioned ice cream tastes wonderful. Combine 1 quart of cream with 1 cup of milk, 1 cup of sugar, 2 teaspoons of vanilla, and ¼ teaspoon of salt. Pour into the inner compartment of the freezer and chill well. Pack the freezer with 1 part of rock salt to each 6 parts of crushed ice, and turn the crank until it will turn no more. That means it's frozen. Wipe the top carefully so that no salt will get in, remove dasher, return top with hole plugged, and repack with ice and salt. Cover with burlap and off to the picnic!

FRUIT ICE CREAM

Make as above, but add 2 cups of crushed sugared fruit before freezing. Favorites are peaches, strawberries, raspberries, apricots, pineapple, and cooked cherries.

DEVILED EGGS

Put the desired number of fresh eggs in cold water and allow to come to a boil, then turn down the heat so they merely simmer, and cook 10 minutes longer. Turn the eggs gently a few times during the cooking so the yolks will stay in the center. Drain, cover at once with cold water, crack the shells, and cool. Remove shells, cut eggs in half, and remove yolks. Mash the yolks smooth, mix with mayonnaise, lemon juice, salt and pepper, and, if you wish, mustard, curry powder, paprika, deviled ham, or seasoned salt. Stuff back in the egg whites, put together in pairs, and wrap in lettuce leaves, then in plastic wrap or foil, and chill. Carry to the picnic in an insulated bag or ice container.

BRAMBLES

These delicious little conceits made by Grammie Hamblet, of Portland, Oregon, are perfect for picnicking or just nibbling indoors or out. Make a batch of your best pie crust, roll it thin, and cut it in 4-inch rounds. Put 1 cup of raisins and 1 lemon through the food grinder, combine with 1 egg, 1 cup of sugar, and a pinch of salt. Put a spoonful of this mixture on each round of dough and fold over, sealing the edges with water. Bake at 375° until brown.

BUTTERSCOTCH CHOCOLATE SQUARES

Combine ¼ cup of butter, 1 cup of dark brown sugar, 1 egg, ½ teaspoon of salt, ¾ cup of flour, ½ teaspoon of double-action baking powder, and 1 teaspoon of vanilla. Bake for 20 minutes at 350° in a buttered 8-inch-square pan, and cool. Spread with 1 package of melted chocolate morsels and sprinkle thickly with toasted chopped filberts. Cut in squares and wrap each one in aluminum foil. These are tops.

WALNUT WAFERS

Another famous Hamblet picnic treat. Combine 1 cup of brown sugar with 1 tablespoon of molasses and 2 well-beaten eggs. Stir in ½ cup of flour, 1 cup of coarsely chopped walnuts, and ¼ teaspoon of salt. Drop by half teaspoons on a well-buttered pan, leaving plenty of space for spreading. Bake them at 350° until brown. Mary Hamblet says: "These are stinkers to get off the pan and must be removed pronto." If they harden too much, stick them back in the oven for a minute or two.

NUT BARS

Brownies and date bars are fine for picnics, too, as are these delicious Viennese cookies. Cream ½ pound of butter with 1 cup of sugar, add 1 egg yolk, 3 cups of flour, ½ teaspoon of salt, 1 teaspoon of cinnamon. Spread on a buttered cookie sheet and brush thickly with slightly beaten egg white, then sprinkle with chopped filberts or almonds. Bake at 350° until lightly browned. Cool and cut in squares.

cook-outs for a crowd

THE WIENER ROAST

This is young America's choice for a cook-out. Simply provide 4 or 5 wieners, or dogs, or frankfurters for each youngster, with a corresponding number of split, buttered hot dog rolls, mustard, and pickle relish. The kids will find their own sharpened sticks and cook their own frankfurters. Sometimes the franks are split and a piece of cheese is inserted, but this is considered a fine piece of foolishness by most of the gang. They'll be happy with hot dogs, plus plenty of marshmallows to roast and something to drink. And if that seems like unbalanced fare, just cram in the vitamins at subsequent meals—no harm will be done.

THE HAMBURGER COOK-OUT

Another favorite with the teenagers. It's just like the **wiener roast** except that hamburgers are cooked on a grate or in a skillet, and the buns are round. Add cookies for dessert, if you wish, and fruit. Or, for a change, have the ground beef formed in the shape of hot dogs and wrapped in bacon. You'll then need the long rolls, of course.

THE STEAK FRY

Here we have a Western term for a cook-out that is actually a misnomer, for the steaks are almost invariably broiled, not fried. What it is is a picnic, usually in the desert or at least quite far afield, and steaks are the *pièces de résistance*. Sliced raw onions, soaked in ice water, vinegar, and orégano, are often the accompaniment, along with plenty of **French sourdough bread,** beans, sliced tomatoes or **salsa fria,** and probably apple or berry pie for dessert. Sometimes, instead of French bread, "pinch-offs" are baked on the spot. These are biscuits, either made from a mix or the **sourdough** kind, which are pinched off, rolled in melted butter, and baked in a Dutch oven.

THE CHUCK WAGON PARTY

Here's another Western custom that is growing more popular year by year. An adaptation of the old chuck wagon used by the cowboys at roundup time, or by the sheep-herders, today's chuck wagon is pretty apt to be a station (or ranch) wagon. Everything is loaded into it, and off it drives to a faraway spot on the prairie. There the wagon acts as a buffet table, and the cooking is done nearby. Again the featured meat is apt to be steaks, and beans are almost always in evidence. Fried potatoes, too, and **sourdough biscuits,** apple pie, and gallons of delicious coffee. Sometimes, if the party is a morning one, fried ham and **sourdough pancakes** are featured. All in all, the chuck wagon party is a fine custom.

THE BURGOO

In Kentucky the burgoo is the favorite way of feeding a mob—and a mighty good way it is, too. We turn to a native daughter of that fair state, Zula Ferguson ("Martha Grayson," food editor of the Los Angeles *Daily News*), for an authentic recipe—she having once chided us for omitting the all-important okra from our version of the dish.

"This inspired combination of soup and stew had its origin around campfires. So, while we have adapted our recipe to use in any kitchen, the burgoo of our childhood, which we still remember nostalgically, was made of wild duck and squirrel in a huge black kettle at the edge of a Kentucky lake where our parents and their friends went 'camping' every fall. With the wild game, beef was simmered in water until all were tender; then vegetables in abundance and variety were added and cooked until done. The burgoo was ladled into tin cups as the famishing horde circled the steaming caldron. Corn bread squares, hush puppies or corn dodgers were served with this one-dish meal which was eaten with a spoon. Two or three cupfuls were the portion of the comparatively dainty. Those with husky appetites did much better than this."

KENTUCKY BURGOO

7 pounds beef shank bone, or 3 pounds beef chuck
1 stewing hen (5 to 6 pounds)
Salt
6 medium potatoes, cut into large cubes
6 medium turnips, cut into large cubes
8 carrots, cut into thick slices
1 large bunch celery, cut into 1-inch pieces
4 medium onions
2 29-ounce cans puréed tomatoes
2 pounds green beans, cut into 1-inch pieces
3 pounds peas, shelled
2 pounds butter beans, shelled
12 ears sweet corn, cut from cob
1 head cabbage, shredded
1 pound okra, cut crosswise into 1-inch pieces
1 cup chopped parsley
1 cup chopped celery leaves
10 small red peppers
1 bell pepper, cut into strips
1 tablespoon rosemary or thyme
Ground black pepper

"Put beef and fowl into water to which 1 tablespoon of salt has been added for each quart. (There should be a little more water than enough to cover meat. Needless to say, you'll need a mammoth kettle; we use our two largest ones.) Bring to a boil, then cook very slowly, covered, until beef and fowl are tender. Remove meat from cooking broth, cool, then cut both beef and fowl into bite-size pieces. Return meat (without bones) to broth, bring to boil, and add vegetables in order given. When liquid comes to a full rolling boil again, add rosemary and pepper; lower heat; cook slowly until all vegetables are done (about 45 minutes). Add salt to taste."

THE FISH FRY

The Southern fish fry is another fine way to entertain a crowd easily and informally. All you need are good fishermen and good skillet tossers. Small fish, caught at the scene of the festivities, are best, whether they are trout, butterfish, catfish, porgies, or whatever. Dip the fish in corn meal or flour, and fry quickly in plenty of fat —butter, lard, bacon fat, or oil. Salt and pepper these crisp golden morsels and serve them with the traditional **hush puppies.** We give you one version of that famous bread:

HUSH PUPPIES

Blend together 3 cups of corn meal, ½ teaspoon of baking soda, ½ cup of buttermilk (the dried kind may be used), 1 teaspoon of salt, and, if you wish, ½ cup of chopped onion. Add enough water to make a thick batter and drop by the spoonful into plenty of hot fat. Cook until a delightful brown on both sides.

underground cookery

There is another type of outdoor meal that certainly requires mention in this book, for it is cooked, if not directly over coals, with the use of coals in its preparation. We mean the closed pit barbecue, the luau, and the clambake. All of these feasts have one thing in common: the cooking of food in underground holes or pits, which have been preheated with hot coals. Cookery of this kind requires experience, so we suggest that you have a private practice session or two before you stage a party, lest the affair be an awful flop. But here's to courage.

OPEN PIT BARBECUE

There are two types of pit barbecue that are usually served to large gatherings. One, the open pit barbecue, should really be left to a professional, as it means cooking whole (or cut-up) beeves and other meat over a huge pit filled with glowing coals. The meat is basted, while cooking, either with a **barbecue sauce** or with a mixture of olive oil, wine vinegar, garlic, and orégano. This is such a big project that a new mop is used to swab on the sauce, and a pitchfork makes a proper tool for turning the meat on the grates or the spit. We're not trying to discourage you, but you see why we suggest an expert.

CLOSED PIT BARBECUE

This, if done for a large crowd, also takes an experienced barbecue cook, but it's a simple and fun job to feed the family and a few friends from a small back-yard pit. If your party is a success, you'll probably want repeats, so it might be wise, after the first try, to make a permanent pit, lining it with fire brick and keeping it covered with a sheet of galvanized iron. Anyway, first dig a hole; one about 4 by 3 feet, and about 2½ feet deep, is a good size. Line it with dry rocks, nice rounded ones about the size of small grapefruit. Line the sides, too, if you can manage it. Next make a great big heaping fire in the pit and keep adding wood as it burns down, until you have a whopping bed of ashes; this will take several hours. Now rake or shovel out the ashes and keep them in reserve, then put a good thick layer of sweet-tasting leaves, ferns, corn husks, grass, or seaweed in the bottom. (Some cooks skip the leaves, by the way.) On top of this put the prepared meat (see below), and another layer of leaves. Next come the hot ashes that you've saved, then a sheet of tin or iron, and a canvas. The top layer is 4 or 5 inches of soil.

The meat is prepared by having it cut in pieces of about 4 or 5 pounds each. Almost any cut of beef will do, though the rump, chuck, ribs, and round are favorites. Marinate the meat in a **barbecue marinade** or use a mixture of 3 parts olive oil to 1 of lemon juice, and season with garlic, orégano, and chili powder. Now wrap each piece in a piece of cheesecloth, douse liberally with more sauce, then wrap in parchment paper or aluminum foil. (The old way was to use burlap or leaves. Cabbage leaves may be used, if you wish, or corn husks.)

Now relax. Your meat will be cooked in anywhere from 3 to 12 hours, depending on how large the pieces are and how hot your stones. It doesn't really matter if the meat stays buried for an extra few hours—better that than have it underdone. Remember that this meat will taste more **braised** than **roasted,** as it's cooked with moist heat. This closed pit barbecue, by the way, is the kind served in Mexico and the Southwest, and is best accompanied by **frijoles, corn,** and **salsa fria.**

THE LUAU

This is the Hawaiian feast that is cooked underground in an *imu.* The luau usually features whole young pig *(kalua),* but other pork, chicken, fish, fruits, and vegetables are also cooked in this manner. It is done in exactly the same way as the **closed pit barbecue,** except that ferns and ti leaves are used for wrapping the food. These packages of food are called *laulaus.* The thing that makes the luau such a festive occasion is the way it's served. The "table" is the ground, spread with huge leaves and with lovely flowers scattered everywhere. Down the center of the table is a stunning arrangement of all kinds of tropical and semitropical fruits and flowers. The guests sit on the ground.

A good menu for a luau would be **broiled shrimps,** *lomi lomi* (salmon), pig, poi, long rice, and bananas and sweet potatoes baked in the *imu* with the pig, and pineapple and other fruits for dessert.

The *lomi lomi* is made by soaking raw pieces of salmon in cold salted water overnight. It is then rinsed, shredded, and mixed with chopped ripe tomatoes and green onions. It is served chilled.

The pig is cooked as is the pit barbecued beef, except that it is rubbed with ginger and painted with soy sauce, or just rubbed with salt, and hot rocks are placed within its body cavity. It is wrapped in leaves and usually laid on chicken wire for easy handling. Sweet potatoes and sometimes wrapped fish, bananas, coconuts, and various vegetables are laid around the pig, it is covered with seaweed or ti or banana leaves, then with burlap and sand. A pig weighing about 75 pounds dressed weight will usually take about 3½ to 5 hours to cook.

Poi is available in tins in fancy grocery stores in this country. Long rice (cellophane noodles), found in oriental markets, comes canned, ready to heat, or dried. In the latter case it is boiled, like noodles. The beverage to be drunk at a luau is most certainly a rum drink, served from pineapple or coconut shells, and leis should grace the neck of every guest.

THE CLAMBAKE

In New England the clambake is just the thing for a big informal gathering at the beach. As for the barbecue and luau, you first dig a big hole and line it with stones. Be careful not to use wet ones or stones from the water, as they are apt to explode. Build a roaring fire in the pit and let it burn fiercely for 2 or 3 hours, then shovel out the coals and put a layer of seaweed in the bottom. On this put chicken wire, then clams. (In New England they usually use "steamers," but any clam, mussel, or cockle will do nicely.) Now comes more seaweed, then a layer of live "chicken" lobsters (about a pound or a little more each). Now more seaweed, then corn and potatoes, and, if you wish, chicken halves. This is all topped with seaweed, which is covered with a tarpaulin weighted down at the edge. Sand on top of this finishes the job. A bake should steam for from 30 minutes to 1½ hours. If chicken is used, it is wise to return hot coals to the top of the seaweed, then add more seaweed before the final covering. It is considered fair to grab a chicken or a lobster from a lifted corner of the tarp and test it for doneness. The way of a bake is to eat clams first, then corn, both with rivers of butter, then lobster, and finally, if there is room, chicken. Bread and beer are the accepted partners.

CAMP
COOKERY

A camping trip may be anything from a couple of nights spent in the open, with a car handy for hauling, to a month's stay in the backwoods, with no means of transportation other than your own two feet. However, it is most apt to mean something between the two—a trip with pack horses or canoe with which supplies and equipment can be carried, at least part of the way. In this book we are not concerned with tents and such supplies, but only with those related to the chow, and that part of it which is cooked over the coals. (If you use a gasoline stove for part of your cooking, you proceed pretty much as you do in your kitchen at home.) Almost all the recipes in this book may be applied to camp life, though we admit that roasting will most probably mean hand-turning of the spit. We therefore recommend broiling, stewing, and frying, as well as a few special recipes, included in this chapter.

✔ GRUB LIST. As for the grub list, it can now be much more extensive than in the past, as some really excellent dehydrated foods are available. They are light and compact to carry, and will be most welcome additions to the fish and game which you expect to be the backbone of your meals. Here is a partial list of them available in any camper's supply store.

Diced carrots, diced potatoes, sliced onions, dried beans, peas, and limas, julienne vegetables, spinach, cabbage, green or red peppers, Boston or chili beans, spaghetti with meat sauce, macaroni and cheese, bouillon cubes, vegetable aspic, rice and vegetable "casserole," fruit juices, fruit, applesauce, bite-size dried fruits, syrup mix, dried milk, buttermilk, cream, and eggs, all kinds of pancake, biscuit, and cake mixes, and innumerable dehydrated soups.

What more could you ask? Well, there are other foods that will prove welcome. They include slab bacon, canned butter, coffee (instant coffee is more economical of space, but you'll have to forgo the thrill of that aromatic pot of Java bubbling over the campfire), tea, instant cocoa, baking powder, baking soda, sugar (or a sweetener, if your pack is small, your sweet tooth large), cheese, salami, chipped beef, ham, rice, prunes, raisins, dates, and other dried fruits, cereals, and pudding mixes. And don't forget salt, pepper, and a couple of spices.

✔ UTENSILS. What to take in the way of cooking utensils depends on two things—how large your party is, and how far you have to hoof it. You will probably do well to visit a reliable sporting goods store and present your problem; just don't be sold on every luxurious camping comfort unless you're sure you can carry it. If you are your own pack horse, keep the equipment light.

You'll want a folding dinner kit apiece, consisting of plate, cup, knife, fork, and spoon. You'll also need a stewpot and probably a coffeepot, a couple of sharp knives, a long-handled fork and a large spoon, and of course a skillet and a pancake turner. A hand grill, or one that can be laid between two rocks or logs, or over a ditch, is also invaluable. If that's all you think you can manage, at least take along some heavyweight aluminum foil. It can pinch-hit for an oven, a baking pan, a drinking glass, or a dish, and is useful for many cooking purposes.

If you have a pack horse, try to include the following:

A portable or reflector oven

A bucket or large stewpot

A baking pan

A pressure cooker (This is invaluable at high altitudes. It will save much cooking time and fuel and will be well worth lugging.)

A Dutch oven

A portable refrigerator

A gasoline stove

There are also a few other musts that have quite a lot to do with cooking:

A flashlight, a plastic pot cleaner, a can opener, matches, detergent, work gloves, dish towels, an ax, fuel if necessary.

✔ LUXURIES. If you've plenty of room, take along a few luxuries. Maybe a tin of anchovies or a fruitcake, or some candy bars or cookies. Meat and fish pastes will taste good, too, and don't take up much room. And you know best whether or not booze is an important part of your camping fun.

✔ CAMPFIRES. Unless your campsite is a more or less permanent one, you'll have to devise some kind of a fire for cooking, as well as one for warmth. It is usually best to have them separate. There are many types of cooking fires, but the simplest are made in one of three ways:

1. Flat rocks of the same height are arranged so that a fire may be laid between them, and pots and pans, or a grate, placed over them. The grate is used for direct broiling, or to hold pots and skillets.

2. Two green logs are placed not quite parallel to each other, and a fire built between them. Small pots and kettles are put at the end where the logs are closest together, the grate and larger pots where the space is greater.

3. A ditch is dug and the fire built in it. It is used in the same manner as the log arrangement, and may be dug wider at one end than the other.

Other devices include cranes or tripod arrangements built over the fire for the hanging of pots, or two forked sticks propping up a crossbar for the same purpose.

The fire is usually made with wood gathered on the spot, using twigs as kindling. The heat may be controlled by raising or lowering the grate or the pots and skillets, or by raking the coals closer to or farther from the cooking center. More important than starting the fire is having the ground scraped clean around it, and being positive that it is completely out when the camp is vacated. If you have ever seen hundreds of acres of magnificent forest transformed into spires of charcoal, you will know why.

✔ CAMP OVENS. If you have a gasoline stove and a *portable oven,* you will know that the oven works very much like a kitchen one, though it may be a bit more difficult to keep at an even temperature. Some campers use the same type of portable oven over a wood fire that has been laid in a fireplace made of stones or logs. However, most campers rely on the Dutch oven or the reflector oven.

The *Dutch oven* is a large cast-iron pot with a cover, which is usually indented so that it will hold hot coals. The bread, biscuits, or whatever, are put on a greased pie tin which is put in the preheated Dutch oven, preferably on a rack. The oven is covered, placed over the coals, and perhaps coals put on top. The timing depends entirely on the heat of the coals and the bulk of the food to be baked. An improvised oven, one that will do nicely for biscuits, may be made by inverting one pan over another of similar or smaller size, and raking the coals around it.

A folding *reflector oven,* available at camp supply stores, is a simple thing to operate. Its open side is placed facing a good hot fire of coals, and the food to be baked is put on the shelf. The reflected heat will hit both bottom and top, assuring an even baking job. A very satisfactory reflector oven may be made with aluminum foil, folded L-shaped, and placed to catch the reflected heat.

✔ MENUS FOR A PACK TRIP. A friend who used to take a yearly two-week trip to the High Sierras with a group of Eagle Scouts used this general eating plan because it had proved so very satisfactory. He took enough fresh food to last 3 or 4 days—this included fresh fruits and vegetables and meat. The dinner meat the first day was hamburgers, the second day stew, and the third steak. From then on they had to rely on fish or game that was caught, or on canned ham, corned beef, and slab bacon. Both fresh and dried eggs were taken, and most of the articles mentioned above. Breakfast was always hot cereal, milk or cocoa, and ham or bacon. Eggs were served while they lasted, then pancakes were substituted, although good scrambled eggs can be made with the dried variety, plus dehydrated onions and green peppers. Lunch was a cold meal —usually sandwiches of salami, peanut butter, or cheese. At this meal candy was served, and perhaps dried fruit or cookies, and, of course, a beverage.

Dinner was a big and wonderful meal, and it's here that my friend's expertise as a cook shone. He made superb soups and stews with what the grub supply afforded. Camp-made bread, pies, cakes, and puddings were featured and everyone ate well. My friend also found that instant puddings were wonderful for emergency desserts, and always took powdered fruit beverages along, either for mid-meal refreshment or for the boys' favorite "ice cream." This was often made when they came upon a clean patch of snow, which they often did in the Sierras. The fruit powder was poured over the snow —result, a delicious water-ice!

Following are a few tried-and-found-good recipes that will add to your regular broiled, stewed, and fried camp dishes.

SIERRA CAMP BREAD

This has been used in the High Sierras for a number of years, and has never failed to make happy campers. Scald 2 cups of milk (usually the dried kind), add 5 tablespoons of sugar and 2 tablespoons of salt, and cool until lukewarm. Dissolve 2 packages of dried yeast in 2 cups of lukewarm water and add to the milk mixture. Add 6 cups of flour and beat smooth, then 5 tablespoons of melted shortening and enough more flour to make easy handling. Knead until the dough is smooth and elastic. Put in a greased bowl or pot, and allow to rise until double in bulk. Divide into 4 loaves, place in greased bread pans, cover, and allow to rise until again double in bulk. In camp this is baked in a portable oven, a Dutch oven, or, if the fire is very hot, a reflector oven. If it is baked at home, have a hot (425°) oven for 15 minutes, then reduce heat to 375° and finish baking for another 30 minutes or so.

FRIED BREAD

Here's another way all campers like the above bread. After the first rising, tear off small pieces of dough about the size of lemons, and pull out into the shape and size of pancakes. Then fry in deep-as-possible fat. Sprinkle with powdered sugar. These are often called "dough gods."

BAKING MIX

This is an almost indispensable adjunct to camping. Make a batch before you leave, and pack it in plastic bags in 2- or 4-cup measurements. You'll use it for biscuits, pancakes, dumplings, and griddle scones. Combine 12 cups of flour, 2 tablespoons of salt, ¼ cup of double-action baking powder, and 1 pound of shortening. Mix until it has the texture of coarse corn meal. Store until ready to use.

BASIC BISCUITS

To 2 cups of **baking mix** add ½ to ⅔ cup of milk (or water plus dried milk). Knead lightly, pat out ¾ inch thick on a piece of waxed paper or foil, and cut in rounds or squares. Put on a buttered sheet pan or sheet of foil, and bake. A portable or reflector oven may be used.

SKILLET BISCUITS

Biscuits may also be baked in a skillet. Grease it well and arrange biscuits with a bit of space between. Put over the grill just long enough to "stiffen" or set, then prop up in front of the fire and cook until brown. The latter process will be hastened if a large sheet of foil is arranged under, behind, and above the skillet, in a manner that will reflect the heat to the biscuits.

BISCUIT VARIATIONS

These variations make quick changes that will relieve the monotony of camp fare.

✔ CHEESE BISCUITS. For each 2 cups of **baking mix** and liquid, add ½ cup of cheese. Bake as for **basic biscuits**.

✔ FRUIT DROP BISCUITS. Add a little extra milk or water to 2 cups of **baking mix**, then add ½ cup of raisins, or chopped dates, figs, or candied fruit peel, and 2 tablespoons of sugar. Drop on pan by spoonfuls, and bake in a reflector oven.

✔ BISCUIT BREAD. Spread biscuit dough about ¾ inch thick in a well-greased skillet, and bake as for **basic biscuits.** When the top is brown, turn carefully and brown the other side. Split and butter.

✔ COFFEE CAKE. To 2 cups of **baking mix** add 2 well-beaten eggs (or reconstituted dried eggs), ½ cup of sugar, and enough milk to make like drop biscuits. Put in well-buttered skillet and sprinkle the top with cinnamon and sugar, then dot well with butter. Bake in a reflector or portable oven.

✔ SWEET BREAKFAST BISCUITS. Make **basic biscuit** dough, break off pieces about the size of golf balls, dip each in melted butter, then roll in brown sugar which has been mixed with chopped nuts. Bake in camp oven.

✔ SCONES. Add 3 tablespoons of sugar to 2 cups of **baking mix;** add liquid. Also add raisins, if desired. Pat out in a circle and cut in pie-shaped wedges. Cook over campfire in a skillet, on a griddle, or on sheet iron, using a small amount of grease. Turn when browned on one side. Split and butter before eating. *Bannocks* are the same, except that they are larger—the size of dinner plates —and the raisins are omitted. They are cut after baking.

✔ CORN BREAD. To 2 cups of **baking mix** add 1 cup of cornmeal, 2 eggs (or reconstituted dried eggs), 1 cup of reconstituted buttermilk (3 tablespoons dry buttermilk to 1 cup water), and ½ teaspoon of baking soda. Add ¼ cup of melted bacon fat or butter, if you want this extra rich. Bake in a thin layer.

PANCAKES

To 2 cups of **baking mix** add 2 tablespoons of dried egg, and enough reconstituted milk (1 cup water, 3 tablespoons dried milk) to make a thin batter. Bake on a griddle or in a skillet. A cup of wild berries and 3 tablespoons of sugar may be added to the batter for a special treat.

DOUGHNUTS

To 2 cups of **baking mix** add ½ cup of sugar, some grated nutmeg,

1 egg, fresh or dried, and enough evaporated or reconstituted dried milk to make a fairly stiff dough. Break off small pieces and fry in as deep fat as the camp can spare. They may be made in fairly shallow fat, if turned as soon as they begin to brown on one side. At high altitudes the fat should be slightly less hot than at sea level —say 350° at five to six thousand feet.

RAISED DOUGHNUTS

Use **Sierra Camp bread** recipe, adding an extra ½ cup of sugar, and some nutmeg or cinnamon. Roll and cut with a doughnut cutter, or pinch off in pieces as for **fried bread.** Allow to rise again before frying.

MEAT PIES

A camp stew may become tiresome if hunting or fishing is poor. That can be easily fixed by adding a topping of biscuits. Simply roll **basic biscuit** dough ¼ inch thick, cut in circles or wedges, and arrange on top of the boiling stew. Put in reflector oven until the biscuits are nicely browned.

DUMPLINGS

Make drop biscuits and add by the spoonful to the top of boiling stew, making sure that the dough will sit on meat and vegetables, not sink in the gravy. Cook rapidly 10 minutes, cover and cook another 10 or 12 minutes. The dumplings may be varied by adding dried parsley, peppers, or green onions.

BISCUIT TWISTS

This is really roughing it, but the biscuits couldn't possibly taste better. Make **basic biscuit** dough. Have some sweet-tasting sticks, their bark peeled. They should be almost as big around as a broom handle. Take a piece of biscuit dough and roll it between your hands into a long thin roll, from ½ to ¾ inch in diameter, and 10 to 12 inches long. Wrap it around the greased stick in a spiral (not too closely spaced), and prop in the ground near the fire. As it begins to brown on one side, turn, so that it is evenly colored. It may be held over the fire, but in that case use a good long stick.

BUTTERMILK BISCUITS

Make **baking mix,** but to the 12 cups of flour add ¾ cup of dried buttermilk. When making biscuits, add ½ teaspoon of baking soda to each 2 cups of mix. Use this mix in any of the above recipes.

CORNMEAL PANCAKES

These are superb served with freshly caught and fried trout, and crisp bacon. Butter, bacon fat, or syrup may lubricate the pancakes, and plenty of stout black coffee is in order. Combine 2 cups of flour, 1 cup of cornmeal, 2 tablespoons of egg powder, ⅓ cup of milk powder, 1 teaspoon of salt, 1 tablespoon of double-action baking powder, and enough water to make the desired thickness. Don't overstir the pancakes—they should be mixed free of lumps, period.

BUTTERMILK PANCAKES

Sift together 2 cups of flour, ⅜ cup (¼ cup plus 2 tablespoons) of dried buttermilk, 2 teaspoons of salt, and 1½ teaspoons of baking soda. Add 2 cups of water, 2 unbeaten eggs, and ¼ cup of melted butter, and stir just enough to moisten the dry ingredients. Cook on a lightly greased griddle, spreading batter with the back of a spoon. Turn when brown, and serve with syrup made from a mix.

CORN PONE

Combine 2 cups of cornmeal with 1 teaspoon of salt, 1 tablespoon of bacon fat, and enough boiling water to make a stiff dough. Let stand a couple of hours, then form into flattish oval cakes and cook on the griddle.

ASH CAKES

Corn pone mixture may be wrapped in foil or in sweet-tasting leaves, and baked in the ashes (or on the grill). Originally they were so baked without benefit of wrapping.

CORN HUSK BREAD

If you're close enough to civilization to have fresh corn along, try this: mix some **corn pone** dough with some green corn that has been cut from the cob, adding a little extra bacon fat. Form in knackwurst-sized rolls, and wrap well in the corn husks, tying the ends like tamales. Steam for 1 hour.

SOURDOUGH STARTER

Mix together 4 cups of flour, 2 teaspoons of salt, 2 tablespoons of sugar, and 4 cups of lukewarm potato water (the water in which potatoes have been boiled). Let stand in a warm spot, covered, but not tightly, for 3 or 4 days, or until fermentation is bubblingly and odoriferously evident (90° is the perfect temperature). If you can't wait the required number of days, add a yeast cake dissolved in ¼ cup of the potato water—the starter should then sour within 24 hours. Be sure you use a large pan or crock for this operation, or you'll have a mess to clean up.

SOURDOUGH PANCAKES

Remove 4 cups of **starter** from the crock and replace with 4 cups of flour and enough water to make as thick as the original. To the 4 cups of starter add 1 teaspoon of baking soda and, if you wish, 2 well-beaten eggs or 1 tablespoon of egg powder. If too thick, add more water, if too thin, more flour—that's elementary. Stir in 2 or 3 tablespoons of melted bacon fat or butter, and cook on a griddle, a sheet of iron, or in a skillet. You'll have the lightest pancakes you ever tasted, and they may be the size of a silver dollar or of a dinner plate. The starter, with or without the additional flour and water, may be kept in the refrigerator for a long time, but it should be "worked" (used) occasionally. Except for the first time, additional sugar and salt should be added when making pancakes or other things.

SOURDOUGH BREAD OR BISCUITS

To 4 cups of **starter** add 1 cup of flour that has been mixed with 1 teaspoon each of baking soda and salt, and 2 tablespoons of melted butter or bacon fat. Mix well, then add more flour to make a stiff dough—about 4 cups. Knead lightly, form in biscuits or loaves, and put in buttered pans. Allow to rise in a warm place until double in bulk, brush with melted butter if desired, and bake at 400° for a few minutes, then reduce heat and cook until done. A medium-sized loaf will take about 45 minutes.

FRENCH
SOURDOUGH BREAD

Soften 1 yeast cake in 1 cup of warm water and combine with 4 cups of flour, 1 cup of **starter** (preferably very sour), 1 teaspoon of salt, 1 cup of warm water, and ½ teaspoon of baking soda, if the starter is extra sour. Mix well and allow to rise in a warm place until double in bulk. Knead lightly, adding a little more flour if necessary, and form in a large round (hearth) loaf. Brush with beaten egg white, allow to rise a short time, and bake at 400° until done—about 1 hour.

Of course, breads aren't the only foods that campers want with fish and game. Their vegetables, as we have said, will be dehydrated and usually cooked according to directions on their packages. **Rice** is another favorite, either just boiled, or **fried**. And then there are beans, both the popular **frijoles refritos** and the following:

BEAN HOLE BEANS

Soak 1 pound of navy or pea beans overnight, then bring to a boil and cook until the skins burst when 2 or 3 are spooned out and blown upon. Pour off the liquid and save. In a pot or kettle with a tight-fitting lid (a Dutch oven is ideal) put a thick slice of salt pork, weighing about 3 or 4 ounces. Pour in the beans, then to the bean water add 1 teaspoon of salt, ½ cup of molasses, and a little freshly ground black pepper. Pour over the beans to cover, and on top put another slice of salt pork, this one skin side up. It should be the same size as the other one. Cover and put in a hole in the ground, prepared as below:

✔ HOT HOLE IN THE GROUND. Dig a hole larger and deeper than the Dutch oven, and line with small stones. Build a fire in the hole and let it burn briskly for 2 hours or more. Remove fire, leaving hot coals at the bottom. Add pot or Dutch oven, cover it with the remaining coals, and cover with soil about 4 inches thick. Let it stay buried for 5 or 6 hours or, better yet, overnight. If you wish to hurry the business, build a fire on top of the soil covering the beans. These beans should taste, according to Yankee tradition, better than any ever made. Mexicans will disagree and stick to their **frijoles refritos.**

CHOWDERS

Chowders are usually made of clams or fish, though a vegetable chowder, from the camp's dehydrated store, is mighty fine fare when served along with grilled meat or game. Chowders start with diced pork or bacon; onions and potatoes are cooked in this, then the fish is added, along with canned or dried milk and water. Fresh-water fish makes just as fine a chowder as does salt; so, too, does salted fish.

✔ OTHER FISH STEWS. Cioppino is a West Coast concoction calculated to transform the day's catch into a gastronomical treat. It includes any or all fish and shellfish, any table wine, tomatoes, garlic, olive oil, and seasonings—usually orégano or basil. Bouillabaisse, the Continental version of cioppino, is sure to have white wine, saffron, and olive oil in *its* make-up. And make-up is just the way they're both done, for there is no set rule for either one.

STEWS

Expert camp cooks can make a stew out of anything and everything, and frequently do. This is a perfect way to use the tougher cuts of game and to "stretch" any piece of meat or poultry. Basically, all stews are the same. The meat or what have you is cut in chunks, dusted with flour, browned in fat, then simmered with vegetables, seasonings, and a liquid until all is a flavorsome and salubrious brew. The vegetables are most apt to be onions, potatoes, carrots, and turnips, but tomatoes, celery, green peppers, corn, beans, and others frequently end up in the stewpot. The dehydrated vegetables made specially for campers are wonderful for stews. See our recipe for **burgoo,** a favorite campers' stew.

BRUNSWICK STEW

The close relative to **burgoo** is made with chicken, squirrels, or rabbits as a base, with corn, beans, bacon, potatoes, onions, and tomatoes all contributing their flavors.

MULLIGAN

This is a plain name for what can turn out to be a fancy ragout, for anything may be added to it, including wine and herbs. Basically, it's the **stew** above, and you and your imagination take it from there.

LOBSCOUSE

Lobscouse is the ship's galley version of **mulligan,** and usually contains salt pork for added richness, and hardtack as a thickener.

SLUMGULLION

Canned corned beef is pretty apt to be the base of this stew—a most welcome one when supplies run low, particularly while aboard ship. It, like **lobscouse,** is thickened with hardtack or pilot biscuits, and sometimes includes bacon.

SALADS AND DESSERTS

Salads pose a pretty problem, so unless you are a woodsman and know your wild greens, you'll have to settle for dehydrated fruits and vegetables. Or, if you have room in your packs, canned tomatoes, string beans, and sauerkraut are mighty refreshing additions to your meals. Also, cabbage keeps well for a week or two, especially if wrapped in damp leaves and then in foil. Cole slaw can really hit the spot.

Desserts can be numerous. Cake mixes are naturals for camping trips, as are prepared puddings and gelatine desserts, and pies or cobblers made from dried fruits. (For cobbler, simply stew the fruit, sweeten, and top with biscuit dough before baking.)

PRESSURE-COOKED GINGERBREAD

Here's a trick you'll welcome in high altitudes, but it tastes just as wonderful at sea level. Serve it warm, with cold applesauce made from that wonderful dried kind. Combine a package of gingerbread mix with ⅔ cup of water; mix until smooth. Fill well-greased custard cups ⅔ full of batter and cover each with foil, tied down securely. Put 3 cups of water in a large pressure cooker with a rack, and put the gingerbread on the rack. Cook 10 minutes at 10 pounds pressure. Let steam return to down position before opening.

CAMP COFFEE

One of the best things about camp food is the wonderful aroma of the coffee cooking over the coals, even if that does mean that some of your coffee flavor is escaping. Camp coffee is best, we think, made in an old-fashioned pot, with the addition of egg or egg shells. So here is how we make it. Break 1 egg, crush the shell, and mix with ½ cup of coffee and ½ cup of cold water. Have 4 cups of water boiling in your pot, add the coffee mixture and stir well, then bring to a boil. Now push to a cooler part of the fire and allow to stand for 3 minutes, then add ½ cup of cold water. Let stand for another 3 or 4 minutes to settle, then serve. For less stout coffee, use 1 or 2 cups more of boiling water.

GALLEY
AND TRAILER
COOKERY

We think that this type of cookery has every right to appear in these pages, because the use of the portable charcoal burner of the hibachi or covered kettle type is such a natural for both boat and trailer. They can be used both on deck and by the roadside. All the charcoal-broiled foods in this book may be so cooked, and the various **partners for the grill,** as well as the **salads** and **breads,** can be easily made with the limited facilities these moving kitchens offer. The trailer has one advantage over the boat—it is easier to stop at a supermarket than to put into port. On the other hand, the trailer cook can't put a line over the side and haul up breakfast or dinner on a hook. Here we offer a series of simple menus that are fitting meals for land or water cruising. In each case, at least one food is cooked outdoors, over the charcoal, usually directly on the grill but sometimes in a skillet, with the coals for heat. This eliminates lingering odors of fried foods in close quarters.

In the following menus, all starred items (*) are cooked on the hibachi, either broiled, fried, or merely heated. The menus are designed for a 16-day cruise or trip, with a reasonable number of stop-offs.

BREAKFAST

Orange slices
Bacon and eggs *

Hot rolls, jam, and butter
Coffee

LUNCH

Tomato soup *
Liver paste, onion, and cream
cheese sandwich

Swedish cucumber salad
Pineapple fingers

DINNER

Cocktails
Raw vegetables and dip
Grilled lamb steaks *

Galette potatoes *
Green beans with bacon
Berries with kirsch

BREAKFAST

Stewed prunes with orange
French toast, * jam

Brown-and-serve sausages *
Coffee

LUNCH

Clam soup *
Olive nut sandwiches

Cheese and fruit
Iced tea

DINNER

Cocktails
Boiled beef *
Potatoes, carrots, turnips,
cabbage

Horseradish sauce
Toasted rye bread
Chocolates
Fruit

third day

BREAKFAST

Melon   Scones,* butter, jam
Boiled eggs   Coffee

LUNCH

Beef broth* Cold beef salad   Oranges
(both from boiled beef dinner) Iced chocolate

DINNER

Cocktails   Cauliflower slaw
Marinated broilers*   Blazing bananas*
Polenta   Coffee

fourth day

BREAKFAST

Orange juice   Toast, butter, jam
Fried polenta*   Coffee
Bacon*

LUNCH

Toasted cheese sandwiches*   Cookies and fruit
Tomato-cucumber salad   Iced coffee

DINNER

Cocktails   Chocolate pot de crème
Lamb chops*   Coffee
Lentils   Celery salad

BREAKFAST

Stewed apricots
Frizzled chipped beef*
Toast

Honeybuns
Coffee

LUNCH

Bean soup
Grilled frankfurters*
Cheese

Cookies
Iced tea

DINNER

Cocktails
Anchovy toasts
Grilled steak,* Béarnaise

Potato cake
Carrot sticks   Tomatoes
Pressure-cooked gingerbread

BREAKFAST

Grapefruit
Scrambled eggs and
    tomatoes*

Toasted muffins,* butter,
    honey
Coffee

LUNCH

Canned Vichyssoise
Bacon and avocado
    sandwiches* on toast

Pickles
Chocolates

DINNER

Cocktails
Broiled duck*
Roasted yams

Glazed onions
Apricot crêpes

seventh day

BREAKFAST

Tomato juice   Poached eggs *
Corned beef hash *   Coffee

LUNCH

Duck salad   Cheese and fruit
Onion and parsley sandwiches

DINNER

Cocktails   Potato salad
Hamburgers *en brochette* *   Beer

eighth day

BREAKFAST

Cornmeal mush, with raisins   Sausages *   Fried Apples *
Butter Honey   Coffee

LUNCH

Sliced hamburgers * on rye   Cookies
    toast   Iced tea
Raw vegetables and dip

DINNER

Cocktails   Heated potato chips
Stuffed eggs   Cole slaw
Broiled lobster * Butter   Pears with chocolate sauce

BREAKFAST

Berries and cream
Grilled finnan haddie *
Fried potatoes *

Toast, marmalade
Coffee

LUNCH

Lobster sandwiches
Cucumbers and tomatoes with
mayonnaise

Cookies   Chocolates
Iced tea

DINNER

Cocktails
Tomato salad
Veal chops, tarragon butter *

Rice with almonds
Butterscotch cream with
crushed brittle

BREAKFAST

Sliced tomatoes
Sausages *

Rye toast   Jam
Coffee

LUNCH

Toasted mushroom
sandwiches *
Iced coffee

Cheese and fruit

DINNER

Cocktails
Broiled liver *
Spinach   Hot rolls

Broiled fruits on skewers *
Coffee

eleventh day

BREAKFAST

Cereal
Ham and eggs *

Hot coffee cake
Coffee

LUNCH

Iced pea soup
Canned chicken and chutney
   sandwiches

Curried almonds
Fruit   Cookies

DINNER

Cocktails
Broiled fish *
Broiled tomatoes *

Chocolate icebox cake
Coffee

twelfth day

BREAKFAST

Grapefruit
Minute steaks *
Toasted buns *

Strawberry jam
Coffee

LUNCH

Onion soup, cheese *
Stuffed eggs

Pickles   Toast
Iced chocolate

DINNER

Cocktails
Grilled Polish sausages *
Broiled eel *

Hot potato chips
Rolls
Fruit shortcake with scones

BREAKFAST

Canned figs
Scrambled eggs * with
green pepper

Corn muffins
Honey   Butter
Coffee

LUNCH

Chicken clam broth *
Tuna-stuffed celery
Cheese-stuffed celery

Toasted crackers * and marmalade
Iced tea

DINNER

Cocktails
Radishes   Green onions
Ham steak *

Broiled sweet potatoes and apples *
Cheese and red wine
Crackers

BREAKFAST

Melon
Broiled kippers *
Scrambled eggs *

Drop biscuits
Butter   Jam
Coffee

LUNCH

Chopped ham and chopped
peanut sandwiches

Carrot sticks   Pickles
Fruit

DINNER

Cocktails
Salted nuts
Steaks, Béarnaise *

Galette potatoes *
Sliced tomatoes
Peaches with kirsch

fifteenth day

BREAKFAST

Orange juice
Sausages and eggs *

Toasted coffee cakes
Coffee

LUNCH

Iced curried chicken soup
Bacon and tomato sandwiches
    on toast *

Chocolates

DINNER

Cocktails
Fish chowder *
Toasted biscuits *

Shrimp salad
Apple pie

sixteenth day

BREAKFAST

Tomato juice
Bacon *
Crisp fried fish *

Toasted muffins   Jam
Coffee

LUNCH

Chicken salad with almonds,
    Curry dressing

Toast   Cheese
Iced tea

DINNER

Cocktails
Broiled lamb chops *
Broiled pineapple *

Fried potatoes
Chocolate pudding with nuts

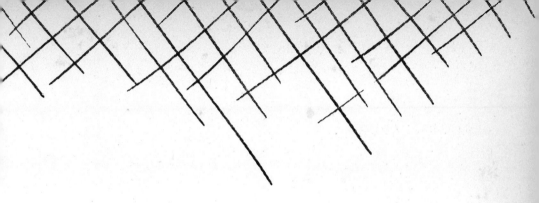

INDEX

Beef, rib roast *(cont.)*
    standing, 51
    standing, timing and
        temperature for, 20–21
    ribs. *See also* short ribs *below*
        deviled, 103
        eye, 53
        prime, 52
        standing, roast, 51
    roast. *See also specific cuts*
        about, 51
        sandwiches, 54
    rump, roast, salted, 53
    shank bone, in Kentucky burgoo,
        205
    short ribs, 103
        deviled, 103
        Korean, 103
        marinated, 103
    sirloin
        boneless top, about, 29
        roast, 53
    skewered, 88
    Spencer roast, 53
        timing and temperature for,
            16, 21
    standing rib roast, 51
        timing and temperature for,
            20–21
    tenderloin
        about, 28
        larded and piqued, 54
        roast, 54
        skewered, appetizer, 119
    tongue
        and beet salad, 180
        tarragon, grilled, 108
Beef steaks
    about, 26–29
    aged, 27
    au poivre, x–xi, 34
    basting, 17
    blue cheese broiled, 32
    boneless loin (strip steak), 28
    Chateaubriands, 28, 30

Beef steaks *(cont.)*
    chuck
        about, 29
        in Kentucky burgoo, 205
    chuletas, 39
    club, 28
    cooking area and, 27
    cuts of, 27–28
    Diane, 33
    doneness of, x, 16
    entrecôte(s)
        about, 28
        Bercy, x, 32–33
        Bordelaise, 32
    filets, 28
    filets mignons, 28, 30–31
        tarragon, 31
    flank, 37
    flank (London broil), 29, 37
        deviled, 37, 38
    grades of, 27
    hamburger, 38
    marchands de vin, 37
    marinated, 36
    meat tenderizer and, 27
    minute, 35
        about, 28
        Charlie's fashion, 35
        deviled, 36
        sandwiches, 35
        smothered in mushrooms, old-
            fashioned, 36
    moyen âge, 33
    porterhouse, 31–32
        about, 28
    rib. *See also* Club steaks;
            Entrecôtes; Minute steaks
        about, 28
        bordelaise, 32
    rump, 29
    Salisbury steak béarnaise, 39
    salt broiled, 34
    sandwiches, 29
        minute steak, 35
    selecting, 26–29

Beef steaks *(cont.)*
  servings of, 26, 28
  sirloin, 31–32
    about, 29
    koon-ko-ki, 98
    teriyaki, 95
    teriyaki, mainland, 96
  skirt steak
    deviled, 38
    orientale, 37
  Spencer, 28
    timing and temperature for, 15
  sukiyaki, 40
  tartare sandwich, Ben Levy's, 126
  T-bone, 31–32
    about, 28
  tenderloin
    about, 28
    broiled, 29–30
    in mixed grill, 104
  tournedos, 28
    Béarnaise, 30
Beet(s)
  roasted, 129
  salad
    olive and, 180
    onion and, 180
    tongue and, 180
Beurre noir, 195
Beverages, for picnics and cook-
    outs, 198–99
Biscuit(s)
  basic, 215
  bread, 216
  buttermilk, 218
  cheese, 215
  fruit, drop, 215
  onion, 176
  skillet, 215
  sourdough, 219
  sweet breakfast, 216
  twist, 217
  variations, 215
Black beans, tipsy, 151
Blender, 8

Blue cheese, broiled steak with, 32
Blue trout (truite au bleu), 78
Bordelaise sauce, 190
  entrecôtes with, 32
Bottle, sprinkling, 4
Brains, broiled, 104
Brambles, 202
Bread, 172–76. *See also* Biscuit(s)
  biscuit, 216
  cheese, 175
    and chili, 174
  corn, 176, 216
    husk, 219
  French, 173–74
    sourdough, 220
  fried, 214
  garlic loaf, 47
  graham, 176
  heated, 172
  onion, 175
    and cheese, 174
  rolls, 174
    stuffed, 174
  Sierra camp, 214
  soufflé, 174
  sourdough, 219
    French, 220
  spider, 175
  spoon, 48
    hominy, 156
  toast, 172
Breakfast, 8. *See also* Camp cookery;
    Galley and trailer cookery
Brine-curing, 136–37
Briquets, 9, 10
Broccoli salad, 180
Broiler
  electrical, 6–7
  hinged, 4–5, 11–12
Broiling
  fire for, 17
  timing and temperature for, 12,
    23–25
Brown sauces, 190–92
Brunswick stew, 221

Brush, basting, 4
Buckwheat groats (kasha), 156
Butter (butter sauces)
    beurre noir, 195
    colbert, 195
    garlic and ginger, 195
    maître d'hôtel, 195
    snail, 196
    tarragon, parsley or rosemary,
        196
Buttermilk pancakes, camp, 218
Butterscotch chocolate squares, 202

Cabbage
    red, salad, 180
    sauerkraut, 167
        salad, 185
        salad, raw, 185
    white
        cole slaw with capers, 181
        cole slaw with chicken, 181
        salad, 180
Cake
    ash, camp, 218
    coffee, camp, 216
    potato, 162
Calf's liver
    steaks, 107
    whole roasted, 107
California lima bean casserole, 155
California sauce, 193
California wine dressing, 187
Camp cookery, 210–23
    ash cakes, 218
    baking mix for, 215
    bean hole beans, 220
    biscuits
        basic, 215
        buttermilk, 218
        skillet, 215
        sourdough, 219
        twists, 217
        variations, 215–16
    bread
        corn, 216

Camp cookery, bread (cont.)
    corn husk, 219
    fried, 214
    Sierra camp, 214
    sourdough, 219
    sourdough, French, 220
coffee, 223
corn pone, 218
doughnuts, 216
    raised, 217
dumplings, 217
fire for, 212–13
grub list, 210–11
meat pies, 217
menus for, 213–14
oven for, 213
pancakes, 216
    buttermilk, 216
    cornmeal, 218
salads, 222
utensils for, 211–12
Capers, cole slaw with, 181
Capretto (kid), whole, 57
Carnitas, 120
Carrot(s)
    broiled, 129
    foiled, 170
    salad, 181
Carryall, 6
Carving boards, 6
Casseroles
    California, 155
    grain, 155–57
        barley and mushroom, 155
        hominy, baked, 156
        hominy spoon bread, 156
        kasha (buckwheat groats), 156
        polenta, 157
        polenta pie, 157
    kidney bean, 154
    noodle and walnut, 164
    olive-rice, 149
    vegetable, 157–62
        corn, simple, 157
        egg and potato, 161

Fish (*cont.*)
  fry, 206
  haddock. *See also* Finnan haddie
    smoke-cooked, 143
  kippered, 137
    salmon, 141
  pâté sandwich, 126
  salmon
    kippered, 141
    lox, 141
    skewered, 91
    smoked, 141
    whole, plank roasted, 77
    whole, roasted, 76
  sandwiches, toasted, 125
  smoked, 137
  split, timing and temperature for, 25
  squares, skewered, 120
  steaks
    timing and temperature for, 25
    variations on, 79
  stew, camp, 221
  teriyaki, 96
  timing and temperature for, x, 25, 75
  trout, whole
    blue (truite au bleu), 78
    pan-fried, 78
  white, skewered, 90
  whole
    foiled, small, 78
    grilled, 75
    grilled, with herbs, 76
    pan-fried, 78
    roasted, foil-, 77
    spitted, 77
    spitted, small, 78
    timing and temperature for, 25
Flaming, 17
Flank steak (London broil), 37
  about, 29
  deviled, 38
Flaring, 3, 5, 12–13, 31

Foil cookery, 170–71
Fork, turning with, 17
Frankfurter(s)
  appetizer broils, 123
  skewered, 90
  wiener roast, 203
French bread, 173–74
  sourdough, camp, 220
French dressing, basic, 187
Fried rice, 148
Frijoles, 150
  con queso, 151
  refritos, 150
Frog's legs, broiled, 80
  appetizer, 123
Frozen meat, timing and temperature for, 15
Fruit(s). *See also specific fruits*
  about, 127
  appetizers, 123
  biscuits, drop, camp, 215
  skewered, 93–94
Fryers, electric deep fat, 7
Frying pans, electric, 7
Fuel. *See also* Fire and fuel
  charcoal, 9–10
  kindling fluid, 10, 11
  wood, 9

Galley and trailer cookery, 224–32
Game
  duck, wild
    broiled, 112
    with olive sauce, 111
    with red wine and gin, 111
    roast, 110
    timing and temperature for, 22
  goose, wild
    with olive sauce, 111
    roast, 110
    timing and temperature for, 22
  hare
    marinated roast, 112
    saddle, roast, 113

Rolled rib roast, 52
Rolls, 174
  stuffed, 174
Rosemary butter sauce, 196
Rotisserie, electrical, 6–7
Rumaki, 121
Rump
  roast, salted, 53
  steak, 29

Salad, 177–86
  apple
    and chestnut, 177
    and cress, 178
    and green pepper, 178
  artichoke, 178
  asparagus
    I, 178
    II, 178
  bean sprout
    I, 179
    II, 179
  beet
    and olive, 180
    and onion, 180
    and tongue, 180
  broccoli, 180
  cabbage. See also cole slaw below
    red, 180
    white, 180
  camp, 222
  carrot, 181
  celery Victor, 181
  celeriac, 181
  cherry, 181
  cole slaw
    with capers, 181
    with chicken, 180
  cucumber, 181
    Chinese style, 182
    orange and, 183
  egg
    and anchovy, 182
    and bacon, 178
  farmer's, 182

Salad (cont.)
  grapefruit and peach, 182
  green bean (string bean), 179
    and artichoke hearts, 47
    and dill, 179
    and white bean, 179
  Japanese, 182
  kidney bean, 179
  lima bean, 179
  melon
    I, 182
    II, 182
  mixed greens
  onion, 183
    and parsley, 183
    -relish, 183
  orange, 183
    and apple, 183
    and cucumber, 183
  parsley, 183
    and green pepper, 183
  pineapple, 184
  potato, 184
  radiccio, 184
  radish, 184
  rice
    I, 184
    II, 184
  sauerkraut, 185
    raw, 185
  string bean, 179
  tangerine, 185
  tomato, 185
    I, 185
    II, 185
    and cheese, 185
    and mushroom, 186
  white, 186
  "yam" or Siamese, 186
Salad dressing
  California wine, 187
  French, basic, 187
  green goddess, 186
  sour cream, 187
  vinaigrette, 186

Salisbury steak béarnaise, 39
Salmon
    kippered, 141
    lox, 141
    skewered, 91
    smoked, 141
    whole
        roasted, 76
        roasted, plank, 77
Salsa fria, Mexican, 197
Salt, x, 5, 17
    -broiled steak, 34–35
    charcoal, 7
    spit roasting and, 19
Sandwiches, 124–26
    beef
        heart, ground broiled, 126
        roast beef, 54
        tartare, Ben Levy's, 126
    cheese, toasted, 124
    fish
        pâté, 126
        toasted, 125
    meat, toasted, 125–26
    for picnics and cook-outs, 199
    sealed toasted, 126
    steak, 29
        minute, 35
Sasaties, 97
Satès, pork, 97
Sauce
    barbecue, 17
    béarnaise, 193
    béchamel, basic, 193
    bigarade, 194
    black pepper, marinated saddle of
        venison with, 117
    bordelaise, 190
    butter. See Butter
    California, 193
    chafing dish for, 8
    champagne, 190
    charcutière, 190
    chasseur, 191
    chateaubriand, 191

Sauce (cont.)
    colbert, 191
    cucumber, 196
    cumberland, 194
    diable, 191
    epicurean, 194
    garlic-lemon, 194
    hollandaise, 192
    malta, 193
    marchands de vin, 191
    mornay, 194
    mousseline, 193
    mushroom, minute steak
        smothered in, old-fashioned,
        36
    olive
        for broiled duck, 66
        duck or goose with, 111
    orientale, 192
    piquant, 192
    poivrade, 192
    red bean, 67
    remoulade, 197
    Robert, 192
    salsa fria, Mexican, 197
    snail butter, 196
    tartar, 196
    teriyaki, 95
    turkey giblet, 71
    vinaigrette, 186
    wine-shallot steak, 195
Sauerkraut, 167
    salad, 185
        raw, 185
Sausage(s)
    appetizer broils, 123
    grilled, 102
    in mixed grill, 104
    skewered, 90
    smoked, 139
Sauteeing, pan for, 7–8
Savoy potatoes, 168
Scallops
    broiled, 83
        appetizer, 123

Turkish Mutton Chops, 47–48
Turnip and potato casserole, 161

Underground cookery, 206–9
Utensils, cooking, 5

Veal
  chops, herbed, 49
  heart, 105
  kidney, 106
    in mixed grill, 104
  larding and barding, 58–59
  shish kebab, 86
  shoulder, boned, with anchovies, 59
  skewered, 90
  timing and temperature for, 23
Vegetables. *See also specific vegetables*
  casseroles, 157–62
    corn, simple, 157
    egg and potato, 161
    eggplant (ratatouille), 159
    potato, 161
    spinach, 162
    turnip and potato, 161
  foiled
    assorted, 170
    frozen, 170
  skewered, 93
  spit-roasted, 132
Venison
  about, 116
  chops, 49–50
    carinated, 50
  leg of, roast, 117
  loin of, spitted, 118
  saddle
    marinated, with black pepper sauce, 117
    roast, 117
  steaks or chops, broiled, 116
  teriyaki, 96
Vermouth marinade and baste, 189

Vertical grill, 3
Vienna sausage appetizer broils, 123
Vinaigrette sauce, 186

Waffle maker, electric, 8
Walnut(s)
  and noodle casserole, 164
  roast, 171
  wafers, 202
Water chestnut
  -chicken liver appetizer, 121
  -lobster appetizer, 121
  -shrimp appetizer, 121
Watercress and apple salad, 178
Weber kettle, 135
Wheeled grills, 2–3
White bean(s)
  cognac, 151
  country style, 43
    cold, 152
  salad, green bean and, 179
White salad, 186
White wine marinade, 189
Wiener roast, 203
Wild rice casserole, 150
Wine
  dressing, California, 187
  red
    duck with gin and, 111
    marinade, 189
    spareribs with, 100
  -shallot steak sauce, 194
  white, marinade, 189
Wine-Shallot Steak Sauce, 37
Wok, 1
Wood as fuel, 9

Yams, 132
  foiled, 170
  skewered, 93

Zucchini
  roasted, 132
  skewered, 93